CONCORDIA UNIVERSITY
DS475.P25   C001 V
BRITISH DIPLOMACY IN NORTH INDIA N

3 4211 000025162

Y0-CLJ-786

WITHDRAWN

WITHDRAWN

BRITISH DIPLOMACY IN NORTH INDIA

British Diplomacy in North India
A Study of the Delhi Residency 1803-1857

K. N. PANIKKAR, M.A. PH.D.

Foreword by
BISHESHWAR PRASAD, M.A. D. LITT.
Vice-Chancellor, Bhagalpur University

Associated Publishing House
New Delhi-5

Associated Publishing House
7717, New Market, Karol Bagh
New Delhi-5

First Published 1968

© K. N. Panikkar

PRINTED IN INDIA
PRINTED AND PUBLISHED BY RAVINDER KUMAR PAUL
FOR ASSOCIATED PUBLISHING HOUSE, NEW DELHI-5

In Memoriam
V.P.S. Raghuvanshi

Preface

JOHN WILLIAM KAYE, commenting on the political developments of India in the nineteenth century, described the British Residency at Delhi as the "headquarters of diplomacy in Upper India". The remark of Kaye points to the significance of a hitherto ignored aspect of Indo-British history—the role of the Political Residents and Agents in the expansion and consolidation of British power in India. In the large number of studies on the political history of India in the nineteenth century, the general tendency has been to focus attention on the decision-making authorities such as the Governor-General, the Court of Directors, and the Board of Control. While the importance of this approach in understanding the British policy is undeniable, it should be admitted at the same time that by itself it does not provide a complete picture of the political developments. Nor does it throw light on the various influences that shaped the British policy in India. For instance, this line of enquiry does not take into consideration the role of the subordinate functionaries in the governmental decisions, which is important for two reasons. First, because it gives a deeper insight into the process of decision-making; and secondly, because it provides a new dimension to the understanding of the political developments.

The British politicals deputed to the various Indian courts were not merely the channel of communication with the rulers, as is often misunderstood, but were, in more sense than one, the diplomatic representatives who performed the dirty spadework, by feeding information and implementing the policy of the Government. They maintained a well-organized system of espionage. The spies were employed inside the palaces, and they submitted daily reports about all important happenings to their masters. Nothing escaped their notice, not even the petty details of the personal life of the princes. It was through their medium that the Company maintained its influence and countermanded the intrigues detrimental to its interests. Through them also, as

Thomas Munro said, the Governor-General was present at every Indian court by proxy. Needless to emphasize that a close scrutiny of their work would provide an intimate knowledge of the diplomatic and political activities of the British in India. In this monograph I have made an attempt to study the working of the British Residency at Delhi from this point of view.

The Residency at Delhi came into existence during the second Anglo-Maratha war when Delhi was occupied by the British in 1803. For managing the British relations with the Mughal Emperor, a military officer was then "appointed to attend to His Majesty in the capacity of Agent or Representative of the British Government". A little later, the states of Rajputana and the Cis-Sutlej also came under his jurisdiction. Though the Resident, at one time or other, had to deal with several states including Afghanistan, Bhawalpur, and the Punjab, the superintendence of British relations with the Mughal Emperor as well as the states of Rajputana and the Cis-Sutlej was his main responsibility.

The extent of the Residency's political jurisdiction then offers a convenient framework to study the dominant theme in the political history of India in the first-half of the nineteenth century, namely the assumption of the *de facto* paramount authority by the East India Company. The British administrators in India had then realized that in order to achieve their end it would be necessary to obliterate the notions of paramountcy associated with the Mughal Emperor. Therefore the Company, while assuming the rights and obligations of the paramount power in its relations with the Indian states, gradually deprived the Mughal Emperor of the various imperial prerogatives enjoyed by him. The significance of this two-pronged policy has been brought out in the following pages by highlighting the Company's attitude towards the Mughal Emperor on the one hand, and its relations with the states of Rajputana and the Cis-Sutlej on the other. The assumption of the paramount authority in respect to the states of Rajputana and the Cis-Sutlej and gradual reduction of the imperial prerogatives of the Mughal Emperor are thus interlinked. The first may be viewed as the positive, and the second as the negative aspect in the Company's quest for paramountcy in India.

A word of explanation may be offered at this point about

the arrangement of the material and chapterization adopted in this book. The first three chapters deal with the affairs of the Mughal Emperor; the fourth and fifth discuss the states of Rajputana; the next is about the Cis-Sutlej states, while the three subsequent chapters return to the affairs of the Mughal Emperor. Thus it is clear that I have neither followed the method of thematic analysis, nor a strict chronological narrative method in the treatment of the subject-matter. It is because of two reasons. First, I have traced the establishment and the organizational and jurisdictional changes of the Residency in its evolutionary process, and then I have examined the developments in the regions under its control. It is to bring out this inter-connexion that the organizational matters of the Residency are discussed along with the narrative which could as well have claimed a separate chapter. Secondly, this is not a study *per se* of Indo-British relations. The analyses of the relationship have been mainly used to illustrate, and thus to adumbrate the role of the Resident and the problems of paramountcy.

This monograph, which was orignally a doctoral dissertation, was prepared under the guidance of the Late Dr. V.P.S. Raghuvanshi, whose knowledge of the political history of India was both deep and incisive. By his premature death the academic world in India has lost a very promising scholar, but to me his death is a personal loss. It is with a heavy heart that I dedicate this book to his loving memory.

I am grateful to Prof. Bisheshwar Prasad, Vice-Chancellor of Bhagalpur Universty, who in spite of his multifarious duties wrote a scholarly foreword to this book.

Shri J.P. Guha whose primary interest is English literature and, unfortunately, not history, has been of help to me in more ways than one. Apart from taking a keen interest in the publication of this book, he offered critical comments in his usual forthright manner, which helped me to avoid several pitfalls.

I am grateful to Shri Vijay Chandra Joshi, to Dr. Ravindra Kumar, to Shri Charan Das Sidhu, and to Shri Satya Dev Jaggi for suggestions.

I wish to express my gratitude to the Director of the National Archives of India for allowing me access to the records in his holdings and, in particular, my gratitude to the authorities of the University of Rajasthan who granted me a scholarship which enabled me to undertake this work.

Finally, I should like to place on record my indebtedness to my friend, Shri M.T.K. Muhammod, who has been a constant source of help and encouragement during the last fourteen years of my life.

Hansraj College,
Delhi University,
Delhi-7

K.N. Panikkar

Contents

	Preface	vii
	Foreword	xii
	Abbreviations	xiii
1.	Introduction	1
2.	Settlement with the Mughal House 1803–1805	5
3.	Appointment of the Heir-Apparent	20
4.	The States of Rajputana	42
5.	Implementation of British Policy in Rajputana	65
6.	The Cis-Sutlej States	99
7.	The Question of the Royal Stipend	115
8.	The Status of the Mughal Emperor	136
9.	The Final Phase	160
10.	Conclusion	180
	Appendix I	186
	Appendix II	191
	Glossary	193
	Select Bibliography	194
	Index	196

Abbreviations

For. Misc.	:	Foreign Department, Miscellaneous Series
P.G.R.	:	Punjab Government Records
Pol. Cons.	:	Foreign Department, Political Consultations
Pub. Cons.	:	Home Department, Public Consultations
Sec. Cons.	:	Foreign Department, Secret Consultations

Foreword

A WHOLESOME turn has come into historical research in India in the last two decades. Initially critical studies were directed to the analysis of events in the eighteenth and earlier centuries, and the last century and half attracted little attention. The most prominent reason for the neglect of the recent most past was the paucity of source material which remained barred for Indian scholars owing to the attitude of the then rulers of India. Even after the Independence it took some time before the archives were opened to the gaze of historians and it was only then that the history of the nineteenth century could admit of examination by Indian historians. A very remarkable development was the collection of the Residency Records at the National Archives as also the half-hearted opening of the records of some of the erstwhile Indian or Princely states. This consciousness of the urgency of making state records available for critical examination naturally prompted some young scholars, particularly in the Universities of Rajasthan, to study the complicated political relations between the Rajput states and the Marathas and subsequently the British. The present study by Dr. Panikkar fills an important gap as it is devoted to the analysis of the mainsprings of British policy towards the states of Rajputana and the Punjab as conducted by the Government of India through the Resident at Delhi. A study of this nature is most welcome for there are very few books on the British relations with the Indian states and even now students have to depend on the garbled, prejudiced version of Sir William Lee Warner, which makes little endeavour to explain the nature of the bondage which was rapidly enmeshing the Indian Princes. Dr. Panikkar's book is a very helpful prelude to another work of this nature which was published in the last few years under the title of "Paramountcy under Lord Dalhousie", as the present study relates to the period 1806 to 1833, which in many senses was the formative age of British dominion in India.

General supposition based primarily on the testimony of Tupper and Lee Warner is that paramountcy, with all its vagueness and comprehensiveness, was a development of the post-1857 period and was the outcome of the assumption of direct rule of India by the Crown of England. Paramountcy has never been defined and the Butler Committee was content with the enigma that paramountcy is paramount. But from the description of Lee Warner one may assume that some of its attributes were control over succession, adoption and regency, as well as appointment of the prime minister. Absolute authority in the matter of external relations of the states, military protection against foreign aggression or internal revolt or disturbances of any kind directed towards the subversion of the Princely power and mal-administration were inherent in the very concept of paramountcy. Whether these were sudden developments after the suppression of the Revolt of 1857 or these had been evidenced earlier have intrigued historians. But if one were to depart from the dogma prescribed by Lee Warner, one would find that all these features are well marked in the earlier years also. Beginning with Bengal and Carnatac, which were the earliest states to fall prey to British diplomacy, and coming to Awadh, Hyderabad, and Mysore, we find that whichever Princely state came under British military protection had to part with its sovereignty in any or all of these matters. It may be correct to hold that in the eighteenth century, after Plassey, the British officers were experimenting in paramountcy within limited spheres, and any state which was brought to their laboratory was meted out similar treatment, so that inevitably, without a principle being enunciated, it was subjected to the pre-eminent control or paramountcy of the British.

Lord Wellesley devised his system of Subsidiary Alliances to give a form to the existing relationship and drew more and more of the Indian Princes into the net. This system involved full control over the foreign or external policy of the subsidiary state and its protection against external aggression which implied submission of inter-state disputes to British arbitration. But it will be wrong to seek explanation of the nature of the subsidiary system in the terms of the treaties then made, and particularly those with Peshwa, Bhonsle or Sindhia. For a precise review of the implications of this system it will be essential to look into the treaty with Awadh and the actual working of the system in the case of Awadh and Hyderabad. There was hardly any aspect of internal administration of these two states—and these were the biggest states of India then—or of Mysore, Baroda, or Travancore, to name only a few of them, which escaped the death grasp of British pre-eminant and blighting control. Revenue administration was reorganized, commerce was affected, ministerial appointments were dictated and the ruler's dealings with his feudatories and even with the members of his family were directed in these states by men like Barlow and Minto who are posed as the strict votaries of the doctrine of non-intervention in the affairs of Indian states.

Lord Hastings interpreted the relationship logically and in his treaties clearly enunciated the principle of the demission of external sovereignty by the Princely states. But even his treaties were not unequivocal when it came to matters of internal administration. There was considerable lacuna between theory and practice. While Hastings deprecated intervention in the internal government of Hyderabad as advocated by Metcalfe in the interest of foreign creditors, he was upholding considerable interference in other matters in the Indian states. Amherst's policy in respect of Bharatpur or Bentinck's dealings with Awadh are a clear testimony of the climate of absolute control. Thus by the year 1834, scarcely any aspect of internal sovereignty of the princes remained untouched by the controlling arm of British paramountcy, but in this period no theory was made out of it and every state was treated as an isolated case, as and when occasion arose for the display of the predominant authority of the supreme military power, the British in India.

Dr. Panikkar has traced the story of this phase of British policy as examplified by the two over-weening Residents of Delhi, Metcalfe and Ochterlony. Both of them had a large canvas to paint and events in Rajasthan and eastern Punjab in the so-called Cis-Sutlej states afforded invitation to them to be aggressively intervening. Jaipur, Jodhpur, Kotah or Alwar and Bharatpur were in a state of semi-chaos at the moment, and for the peace and tranquillity of these states as well as the bordering British territories it was essential that symptoms of unrest and disorder should be immediately and conclusively eliminated. The Calcutta Government or the India House in London might occasionally demur and swear by the notion of non-intervention, but finally the local authority had its way, and in this manner British paramountcy was clearly exercised in the region of North India. The Mughal Emperor was a mere cipher and his treatment can afford no proof of the emphatic nature of British paramountcy; but Rajput and Sikh states provided the object lesson and it was on the experiments made then in their cases that in the future the foundations of the edifice of paramountcy were solidly laid, and Canning or Curzon could say that the Paramount authority has itself laid certain limits otherwise Paramountcy is unlimited and has sway over every phase of the administration of the Princely states or conduct of their rulers.

I greatly welcome the advent of Dr. Panikkar's study which will, I am sure, reveal the true nature of an important phase of British Indian administration.

Bhagalpur University,   Bisheshwar Prasad
Bhagalpur-7
June 4, 1968.

I
Introduction

THE EMERGENCE of the East India Company as a territorial power in the second half of the eighteenth century ushered in a new force on the political horizon of India. Beginning as suppliant merchants in the coastal regions, the British gradually acquired a domineering position, eliminating their European rivals, concluding alliances with powerful Indian states like Hyderabad and Awadh, and successfully resisting the might of the Marathas and of the Sultan of Mysore. By the end of the century they had, in fact, become strong contenders for the sovereignty of India.

During this process of political development, the Company's interests demanded the maintenance of influence and representation at the various Indian courts. The Governments at the Presidencies could not fulfil this task in the absence of proper agencies to project the policy of the Company and to countermand the intrigues and activities of other powers detrimental to their interests. The institution of Residency was devised in the wake of this necessity. To begin with, the Residents were deputed to the courts of Murshidabad, Lucknow, Hyderabad, and Poona. The appointment of Samuel Middleton in 1764 at the court of Murshidabad was the first formal appointment of a British Political Resident.[1] Francis Sykes and Richard Becher at Murshidabad, John Holland at Hyderabad, and Nathaniel Middleton at Lucknow followed him. The contribution of these functionaries in enhancing the prestige and influence of the British prompted the Government to extend the system to the other states as well.

The politics of North India with Delhi as its epicentre had assumed increasing importance in the last quarter of the eighte-

[1] National Archives of India, *Select Committee Proceedings*, 1764, Vol. 19, pp. 645-46.

enth century. Though Shah Alam II, the Mughal Emperor, had by then ceased to be a power of any note, his name and authority were of considerable weight in Indian politics. The British Government, therefore, looked upon his activities and the endeavours of other powers to command control at Delhi with a sense of scepticism and disapproval. In 1776 Shah Alam had vainly tried to forge a combination of the Rohilas, the Marathas, and the Sikhs against the Nawab of Awadh. This attempt of the Emperor to head a coalition of the most powerful martial races in the country had induced Warren Hastings, the then Governor-General, to take active interest in Delhi politics. The failure of these powers to execute their plan and the preoccupations of the British Government with the first Anglo-Maratha war prevented the contemplated interference. He, however, wanted to forestall any possible ascendancy of the Marathas, the Sikhs, and the Jats at Delhi.

The death of Najaf Khan, the minister of Shah Alam, in April 1782 and the chaos and confusion that followed provided a welcome opportunity for the British Government to make its influence felt at the Mughal Court. Najaf Khan had efficiently managed the royal affairs and had succeeded in introducing certain regularity in the administration and cohesion among the ranks of the nobles. But soon after his death the factious spirit again asserted itself. Mirza Shafi Khan, his grand nephew, Afrasaib Khan and Najaf Quli Khan, his chief slaves, and Muhammad Beg Hamdani, one of his generals, vied with one another for power. The outcome of this struggle was uncertain as the contending parties were almost evenly balanced. The Sikhs, the Jats, and the Marathas, always eager to fish in the muddy waters of Delhi, discerned in this contest a possible opportunity to control Delhi and the Emperor. Hastings also realized the possibilities afforded by this situation for the British Government to interfere and check the ascendancy of other powers at Delhi. With this aim in view he deputed Major James Browne in 1782 as his agent to secure reliable information about Delhi affairs.[2]

Browne reached Delhi on December 11, 1783. His chief

[2] Hastings to Browne, August 20, 1782, Krishna Dayal Bhargava: *Browne Correspondence*, pp. 1-5.

duty was to collect information about "the character, connection, influence and power of the several competitors for the possession of the king's favour and the exercise of his authority", and about the relation the independent chiefs had with the Emperor.[3] He was to keep a close watch on the design and activities of all foreign agents, especially of the vakil of the Sultan of Mysore Browne was, however, not vested with any discretionary powers, and was instructed to refer all matters to the Governor-General for his decision. His appointment was purely temporary, but Hastings was prepared to establish a permanent Residency, if the Emperor so desired.

Browne remained in office for about two years. Within this period the political situation in Delhi had undergone kaleidoscopic changes. Mahadaji Sindhia, who after the treaty of Salbhai had extended his activities to the North, gained complete control over the Emperor, notwithstanding Major Browne's opposition. The Emperor appointed him the *vakil-i-mutlaq* (Regent Plenipotentiary) in December 1784. He then assumed the role of the imperial protector, took charge of the administration, and ruthlessly suppressed all opposition. Sindhia's assumption of power at Delhi was none too unpleasant to the British as he recognized the obligation to the British Government for the predominant position he enjoyed in the North. In these circumstances the presence of an Agent at Delhi was of no consequence and Browne was, therefore, recalled to the Presidency without any delay.[4]

The Emperor was not happy at the withdrawal of the British Agent. He considered it a slight on his authority and an "evasion of the common externals of respect and consideration" due to him, especially because the British Government maintained their representatives at the courts of the various Indian powers: the Sultan of Mysore the Nawab of Awadh, the Nizam of Hyderabad, and the Marathas, all of whom the Emperor regarded as his subjects.[5] Browne also regretted the decision of

[3] *Ibid.*
[4] Macpherson to Browne, March 1, 1785: *sec. cons.*, March 1, 1785, No. 7.
[5] Browne to Macpherson, March 19, 1785: *sec. cons.*, April 9, 1785, No. 4.

the Governor-General to abolish the Agency. He sincerely believed that the interests of the British Government warranted its continuation. All important powers of the country had their vakils at Delhi. The Imperial Court was the centre of intrigues and negotiations. Tipu Sultan had offered a tribute of twelve lakhs of rupees to the Emperor when he received *sanads* for the *subedari* of Arcot. Bussy, the French General, had promised necessary troops for expelling the British from India. These intrigues of the various powers to use the Emperor as a stalking-horse, Browne contended, could be forestalled only by the vigilance of an Agent stationed at Delhi. The Governor-General was, however, not convinced by this argument and decided to terminate the Agency. Browne was, therefore, asked to comply immediately with the former orders of the Government and accordingly he left Delhi on April 20, 1785.[6] The intercourse with the Emperor was then entrusted to the Agent with Sindhia, who maintained a vakil at Delhi for gathering all necessary information.[7] This arrangement continued till 1803 when the Residency was established at Delhi on a permanent basis.

---

[6] Browne to Macpherson, April 20, 1785: *sec. cons.*, May 12, 1785, No. 2.
[7] Macpherson to Shah Alam, March 1, 1785: *sec. cons.*, November 1, 1785, No. 7.

2
Settlement with the Mughal House 1803-1805

LORD WELLESLEY, who assumed the Governor-Generalship of India in 1798, gave a new orientation to British policy towards Indian states. Since the departure of Warren Hastings, the British Government in India was consciously pursuing a policy of non-intervention which considerably weakened many Indian powers due to their mutual aggrandizement and recriminations. Though this could in a way serve the British imperial interests, it provided vast opportunities for the more powerful Indian states like the Marathas and Mysore to strengthen their resources and consolidate their position at the expense of the unprotected weaker powers. Wellesley saw the dangers inherent in this policy. The influence and power of the British in Indian politics, he argued, had already advanced to a stage from where a retrograde step would adversely affect their prospects. Though he could not carry the Home authorities with him in all his endeavours, his tenure of office was a period of unprecedented territorial expansion for the British Government in India. The most formidable enemies that he had to deal with were the Marathas and a major area of conflict was North India. The internal dissensions in the Maratha camp, the bane of Indian feudalism in the eighteenth century, helped Wellesley to force a subsidiary treaty on the Peshwa, Baji Rao II. With this treaty the Peshwa passed under the surveillance of the British and it ultimately precipitated the second Anglo-Maratha war in 1803.

The capture of Delhi and the alienation of the Mughal Emperor from the Marathas were considered by Lord Wellesley the "principal object of the war and an indispensable condition of peace".[1] The Marathas had virtually controlled Delhi

[1] Governor-General-in-Council to the Secret Committee of the Court of Directors, July 13, 1804.

affairs since 1784. Though bereft of the old glory and grandeur the Mughal Emperor was still regarded with special sanctity by Indian public. The old and infirm Emperor was the symbol of the imperial power in the eyes of the people. Almost every ruler in India still struck coins in the name of Shah Alam. Princes and nobles still applied to the Emperor for *khilats* and titles and displayed the insignia of rank which they or their ancestors derived from the throne of Delhi.[2]

Lord Wellesley was conscious of the unique position of the Emperor and feared that "Shah Alam might form a dangerous instrument in the hands of any state possessing sufficient power, energy and judgment to employ it, in prosecuting views of aggrandizement and ambition". The power which Wellesley had in mind was none other than the French. Mons. Perron and other French generals in the service of Sindhia were active and powerful in Delhi and were actually scheming to restore the authority of Shah Alam in order to thwart British imperial designs. A possible ascendancy of the French in the Mughal Court could be averted, so held the Governor-General, only by securing "the person, family and nominal authority of Shah Alam" and by taking him under the protection of the British Government.[3]

In pursuance of this policy the British Government offered protection to the Mughal Emperor while the war was in progress.[4] The Emperor was assured "every demonstration of respect and every degree of attention" and an adequate provision for the support and maintenance of the royal household.[5] Shah Alam was favourably disposed towards this offer.[6] He was,

[2] Wellesley wrote: "Notwithstanding His Majesty's total deprivation of real power, dominion and authority, almost every state and every class of people in India continue to acknowledge his nominal authority." *Ibid.*

[3] Montgomery Martin (ed.): *The Despatches, Minutes and Correspondence of Wellesley*, iv, p. 157.

[4] Lord Wellesley to Shah Alam, July 27, 1803: *Sec. Cons.*, March 2, 1804, No. 6-A.

[5] This communication was made through Syed Reza Khan who was the agent of the Resident with Sindhia at the Court of Delhi. Colonel Collins was then the Resident with Sindhia. Lord Lake to G.G., August 8, 1803: *sec. cons.*, March 2, 1804, No. 53.

[6] H.M. to G.G., dated nil: *sec. cons.*, March 2, 1804. No. 54.

however, firmly under the control of Mons. Perron and is stated to have expressed his intention of taking the field against the British.[7] But the defeat sustained by Sindhia's army on September 11, 1803 at Delhi put an end to the French machinations. Now that the British became the masters, Shah Alam was eager to avail of the protection earlier offered by them. The Governor-General considered the emancipation of the Emperor from the thraldom of the Marathas a happy and important result of the war. He wrote to Shah Alam: "Among the inestimable benefits resulting from the brilliant victories obtained by the British troops over the armies of Daulat Rao Sindhia and of Mr. Perron, I have derived the most cordial satisfaction in accomplishing the deliverance of Your Majesty and your royal family from the indignities to which Your Majesty and your household have been subjected by the violence, injustice and rapacity of those who have forgotten the reverence due to your royal person and illustrious house."

Lord Lake, the Commander-in-Chief of the British army, was received by Akbar Shah, the eldest son of the Emperor, and was escorted to the palace where he met the Emperor on September 16, 1803. The miserable plight of the blind old Emperor evoked sympathetic sentiments in the mind of the General who treated him with kindness and consideration. His Majesty and his whole Court gave him an enthusiastic reception and convinced him by expressions of cordiality and friendship that the change in their fortunes was agreeable and advantageous to them. They were profuse in congratulating him for the magnificent victories of the British arms over the Marathas and expressed their appreciation by bestowing *khilats* and titles. At a reception accorded to him on the 20th, the *Sumsam-ud-Daula, Asugar-ul-Mulk, Khan-Dauran Khan Bahadur, Sipeh Salar Fatteh Singh* ("the sword of the state, the hero of the land, the lord of the age and the victorious in war"), the second most important title of the Empire, was conferred on him. The Emperor regretted that he could not confer the highest title as it had already been given to Mahadaji Sindhia. The Governor-General warmly reciprocated these friendly gestures by granting six lakhs of

---

[7] Lord Lake to G.G., September 1, 1803: *sec, cons.*, March 2, 1804, No.63.

rupees to Shah Alam for his immediate requirements.[8]

The capture of Delhi and the unconditional acceptance of British protection by Shah Alam presented the problem of providing proper facilities to the Emperor and his household, commensurate with their former dignity and status, but at the same time without sacrificing the advantages achieved by the military successes. The Government had at the very outset decided "to appoint a civil or military officer to attend His Majesty in the capacity of Agent or Representative of the British Government."[9]

The person selected by Lord Lake to perform this duty was David Ochterlony who was appointed the acting Resident and Chief Commandant at Delhi with a garrison of one battalion and four companies of native infantry and a corps of Mewattis under his command.[10] The Residency at Delhi thus came into existence on September 24, 1803 and the Resident was placed under the control of the Commander-in-Chief who was vested with the authority to conduct both military and political affairs in Hindustan.

David Ochterlony, generally known in Indian courts as "Loony Akhtar" who had come to India at the "unusually mature age of nineteen" took a fancy to the Indian way of life. He lived almost like a nawab with several wives and a train of attendants and underlings.[11] During his journeys he moved with a large retinue of elephants, palanquins, covered carriages, and

[8] G.G. to H.M., October 8, 1803, *op. cit.,* para 9.
[9] G.G. to Lake, July 26, 1803: *sec. cons.,* March 2, 1804, No. 6.
[10] Lake to Wellesley, September 23, 1803: *sec. cons.,* March 2, 1803, No. 119. There does not seem to be any clear-cut written instruction to Ochterlony at the time of his appointment either from Lord Lake or from the Governor-General regarding his duties and responsibilities. The Governor-General, of course, had directed Lake to give "proper instructions for the regulation of his conduct towards His Majesty and the royal family founded on the actual circumstances of their situation." The instructions rendered by Lake, if any, were verbal. Though he was to manage British relations with the Mughal Emperor, military exigencies mainly prompted Lord Lake to leave him behind at Delhi.
[11] In Delhi Ochterlony went for evening stroll every day with his thirteen wives on thirteen elephants. Edward Thompson: *Making of the Indian Princes,* p. 184.

SETTLEMENT WITH THE MUGHAL HOUSE

so on, imparting to them the splendour of oriental royal processions. He was, according to Bishop Heber, "a tall and pleasing-looking man, but was so wrapped up in shawls, kincobe, fur, and a Mughal fur cap, that his face was all that was visible."[12] He found his place in India most easily, as if by manner born to it. This made him a most agreeable person to deal with the dispirited but nostalgic Mughal Emperor, whereas his military talents and experience recommended him to the discharge of the onerous duties that devolved on the Resident in the wake of the military campaigns as well as the organization of the Residency.

Ochterlony had hardly found his place in the new office when he was called upon to defend Delhi against the onslaught of Holkar. Even though Lake had successfully dealt with Sindhia in the fierce battles at Laswaree and Assaye, Holkar, realizing his mistake a bit too late, "stepped on the saddle" to vanquish the British. After his lightning successes at Tonk and Rampura, he reached Delhi on October 8, 1804. Ochterlony found himself in a very precarious situation. With a limited number of soldiers and artillery, thoroughly inadequate to match the vast army of Holkar, the defence of Delhi looked like a lost game. The city was unprotected except by a wall badly constructed and in many places without a parapet. Added to all this, the attitude of the Emperor and the royal family was one of disguised hostility.[13] The appeals of the Resident to the Emperor for help were brushed aside on one pretext or the other.[14] But Ochterlony did not despair and tried to muster all available forces for the defence of the imperial city. Holkar had about seventy thousand men with him, whereas Ochterlony had merely one thousand

[12] Reginald Heber: *A Journey Through the Upper Provinces of India*, ii pp. 392-3.
[13] The British got hold of some letters from His Majesty's *Najibs* (a body of irregular infantry), which apparently appeared to be from a mistress to her lover but conveyed best wishes and hopes for the success of Holkar. Ochterlony also found that the *Najibs* were in the habit of passing on secret information to Holkar. Ochterlony to Edmonstone, Secretary to Government, November 30, 1804: *sec. cons.*, January 31, 1805, No. 216.
[14] Ochterlony to Edmonstone, November 30, 1804: *sec. cons.*, January 31, 1805, No. 218.

four hundred regular sepoys, one thousand one hundred irregulars, and eleven guns at his command.[15] With this meagre force, ably assisted by Colonel Burn, the Officer-in-Command of the garrison, he defended the city for eight days against a tremendous cannonade.[16] Foiled in his attempt to conquer Delhi, Holkar marched towards Panipat on October 15, 1804. Ochterlony and his brave men breathed a sigh of relief.

The defence of Delhi was the first major undertaking of the Resident after he had taken charge in 1803. The importance of this gallant operation can hardly be overrated. After the disasters at Tonk and Rampura, the morale of the British army was quite low. It would undoubtedly have been disastrous for British prestige and interests, had Delhi passed into the hands of Holkar. Ochterlony did a gallant job of it and was applauded by the Commander-in-Chief.[17]

Arrangement with the Mughal Emperor

It was at this time that the Governor-General applied himself to the task of finalizing an arrangement with the Mughal Emperor. Colonel William Scott who was appointed the Resident on February 25, 1804[18] to succeed Ochterlony, submitted a proposal to this effect before joining at Delhi.[19] His views, were not accepted in *toto* by the Governor-General but they formed the basis of the subsequent arrangement.

According to Scott, the conquest of Delhi and the country contiguous to it was made directly from the Marathas and not from the Emperor. Naturally the British Government possessed over the conquered territory indubitable rights which, accrued from conquest. This excluded all consideration of the rights of the former occupants or sovereigns.[20] He suggested the

[15] Huge Pearse: *Life and Military Services of Viscount Lake*, p. 304.
[16] Ochterlony's soldiers were on duty day and night. To boost up their spirits, Ochterlony distributed sweetmeats and promised them half a month's wages after they repulsed the enemy. Montgomery Martin: *Indian Empire*, i, p. 401.
[17] William Thorne: *Memories of Lord Lake*, p. 383.
[18] Scott to Edmonstone, March 12, 1804: *pol., cons.*, May 17, 1804, No. 121.
[19] Lake to Wellesley, September 4, 1804: *sec. cons.*, March 7, 1805, No. 9, Encl. 1.
[20] *Ibid.*

SETTLEMENT WITH THE MUGHAL HOUSE

payment of an allowance adequate for the support of His Majesty and the royal family, either in the from of money or in the from of territory or partly in both. The Emperor could be allowed to retain a certain portion of his former possessions in the vicinity of Delhi and to exercise authority within that limit under the superintendence and control of the British Resident at his Court. He would have liked to bring under the management of the British Government the entire country appropriated by the Marathas for the support of the royal family, but for respect for public opinion. All appointments to public offices were to be made by His Majesty and all acts of public authority to be issued in the royal name, but not until the British Resident had agreed to them. The British military force stationed in the territory assigned to the Emperor was to be at the disposal of the Resident.[21] The Emperor was to be left free regarding the distribution of money among the several members of his family, but the British Government was to be informed of the expenditure and the minister was required to present annually a detailed statement of all expenditure for the inspection of the Resident. He suggested the payment of a sum not less than thirty-six lakhs of rupees annually for the expenses of the Emperor.[22]

Scott did not live long enough to receive the Governor-General's reaction to his proposals. He died on September 27, 1804, on his way to Delhi from Lucknow to assume the charge of his new assignment. Consequently, Divid Ochterlony was confirmed on November 7, 1804 as the Resident in a permanent capacity.[23]

Ten days after this appointment, the Secretary to the Government despatched the first note of instructions to the Resident regarding the affairs of Delhi in which the guiding principles for the settlement with the Mughal Emperor were elaborately discussed.[24] In general, the Government was in agreement

---

[21] Lake to Wellesley, September 4, 1804: *sec. cons.*, March 7, 1805, No. 9, Encl. 1.
[22] *Ibid.*
[23] Edmonstone to Ochterlony, November 7, 1804: *sec. cons.*, November 29, 1804, No, 299.
[24] Edmonstone to Ochterlony, November 17, 1804: *sec. cons.*, November 29, 1804, No. 302.

with the principles and broad features of Colonel Scott's proposals. It was considered by the Government that the manner in which the Emperor and the royal family came under British protection, imposed no other obligation on the Government, except "to relieve them from the embarrassment, distress and degradation to which they were exposed under the oppressive control of the Marathas."[25] The mode of effecting this improvement, although entirely a question of expediency and convenience for the British Government, could show due regard for the prejudices and feelings of the Emperor. This is what Scott also had in view.

The most suitable arrangement according to the Government, was "to continue the assignment for the expenses of the royal household of all the territories and resources assigned for that purpose under the authority of the Marathas, excepting such as may be situated within the Doab and such as it may be necessary to maintain on the right bank of the Jamna, for the security of the navigation of that river and for the protection of the frontier." Should there be "difference between the produce of those territories and resources and the amount which may be deemed to constitute an ample provision for the dignity and comfort of His Majesty and the royal family," it could be supplied by pecuniary payments.[26] The Governor-General did not visualize that these territories and resources would yield a revenue sufficient enough to maintain the Emperor and the royal family in a condition of dignity, affluence and comfort. It was left to the Resident to suggest a reasonable amount to meet the expenses of the royal household. But he was positive "that the money should be fixed and not liable for fluctuation according to the actual produce of the assigned territories and resources, excepting in special cases to be referred specifically on their occurrence to the decision of the British Government."[27] No written engagement was to be executed with the Emperor[28] as he was not directly involved in the military operation at Delhi.

[25] Edmonstone to Ochterlony, November 17, 1804, *op. cit.*
[26] *Ibid.*, para 5.
[27] Edmonstone to Ochterlony, November 17, 1804, *op. cit.*, paras 6 to 10.
[28] *Ibid.*, para 20.

SETTLEMENT WITH THE MUGHAL HOUSE

He was looked on as a prize of war.[29] The Resident was entrusted with the task of evolving the details of the arrangement within the framework of the general principles laid down by the Government.[30] In deference to the former dignity of the Mughal House Ochterlony suggested an annual payment of Rs. 15,55,000 to the Emperor and the royal household and a sum of Rs. 10,000 to His Majesty on all important festivals.[31] He was, however, not in favour of assigning any territory to the Emperor.[32] He repeatedly urged the Government not to adopt such a course as the Emperor could not evidently manage the territory and ultimately his underlings would be the real beneficiaries.[33] Lord Lake, too, had evinced the same opinion very much earlier.[34] The Supreme Government at Calcutta was, however, in favour of assigning the territory to the Emperor. Ochterlony, at last, under sheer desperation suggested that at least the control of the assigned territories should vest with the Resident.[35] which was ultimately agreed to by the Government.[36]

On the question of the stipend the proposal of Ochterlony

---

[29] Lake to Wellesley, September 4, 1804, *sec. cons.*, March 7, 1805, No. 9, Encl. 1, para 2, and Edmonstone to Ochterlony, November 17, 1804, *op. cit.*, para 2.

[30] Edmonstone to Ochterlony, November 17, 1804; *sec. cons.*, November 29, 1804, No. 302, para 19.

[31] Ochterlony to Edmonstone, November 30, 1804, *sec. cons.*, January 31, 1805, No. 218. The distribution of the amount suggested by Ochterlony per month was as follows: His Majesty's private expenses: Rs. 1,00,000 ; the heir-apparent: Rs. 10,000; Mirza Izzat Buksh, the second son by His Majesty's favourite wife, Mubarak Mahal: 5,000; Mirza Monym Bukht: 1,000; His Majesty's brother: 500; nearly fifty younger sons and daughters of His Majesty @ 200 each total 10,000; Shah Nawaz Khan: 2,500. Total; Rs. 1,29, 000 p.m.

[32] Ochterlony to Edmonstone, November 30, 1804: *op. cit.*, & Ochterlony to Edmonstone, December 1, 1804: *sec. cons.*, January 31, 1805, No. 227.

[33] Ochterlony to Edmonstone, December 8, 1804, *sec. cons.*, January 31, 1805, No. 230.

[34] Lake to Wellesley, September 4, 1804, *sec. cons.*, March 7, 1805, No. 9, Encl. 1, Marginal note by Lord Lake.

[35] Ochterlony to G.G., February 9, 1805: *sec. cons.*, March 28, 1805, No. 168.

[36] Lumsden, Chief Secretary., to Ochterlony, May 23, 1805: *sec. cons..* June 20, 1805, No. 422.

was not accepted in its entirety. After due consideration of the various suggestions at hand the Government decided to pay a monthly sum of Rs. 90,000 to the Emperor.[37] This decision differed from the proposal of Ochterlony mainly in respect of the provision allotted to His Majesty for his private expenses. The Government reduced Rs. 40,000 under this head from the amount proposed by him. The total difference was only Rs. 39,000 as a provision of Rs. 1,000 was made by the Government for Syed Reza Khan. The Governor-General also approved of a provision for the enhancement of the stipend to one lakh of rupees in future, if the revenue from the assigned terrritory would admit of it.[38] In addition to the stipend, the Emperor was to receive a sum of Rs. 10,000 on the occasion of religious festivals like *Jeshur, Id, Naurauz, Basant, Holi,* and *Ramzan.*[39]

This arrangement fully explains the British attitude towards the Emperor. As early as 1803 Wellesley had suggested the removal of the Emperor to some station in the south-eastern provinces, preferably Monghyr, if it could be effected without injuring his feelings.[40] Though this was not pressed into execution, it suggests the working of the Governor-General's mind. The removal of the Emperor from the imperial palace would have put an end to all his pretensions and prerogatives of sovereignty by a single stroke. When this could not be carried out in the manner then contemplated, the settlement of 1805 almost attained the same goal. The grant of a fixed allowance sufflcient for the convenience and comfort of the royal household, relegated the Emperor to the position of a stipendiary and in conseqince the British Government assumed the role of imperial protector.[41]

[37] Lumsden to Ochterlony, May 23, 1805, *op. cit.* The amount was to be distributed as follows: To His Majesty for his private expenses: Rs. 60,000; To the heir-apparent exclusive of the revenues of his Jagir: Rs. 10,000; To Mirza Izzat Buksh : Rs. 5,000; To Mirza Monym Bukht: Rs. 1,000; To His Majesty's brother : Rs. 500; To His Majesty's fifty younger sons and daughters : Rs. 200 each, total Rs. 10,000; To Shah Nawaz Khan: Rs. 2,500; To Syed Reza Khan. : Rs. 1,000. Total Rs. 90,000.
[38] Lumsden to Ochterlony, May 23, 1805, *op. cit.*
[39] *Ibid.*
[40] Wellesley to Lake, July 27, 1803: *sec. cons.*, March 2, 1804, No. 6.
[41] Wellesley to Shah Alam, October 8, 1803: *sec. cons.*, March 2, 1804, No. 115.

SETTLEMENT WITH THE MUGHAL HOUSE

While establishing the relationship of the protector and the protected, the Government was not unmindful of the former glory of the Imperial Mughals. Any injury to the feelings of the Emperor was to be avoided by all possible means without sacrificing the interests and prestige of the British. Colonel Scott had recommended a high degree of respect and conciliatory attitude towards him. He had even gone to the extent of suggesting that the Resident should endeavour to support and exalt the imperial dignity and authority, transact all business as far as possible with the responsible ministers and avoid, except in the last extremity, personal altercation with the Emperor.[42] Shah Alam was allowed to maintain a royal durbar and other manifestations of royalty inside the palace. The Resident was instructed not "to interdict or oppose any of those outward forms of sovereignty to which His Majesty has been accustomed, as the Governor-General was desirous of leaving His Majesty in the unmolested exercise of all his usual privileges and prerogatives."[43] He was also instructed to observe towards the Emperor all the forms of respect considered to be due to the Emperor of Hindustan and to promote the ease and comfort of the royal family.[44]

The paradoxical nature of this relationship was too apparent. The stipendiary position of the Emperor made him subservient to, and dependent upon, the British Government. As such, he was to be a nonentity in the political life of the country. At the same time he was to receive the respects due to the Emperor of Hindustan inside the palace. He could hold durbar, enjoy immunity from law, and could maintain all the facade of sovereignty. The limitation of his prerogatives to the four walls of the palace was certainly difficult to accomplish, and this both the Government and the Emperor realized in the near future.

Reaction of the Emperor

The Emperor was very much disappointed at the provision

---

[42] Lake to Wellesley, September 4, 1804: *sec. cons.*, March 7, 1805, No. 9, Encl. 1, para 16.
[43] Edmonstone to Ochterlony, November 17, 1804, *op. cit.*, para 20.
[44] *Ibid.*, para 21.

made for his maintenance and dignity.⁴⁵ Ochterlony knew very well that even the arrangement proposed by him would fall very short of the of the Emperor's expectations.⁴⁶ The Government did not take a serious view of the Emperor's disappointment and considered it as arising from his unreasonable expectations rather than due to the insufficiency of the provision made for him.⁴⁷ The Governor-General, however, considered the entire arrangement as a temporary one.⁴⁸

The Emperor agreed to distribute the stipend according to the instructions of the Government but desired that the amount be handed over to him directly without any intimation to the other members of the royal family. The object of this solicitation was to appropriate a larger share for his personal expenses and make his dependents feel their obligations to him rather than look to the British Government as the benefactor.⁴⁹ Ochterlony promised to comply with this request.⁵⁰ The Emperor further pressed that the amount of Rs. 10,000 sanctioned for each of the seven festivals in a year be commuted into Rs. 6,000 per mensem. This would enable him to distribute this sum in small portions to the members of the royal family, exclusive of his immediate offsprings.⁵¹ Ochterlony knew that this was "a sacrifice on the part of His Majesty for the conciliation of individuals in the *zenana*", and hoped that this small addition to his stipend could be made without affecting the amount reserved for the various festivals.⁵² The Governor-General permitted the Resi-

⁴⁵ H.M. to G.G., dated nil: *sec. cons.*, July 29, 1805, No. 158.
⁴⁶ Ochterlony to G.G., July 1, 1805: *sec. cons.*, July 29, 1805, No. 157.
⁴⁷ Lumsden to Ochterlony, July 29, 1805, *sec. cons.*, July 29, 1845, No. 6.
⁴⁸ The Chief Secretary to the Government wrote very categorically: "The extent of the provision assigned for His Majesty's personal expenses has been regulated by the state of our resources under immediate pressure of the exigencies of war and the Governor-General-in-Council will be disposed to augment that provision when these exigencies shall cease to exist." *Ibid*.
⁴⁹ Ochterlony to G.G., August 26, 1805: *sec. cons.*, February 13, 1806, No. 80.
⁵⁰ Ochterlony to G. G., August 26, 1805: *sec. cons.*, September 12, 1805, No. 18.
⁵¹ Ochterlony to Cornwallis, August 26, 1805, *op. cit.*
⁵² Ochterlony to Barlow, Vice-President-in-Council, August 26, 1805: *sec. cons.*, September 12, 1805, No. 17.

SETTLEMENT WITH THE MUGHAL HOUSE

dent to comply with the wish of the Emperor and a monthly sum of Rs. 6,000 was added to the stipend.[53] But this did not satisfy the heir-apparent and his mother to whom the amount was handed over for distribution in the *zenana*.[54]

The Emperor had by now realized the position to which the British Government had relegated him, and he therefore desperately struggled to assert his superiority over the British. To Shah Alam, who still remembered the resplendent glory of the great Mughals, the stipendiary position under the protection of the British was an anathema. The non-payment of the six lakhs of rupees earlier promised by Wellesley further embittered his feelings. The stipend allotted to the Emperor, though a comparatively resonable amount for his personal expenses, was not as large as it appeared to be, for, he was not only to provide for his immediate dependants, but also for the whole "tribe of relatives or royal collaterals" who resided in the fort as virtual prisoners, depending entirely on him for support and clinging tenaciously to their royal privileges. Ochterlony, who was "convinced that His Majesty's satisfaction was a grand object in the Governor-General's wishes"[55] noticed with alarm the growth of disaffection and dissatisfaction inside the palace.

The members of the royal household, who were aware of the liberal provision assigned to the Nawab of Bengal, expected an augmentation of the allowances on the conclusion of the war and the consequent improvement of the financial condition of the Government.[56] Ochterlony at the earliest opportunity apprised the Government of their expectation and suggested the payment of at least fifteen lakhs of rupees per annum. This he believed would afford them the greatest satisfaction and impress on them the most favourable opinion of British munificence.[57]

Removal of Ochterlony

While Ochterlony was thus trying to settle the complica-

---

[53] Ochterlony to Edmonstone, June 13, 1806; *see. cons.*, February 6, 1806, No. 54.
[54] *Ibid.*
[55] Ochterlony to G.G., May 30, 1805; *sec, cons.*, May 16, 1805, No. 24.
[56] Ochterlony to Edmonstone, June 13, 1806, *op. cit.*
[57] Ochterlony to Edmonstone, June 13, 1806, *op. cit.*

ted affairs of the royal palace, the news of his removal and the appointment of Archibald Seton as the Resident in January 1806 came to him as a bolt from the blue.[58] He felt highly embittered and took his removal as a reflection on his character as a public servant.[59] In a frantic letter he complained to his benefactor,[60] Lord Lake, to whom he owed his appointment of the Resident after the fall of Delhi. Lord Lake immediately wrote to the Governor-General requesting him to reconsider the whole matter. He testified in strong terms to the "uncommon activity, intelligence and gallantry of Ochterlony."[61]

The Governor-General, however, had made up his mind. By now the character of the office of the Resident at Delhi had considerably changed. In 1803 when Ochterlony was appointed the Resident, "that situation required to a peculiar degree the exercise of military knowledge and talents."[62] Now the political interests of the British Government in Hindustan exclusively devolved on the Resident at Delhi. Consequently, that situation involved the performance of civil and political duties of a very extensive and important nature. So the Governor-General thought it necessary to appoint an experienced civil servant to that office.[63]

Ochterlony was repeatedly assured by the Government that his removal did not amount to any disapprobation of his management of public affairs. But he did not feel quite at ease with the change. It is true that when he was appointed in 1803 the duties of the Resident were more military than civillent

[58] Adam to Ochterlony, January 27, 1806: *sec. cons.*, March 6, 1806, No. 3.
[59] Ochterlony to Lord Lake, February 12, 1806: *sec. cons.*, March 6, 1806, No. 2.
[60] *Ibid.*
[61] Lord Lake to G. G., February 14, 1806: *sec. cons.*, March 6, 1806, No. 1. Lord Lake wrote to the Governor-General, "I feel it unnecessary to enter into a further detail of the important services of this valuable officer, who in every situation that I have known him has been alike distinguished for zeal, honour and ability and I consider it a duty on the present occasion to state that there is no individual to whose personal exertion I have been more deeply indebted for that success which has attended my late efforts in the public service."
[62] Edmonstone to Ochterlony, February 20, 1806: *sec. cons.*, February 27, 1806, No. 60.
[63] *Ibid.*

SETTLEMENT WITH THE MUGHAL HOUSE

with the transfer of political powers from Lord Lake to the Resident at Delhi on the conclusion of the second Anglo-Maratha war, this charge became very important, as the management of British relations with the states of Rajputana and the Cis-Sutlej states devolved on the Resident at Delhi.[64] In the opinion of the Government a senior civil servant with a mature understanding of political affairs was preferable to a military officer. But Ochterlony as the Resident at Delhi neither showed any lack of understanding of the policy of the British Government, nor any indifference to its true interests. Military exigencies also did not demand his presence in any other part of the country. In fact, the Governor-General found it difficult to offer him an equal situation in the army.[65] It may be mentioned that later on Ochterlony was given political assignments at Ludhiana, Delhi, and Rajputana in turn. The character of these assignments was then equally important, if not more as the 1806 appointment. The question naturally arises why the Governor-General was prompted to remove him from the post at Delhi without strong justification. After the exit of Wellesley a marked bias was evident in the Supreme Government against military officers holding civil posts. Sir George Barlow, a civilian from Madras, naturally preferred a civilian to a military officer to manage the important office of the Delhi Resident. Consequently, Seton took charge of the Residency on June 25, 1806.[66]

---

[64] *Ibid.*
[65] G.G.'s minute, June 5, 1806: *sec. cons.*, June 5, 1806, No. 46.
[66] Seton to Edmonstone, June 25, 1806; *pol. cons.*, July 17, 1806, No. 21.

3
Appointment of the Heir-Apparent

SHAH ALAM died on November 19, 1806 and his eldest son, Akbar Shah, succeeded to the throne on the very next day.[1] The accession of Akbar Shah II created a plethora of complicated problems. The most important of these was the question of the appointment of the heir-apparent. The natural choice to the office, according to the law of primogeniture upheld by the British Government, fell on Abu Zafar, the eldest son of the Emperor. He was easily the best among the royal children: an accomplished poet and a skilled calligraphist; a good marksman and archer; and indeed without major blemishes in character. Akbar Shah, however, was not favourably inclined to his nomination primarily due to the influence of his favourite wife, Mumtaz Mahal, who possessed an inordinate passion for power and an unique capacity for intrigue. She wanted her son, Mirza Jahangir, to occupy the position of the heir-apparent, and in order to satisfy her desire the Emperor decided to overlook the claims of Abu Zafar. Consequently, Jahagir was honoured with a few articles which belonged to the rank and station of the heir-apparent. This was naturally construed by the palace circles as a clear indication of the Emperor's preference in the matter of succession.[2]

On December 17, 1806, in a letter to the Resident the Emperor expressed in laudatory terms the excellent qualities of Mirza Jahangir, which induced him to bestow honours upon the Prince and prefer him for appointment as the heir-apparent to

---

[1] Rumours were afoot about the intentions of Mirza Izzat Buksh, the second son of Shah Alam, to contest the title to the throne against his elder brother. The Resident immediately took necessary military precautions for the suppression of any breach of peace. There was, however, no untoward incident and the succession of Akbar Shah was a smooth affair. Seton to Edmonstone, November 26, 1806: *sec. cons.*, December 18, 1806, No. 21.

[2] *Ibid.*

his elder brother.³ This move, according to Seton, had disastrous implications. It could give rise to intrigues and mutual jeolousy among the royal princes, and create the possibility of internicine feuds, notorious in the annals of the Mughal House. The Resident thought it to be a bounden duty of the British Government as the paramount power to forestall such a possibility. He advised the Emperor to refer the matter to the Governor-General and secure his concurrence before the Emperor took a final decision on this important issue. He should not be, Seton thought, swayed by his partiality to the Prince, or by the intrigues of Mumtaz Mahal.⁴ He, however, did not consider the Emperor to be bold enough, in spite of the petty coat influence and the intrigues in the palace, to take a final decision till the sentiments of the British Government were made known to him.⁵ The Governor-General also thought it "extremely improbable that the Emperor would take a positive step in this matter without previously ascertaining the wishes of the British Government."⁶ The prediction of the Resident and the belief of the Governor-General came true when the suggestion of the Resident was accepted by the Emperor.⁷ He agreed to refer the matter to the Governor-General for advice before taking a definite step.⁸ The Governor-General, prompted as he was by a "sincere regard for the law of primogeniture and the peace and welfare of the royal family," was not in favour of anyone else besides the eldest prince "on whom the station and dignity of the heir-apparent devolved by right."⁹ But the Muslim law extends no recognition to the principle of primogeniture in the matter of succession to the state. The Emperor therefore

[3] H.M. to Seton, received on December 11, 1806: *sec. cons.*, January 8, 1807, No. 14.
[4] Seton to H.M., December 18, 1806: *sec. cons.*, January 8, 1807, No. 14.
[5] Seton to Edmonstone, December 19, 1806: *sec. cons.*, January 8, 1807, No. 13.
[6] Edmonstone to Seton, December 18, 1806: *sec. cons.*, December 18, 1806, No. 25.
[7] Seton to Edmonstone, December 23, 1806: *sec. cons.*, January 8, 1807, No. 16.
[8] H.M. to Seton, December 23, 1806: *sec. cons.*, January 8, 1807, No. 17.
[9] Edmonstone to Seton, January 2, 1807: *sec. cons.*, January 8, 1807, No. 15.

insisted on his right to nominate his successor, a practice sanctioned by usage and law. The British Government was in no case prepared to countenance a measure that would disrupt the cordial relations of the royal princes and threaten the peace of the royal family. Understandably enough, the Emperor resented the attempt of the British Government to impose an alien rule in a matter which to his mind was purely a family affair. He considered it his right to decide all matters connected with the royal family,[10] whereas the Governor-General did not entertain any doubt about the right of the British Government to interfere in the affairs of the Emperor, either personal or political in nature.[11]

These conflicting attitudes considerably strained the relations between the British Government and Akbar Shah. All requests and representations of the Emperor were turned down in a manner which convinced him about the futility of such endeavours. The royal palace now became the arena of active intrigues in which Mumtaz Mahal, Qudsia Begam, the Emperor's mother, and Daulat-ul-Nisa Begum, his paternal aunt, were the major participants. This junta, bent on securing the office of the heir-apparent for Mirza Jahangir, had a pernicious influence on the Emperor. They indulged in vigorous manoeuvres to discredit Abu Zafar in the eyes of the British Government and removing him from the run by fair or foul means. Overcome by their vile influence, the Emperor accused Abu Zafar of having seduced one of his wives during the time of Shah Alam.[12] The Resident was mortified to learn of so foul and odious an accusation preferred by a father against his son. He received this information very cautiously as he was aware that the palace faction was avowedly hostile to the succession of Abu Zafar.[13] He decided to ascertain the truth of the charge and insisted upon the Emperor "to institute an investigation as it appeared necessary to forbear condemning without clear conviction of guilt."[14] He urged that the Prince should get the justice and

[10] H.M. to G.G., January 5, 1807: *sec. cons.*, January 8, 1807, No. 18.
[11] Edmonstone to Seton, December 18, 1806, *op. cit.*
[12] Seton to Edmonstone, February 7, 1807: *sec. cons.*, February 26, 1807, No. 25.
[13] *Ibid.*
[14] Seton to Edmonstone, March 19, 1807: *sec. cons.*, April 9, 1807, No. 1.

APPOINTMENT OF THE HEIR-APPARENT

opportunity to which even the meanest and most guilty of the Emperor's subjects were entitled. He suggested that the Prince himself could be examined and his explanations compared with the sworn dispositions of the respectable, disinterested, and well-informed persons in the palace. He offered his assistance in the enquiry and even to conduct it in the presence of any person appointed by the Emperor in case he agreed. The Emperor was not prepared to sanction such an enquiry "as the relation in which the Prince stood with respect to His Majesty, precluded the possibility of having recourse to the ordinary forms observed in similar cases."[15] The refusal of the Emperor to provide an opportunity to the Prince to defend himself betrayed the hollowness of the charge.

Seton, however, exerted to verify the validity of this accusation. In course of his personal investigation he found that neither the Europeans nor the citizens of Delhi, not entangled in the intrigues of the palace, knew anything about it. Colonel Ochterlony, the former Resident, who invariably received detailed information of all the occurrences in the palace was also ignorant about it, though he had heard about the illicit relations of Abu Zafar with one of the female attendants of Mumtaz Mahal.[16] The accusation preferred against him was nothing but a product of the palace machinations and intrigues. The Resident, therefore, declined to accept it as a valid ground for quashing the legitimate claim of the Prince.

The palace junta refused to be outwitted so easily. To defeat the intentions of the British Government to uphold the rule of primogeniture, they obtained a declaration from Abu Zafar to the effect that considering the Emperor's preference for his brother, Jahangir, he had "voluntarily and cheerfully resigned his claims to be the heir-apparent".[17] This was conveyed to the Resident in the form of a paper signed and sealed by the Prince through Abul Kasim, the confidential messenger of the Emperor. The Resident, well posted with the intrigues of the palace, refused to accept the deed as really voluntary on the part of the Prince. He had also become apprehensive of the intentions of the Empe-

---

[15] *Ibid.*
[16] *Ibid.*
[17] *Ibid.*, para 6.

ror and decided to ascertain the truth from Abu Zafar by obtaining an interview from him. The Prince declared that he had executed the paper voluntarily, and that he was far from repenting of it. The Resident was still not satisfied and decided to interview the Prince once again at a later date in order to give him ample time for reconsideration.[18] The result of the second interview, too, was nothing different from the first, as the Prince was not inclined to revise his former decision.[19] The Resident, however, was not convinced and believed that the resignation was obtained under the direct pressure of the Emperor. His belief came true when he was informed ultimately by the Prince that the deed of relinquishment was obtained from him under pressure and compulsion.[20]

In spite of energetic endeavours by the Resident, the Emperor was not prepared to set aside the deed of relinquishment executed by the Prince. His mind was made up in favour of Mirza Jahangir. To the Resident, however, the entire matter stood on a different footing. Even if Abu Zafar relinquished his claims, he did not consider Jahangir as the next incumbent. He proposed to the Emperor to consider Mirza Buland Bukht, the second son, in case Abu Zafar was not desirous of being considered for the office. The reaction of the Emperor to this proposal was more derogatory to himself than to the person whom it was meant to vilify. The Emperor confessed that Buland Bukht was illegitimate and could not therefore be considered for the exalted office of the heir-apparent.[21] But the British Government did not regard illegitimacy as a serious disqualification for succession to the Mughal throne for it was overlooked more than once in the past.

Akbar Shah was now convinced beyond any shadow of doubt about the futility of his attempts to get the concurrence of the British Government to his wishes on the question of *walli ahdi*. He, therefore, decided to invest Mirza Jahangir with the dignity of heir-apparent on April 23, 1807 without waiting

[18] *Ibid.*, para 9.
[19] *Ibid.*, para 10.
[20] *Ibid.*, para 12.
[21] It was said that the mother of Buland Bakht had become pregnant even before she was admitted to the palace.

APPOINTMENT OF THE HEIR-APPARENT

for the acquiescence of the British Government, and requested the Resident to arrange the payment of the allowance of the heir-apparent to Prince Jahangir.[22] This unilateral decision, bold but lamentable, met with the undaunted opposition from the British Government. The appointment of an heir-apparent at this stage when the Emperor was in perfect health was deemed unnecessary as well as inconsistant with the usages of the Mughal House.[23] The Resident therefore induced the Emperor to postpone the investiture at least, if he was not prepared to abandon it altogether.[24]

The Emperor then tried to win the support of the Resident to his cause through the medium of the ladies of the palace. On March 20, 1807, three days after the announcement of the Emperor's decision, Qudsia Begam, Daulat-ul-Nisa Begam, and Mumtaz Mahal met the Resident in the presence of the Emperor.[25] The purpose of this meeting was to impress upon him the intensity of the feelings of the Emperor on the whole issue. During her long conversation, Qudsia Begam dwelt upon the comparative situation of the British Government and the Emperor and pleaded for the fulfilment of the various demands of the latter.[26] The Resident vehemently opposed them. He intimated the ladies that the attempts to elevate Mirza Jahangir to the status of the heir-apparent was inexpedient and "inconsistent with the principles of justice and established usage."[27]

The Emperor, though convinced about the justness of his

---

[22] H.M. to Seton, received on March 17, 1807: *sec. cons.*, April 19, 1807, No. 3.
[23] G.G. to H.M., April 4, 1807: *sec. cons.*, April 9, 1807, No. 7.
[24] Seton to Edmonstone, March 19, 1807, *op. cit.*, para 16.
[25] Seton to Edmonstone, March 21, 1807: *sec. cons.*, April 9, 1807, No. 5, para 2.
[26] The demands of the Emperor as expressed by Qudsia Begam were as follows:—(i) Prince Jahangir to be acknowledged as the heir-apparent by the British Government. (ii) The stipend of Rs. 7,000 per month attached to the office of the heir-apparent and enjoyed by His Majesty while he held this office, to be restored. (iii) The stipend formerly enjoyed by the late Shah Nawaz Khan as Khilledar to be restored, and be at the disposal of His Majesty. (iv) An augmentation to be made to the royal stipend. *Ibid.*, para 3.
[27] *Ibid.*

cause, was helpless in the face of this opposition.[28] He neither the means nor the courage to oppose the wishes of the British Government. He therefore agreed to postpone the investiture till the beginning of *Rabia-ul-Awal*, hoping to obtain the compliance of the Governor-General by that time.[29] The Resident, however, insisted that none other than Abu Zafar could be named as the heir-apparent, in case it became necessary.[30]

The attitudes of the Emperor and the British Government on the question of *walli ahdi* brought into sharper relief the status of the Emperor in relation to the British Government. Lord Wellesley had undoubtedly relegated him to the position of a stipendiary and made the British Government appear as his protector and not as his servant as was the case with the Marathas and the French. But due regard was shown towards his personal comfort and feelings. The Governor-General, though with reluctance, allowed him a certain ostentation of sovereignty inside the palace. In the Durbar the representative of the British Government stood before him in obeisance, but outside the palace the British Government was the sovereign power. The Emperor, in fact, had become a complete nonentity in the political life of the country.

As far as Shah Alam was concerned, he, however, did not resign to the superior status of the British Government. He accepted British protection in 1803 as no other convenient alternative was open to him, and he felt that it did not mean an abject submission to the British authority. His intention was to preserve the status of paramountcy, at least in name, which his ancestors had enjoyed for more than two centuries. Lord Wellesley was opposed to the acceptance of any other position for the British Government than that of a benevolent protector. The Emperor, had neither the boldness nor the resources to assert his intentions or offer opposition to the wishes of the British Government though he was aware of the attitude of the Governor-General. But in all his communications he addressed the Governor-General "his most favoured son and devoted servant". Lord Wellesley did not object to it as it was considered a source of satisfaction

---

[28] H.M. to G.G., March 21, 1807: *sec. cons.*, April 9, 1807, No. 6.
[29] *Ibid.*
[30] *Ibid.*, para 12.

APPOINTMENT OF THE HEIR-APPARENT

to the Emperor. Colonel Ochterlony, with all his veneration for the past glory of the Timurids, did not realize the possible consequences of the indulgence allowed to Shah Alam and sound the Government about his true intentions.

In effect, the Emperor gained by implication all that Wellesley wanted to deny. By addressing the Governor-General as his servant, he claimed a superior status. The title conferred on Lord Lake, the second highest in the Empire, also signified a similar situation. The Emperor had then proclaimed that the highest title could not be conferred on Lake as it had already been bestowed on Sindhia. By this he meant to treat the British on par with the Marathas who were considered only servants and not superiors. In practice, however, the Emperor was only a stipendiary without any freedom of action. But a certain show of sovereignty enjoyed by him gave a different impression. Shah Alam tenaciously clung to it and Akbar Shah attempted to give it a wider interpretation.

Akbar Shah was vigorous, energetic, and, above all: ambitious. Unlike his father, who had all his faculties completely impaired, he was in the prime of his life. The British yoke imposed on his predecessor was extremely galling to him. He had dim recollections of the days when his ancestors ruled over the country like mighty potentates and entertained hopes of restoring the past glory and independence of his House. The ladies of the palace, particularly Mumtaz Mahal and her adherents, did much to inflame his ambition.

The issue of the appointment of the heir-apparent, Akbar Shah realized, could be used as a means to assert his imperial pretensions. Hence his determination not to accept any person other than Mirza Jahangir as the heir-apparent. He communicated this decision to the Governor-General along with his intention to execute it without further delay.[31] This move of the Emperor was incompatible with his real situation, as conceived by the British Government, and it was necessary in the interest of the Government to restrain him.[32] "The consequence of yielding in any degree to such pretensions", wrote Edmonstone, "must be of a nature highly embarrassing and even

---

[31] H.M. to G.G., April 2, 1807: *sec. cons.*, April 9, 1807, No. 1.
[32] Edmonstone to Seton, April 6, 1807: *sec. cons.*, April 9, 1807, No. 8-C.

dangerous to the British Government and this consideration alone constitutes a forcible argument for resiting with firmness all the demands which His Majesty has lately preferred in a manner highly objectionable. It is evident that the argument of respectful persuasion, urged under an apparent admission of His Majesty's imperial rights are calculated rather to encourage than to restrain his pretensions and it becomes necessary that His Majesty should be required to submit to that condition of dependence on which the royal household has been placed by the revolution of affairs.[33] The Resident was, hence, instructed to oppose sternly all attempts of the Emperor to adopt Mirza Jahangir as the heir-apparent. It was, however, believed that he would not conduct the investiture against the declared opposition of the British Government.[34]

The attitude adopted by the Emperor in this issue questioned the very foundation of the principles governing the relations between him and the British Government, which the latter was eager to maintain. The Governor-General was convinced that the Emperor was endeavouring to shake off his dependence upon the British power and to assume in some degree the exercise of regal authority.[35] The intentions of the Emperor to be enthroned in the city of Agra, from which he was dissuaded with great difficulty by the Resident, and to make distant excursions from Delhi,[36] were considered a part of his strategy to assert his sovereignty.[37] The Government felt that the attempts of the Emperor to obtain a degree of ascendancy and latitude of independent action could "lead to consequences of the most serious embarrassment and even danger to the interests of the British Government in India."[38]

The Governor-General attributed this change in the attitude of the Emperor partly to the passive and submissive conduct of Seton. He was apprehensive that "the general tenure of the Resident's demeanour towards His Majesty might

[33] *Ibid.*, para 3.
[34] *Ibid.*, para 5.
[35] Edmonstone to Seton, April 9, 1807: *sec. cons.*, April 9, 1807, No. 8-D.
[36] Seton to Edmonstone, March 23, 1807, *sec. cons.*, April 9, 1807, No. 8-B.
[37] Edmonstone to Seton, April 9, 1807, *op. cit.*
[38] *Ibid.*

have tended to encourage in his mind notions of sovereignty and independence inconsistent with his real condition and calculated to excite latent projects of ambition."[39] This necessitated marked change in the conduct and behaviour of the Resident towards the Emperor. Firm attitude, decided address, and strict vigilance were suggested. Seton was instructed to observe due distinction between the reality of passive submission and the forms of external respect and to maintain effectual control without violating the laws of decorum.[40] He was to impress on the Emperor the expectations of the British Government regarding his conduct and behaviour in the light of "the present condition of His Majesty and the royal family" as compared to "the state of distress, degradation and control from which they have been permanently relieved by the arms and humanity of the British power."[41] The medium of Qudsia Begam, Daulat-ul-Nisa Begam, and Mumtaz Mahal who had decided influence on the Emperor,[42] could be conveniently used for this purpose. In case this did not produce the desired effect, the Resident was empowered to "suggest an arrangement for establishing an effectual control over the conduct of the Emperor, if the circumstances so warranted."[43] With all his conciliatory policy, even Sir George Barlow did not favour relaxation in British control over the Mughal House.

The admonition to Seton for his conduct and demeanour towards the Emperor shocked him beyond expectation. In the performance of public duties, his devotion was exemplary. He scrupulously discharged his responsibilities with full regard to the policy of the Government and avoided all that appeared inconsistent with it.[44] It is, however, true that he showed consideration bordering at times on veneration for the Mughal House and its unlucky master. He could not succeed in reconciling the Janus faced policy of submission and obeisance inside the palace, where the Emperor held the mock Court, and virtual

---

[39] Ibid.
[40] Ibid.
[41] G.G. to H.M., April 4, 1807: *sec. cons.*, April 9, 1807, No. 7.
[42] Edmonstone to Seton, April 9, 1807, *op. cit.*
[43] *Ibid.*, para 10.
[44] Seton to Edmonstone, April 21, 1807: *sec. cons.*, May 7, 1807, No. 1.

non-recognition outside. His was, in fact, an ardous task rendered the more difficult by the double standards adopted by the Supreme Government at Calcutta. The meek, straight-forward, and kind-hearted Seton was toiling in the Residency from the early hours of the day till midnight, foregoing very frequently breakfast and lunch[45] for evolving an acceptable solution for the tangled affairs of the royal family. With the disappointed and disgruntled Emperor, craving always for more money and freedom of action, an avaricious and unscrupulous swarm of people inside the palace lying in wait for attaining their self-interests by hook or by crook, and an unruly and rebellious prince with ambitions of high office—Seton had all the difficulties in the world to face. His generosity and sympathy towards the House of Timurids stood in his way of suggesting and adopting a stern attitude. He was striving to find out a feasible solution that would uphold the interests of the Government that he served and at the same time not injure the feelings of His Majesty. The reprobation of the Government gave him a serious jolt. He believed that his "attentive and respectful manner" towards the Emperor made a favourable impression and "tended to establish in his mind, a species of influence which under certain circumstances, might be found beneficial."[46] He wrote: "I believe the Emperor to be persuaded that I have his happiness and interest much at heart and it forcibly strikes me that this conviction would greatly facilitate the success of any remonstrance which it might become my duty to make to him, even though they should be contrary to his wishes."[47] The apprehension of the Governor-General was precisely the same. He was wondering whether the Resident entertained more consideration for the happiness and prosperity of the Emperor than was actually necessary.

The British Government, it appeared, was in a precarious situation. In principle it had decided to put an end to the fiction of the sovereignty of the Mughal Emperor in its all possible implications. A blatant exercise of power, however,

---

[45] Metcalfe to Sherar, October 25, 1806; John William Kaye: *The Life and Correspondence of Charles, Lord Metcalfe*, i, p. 147.

[46] Seton to Edmonstone, April 24, 1807: *sec. cons.*, May 14, 1807, No. 1.

[47] *Ibid.*

APPOINTMENT OF THE HEIR-APPARENT

was not contemplated. The prerogatives of sovereignty enjoyed by the Emperor were intended to be discouraged by slow degrees. During the interregnum between Lord Wellesley and Hastings, the implementation of this policy was not very clear. The goal was marked but not the means. This became evident from the incongruity in the spirit of the instructions of the Governor-General to the Resident and also from his letter addressed to the Emperor. On April 4, 1807 the Governor-General, in a letter to the Emperor, expressed his anxiety to fulfil the wishes of the latter and entreated him to act in conformity with the wishes of the British Government.[48] On April 6, 1807 in his instructions to the Resident, the Governor-General chose very strong words to express the opposition of the Government to the proposed intentions of the Emperor.[49] Had he adopted the same spirit, if not the same language, in his letter to the Emperor, it would have more easily induced the latter to act in conformity with the wishes of the Government. It would also have simplified the delicate task of the Resident, especially because the Emperor was labouring under an illusion that the opposition to his scheme had emanated from Seton. A meek and submissive letter to the Emperor on the one hand, and admonition, though mildly expressed, to the Resident on the other, clearly indicate some vacillation on the part of the Supreme Government.

Mission of Shah Haji

The mission of Shah Haji and Raja Sher Mal to Calcutta was the direct outcome of this policy. The apparent incongruity in the representation of the Resident and the letters of the Governor-General produced an impression in the mind of the Emperor that a direct appeal to the Governor-General would help to fulfil his ambition. Mumtaz Mahal and her adherents vigorously persuaded him to adopt such a line of action. Disappointed by the staunch opposition of the Government to his earlier effort to gain superiority, the Emperor was only marking time to try again. The first anniversary of his accession to the throne

---

[48] G.G. to H.M., April 4. 1807, *op. cit.*.
[49] Edmonstone to Seton, April 6, 1807, *op. cit.*.

provided the needed opportunity. On this occasion the Emperor intended to bestow *khilats* on "all the principal sardars connected with the Court of Delhi."[50] This was to commence by sending honorary dresses to the Governor-General and the Nawab Vazir of Awadh. Shah Haji, one of his confidential servants, was selected by the Emperor to present the *khilat* to the Governor-General at Calcutta.[51]

The object of this mission was threefold: to assert the sovereignty of the Emperor; to obtain the consent of the Governor-General to the appointment of Mirza Jahangir as the heir-apparent; and to effect an augmentation of the royal stipend.

The intention of the Emperor to distribute *khilats*, which is a prerogative of the sovereign power, was viewed with dubious suspicion and disapproval by the British Government as it could have implications incompatible with the real status of the Emperor.[52] Moreover, there was no precedent for it ever since Shah Alam accepted the protection of the British Government. According to the Governor-General, it was, "highly objectionable to grant *khilats* to princes and chiefs who were wholly unconnected with the throne of Delhi, but by nominal relation which in reality has long ceased to exist."[53]

The opposition of the Government to the proposed mission greatly distressed the Emperor. The endeavours of Seton to soothe his feelings by adverting to the innumerable hazards, particularly financial, involved in the execution of the mission did not prove effective.[54] He believed that the suspension of the mission would adversely affect his dignity and status as the mission had already gained wide publicity throughout the country. The Resident suggested that a declaration of the postponement of the mission could obviate any such untoward impression.[55] The Emperor, on the other hand, was convinced that a direct representation to the Governor-General would help to straighten his tangled affairs. He therefore made a counter-proposal.

[50] Seton to Edmonstone, June 14, 1807: *pol. cons.*, July 2, 1807, No. 14.
[51] Seton to Edmonstone, October 28, 1807: *pol. cons.*, November 16, 1807, No. 17.
[52] Seton to Edmonstone, June 14, 1807, *op. cit.*
[53] Edmonstone to Seton, July 2, 1807: *pol. cons.*, July 2, 1807, No. 15.
[54] H.M., to Seton, dated nil, *pol. cons.*, November 16, 1807, No. 19.
[55] Seton to H.M. October 25, 1807: *pol. cons.*, November 16, 1807, No. 20.

APPOINTMENT OF THE HEIR-APPARENT

He sought to depute Shah Haji in a private capacity and was asked not to carry the *khilat*, but to enquire about the health of the Governor-General, which is a form of expression of goodwill and friendship generally observed by the rulers throughout India.[56] This could deprive the mission of only one of its three aims viz., the assertion of sovereignty. The two others—the appointment of Mirza Jahangir as the heir-apparent and the augmentation of the royal stipend—could still be urged at Calcutta. This presumably induced the Emperor to drop the idea of investiture.

Seton was inclined to permit the mission in its changed character as it could be of help in removing certain misconceptions from the mind of the Emperor.[57] The palace junta had succeeded in convincing the Emperor that the Resident was the source of all mischief and opposition, and he was led to believe that the Governor-General was not even acquainted with his various demands.[58] The mission of Shah Haji could provide an opportunity to convince the Emperor that the Supreme Government at Calcutta in no way differed from the Resident. This would enhance the prestige of the Resident and would also facilitate his intercourse with the Emperor.[59] The Resident therefore requested the Governor-General not to object to the mission in its changed character. The Governor-General consented to it provided the Emperor did not insist on a formal reception of his agents as the representatives of an imperial power. They were welcome in a private capacity.[60] Accordingly, Shah Haji and Raja Sher Mal reached Calcutta on June 1, 1808.[61]

After reaching Calcutta, Shah Haji's endeavours were

[56] H.M. to Seton, dated nil, : *pol. cons.*, No. 16, 1807, No. 19.
[57] Seton to Edmonstone, November 1, 1807, *pol. cons.*, November 23, 1807, No. 20.
[58] When Seton informed the disapproval of the Government to the mission, the Emperor wrote to him: "State your answer in order that it may appear why our orders are not attended to by you and why you do not act according to our royal commands." H.M. to Seton, October 27, 1807: *pol. cons.*, November 16, 1807, No. 10.
[59] *Ibid.*
[60] *Letters to the Court of Directors (Pol.)* August 1, 1809.
[61] Monckton, Persian Secretary, to Seton, March 8, 1809: *pol. cons.*, March 13, 1809, No. 103, para 1.

directed to give a public character to the mission. He declared his intention to invest the Governor-General with a *khilat* on behalf of the Emperor in a manner calculated to represent the exercise of imperial authority by His Majesty. The acceptance of the *khilat* by the Governor-General would mean a solemn manifestation of the vassalage and submission of the British Government to the throne of Delhi.[62] This was to be followed by the conferment of honorary dresses to all the principal chiefs and princes of India. This, indeed, was a disavowal of the Emperor's earlier professions about the object of the mission. The Government considered it an extremely disingenuous move and, therefore, the attempts of Shah Haji to give the mission a public character were systematically resisted. His endeavours to appear before the public as a recognized ambassador of the Emperor met the same treatment. He was received as a confidential servant of the Emperor, accorded the honour of a private audience, and provided with accommodation at the public expense.[63] The Governor-General refused to accept the honorary dress in person, which was later received by the Persian Secretary on his behalf. The shawls from Qudsia Begam and Mumtaz Mahal were also refused as the Resident was not informed about these presents.[64] These, however, were accepted later on as the Governer-General did not find any material objection to that.

When Shah Haji's efforts to establish the status of the Emperor as the sovereign power were decidedly prevented by the Government, he turned his attention to the accomplishment of the other objects of the mission. In an interview with the Persian Secretary on June 23, 1808 he presented the various demands of the Emperor. The appointment of the heir-apparent and augmentation of the royal stipend were the most important of them. These demands, when earlier forwarded through the Resident, had already been refused by the Government. The subsequent endeavour to press them through the medium of a confidential servant was considered an attempt to ignore the

[62] *Ibid.*
[63] *Ibid.*
[64] Report of the Persian Secretary's conference with Shah Haji, June 23, 1808: *pol. cons.*, March 13, 1809, No. 102.

authority of the Resident. Morever, the Emperor had not proclaimed these intentions before the departure of the mission from Delhi. The acceptance of these demands in this manner would have been harmful to the influence and authority of the Resident, and consequently, injurious to the interests of the British Government. Shah Haji and Raja Sher Mal were therefore dismissed without any positive assurance. The Governor-General, however, addressed a letter to the Emperor promising to intimate his sentiments through the Resident.[65] Seton was also instructed to appraise the Emperor about the propriety of the conduct of the British Government in order to obviate any misunderstanding in his mind. Thus the mission of Shah Haji ended unsuccesssfully.

An important result of the mission was that it helped to highlight the authority of the Resident. The terms earlier accepted by the Resident were the *ultra ne plus* for the Government. The shawls presented on behalf of Begam and Mumtaz Mahal were initially refused as these presents were not in the knowledge of the Resident. Shah Haji was also told about the impropriety and irregularity of sending letters and presents to the Governor-General without informing the Resident.[66] The mission could obtain merely a letter to the Emperor containing nothing but the customary form of address and promises of goodwill.[67] Shah Haji was not even informed about the reaction of the Government to the various demands of the Emperor. The intimation of the same was, however, promised through the Resident. This clearly indicates the determination of the Government to consider the Resident as the only acceptable channel of official communication. As a result, any doubt about the representative character of the Resident, as Seton himself had foreseen, was removed from the mind of the Emperor. It was now clear that nothing could be obtained from the Government without the knowledge of the Resident. It was precisely for this reason that the Government did not untimate its decision to the Emperor regarding his demands.[68]

[65] G.G. to H.M., March 8, 1809: *pol. cons.*, March 13, 1809, No. 104.
[66] Monckton to Seton, March 8, 1809: *pol. cons.*, March 13, 1809, No. 103, para 8.
[67] G.G. to H.M., March 8, 1809, *op. cit.*

In a sense the mission is an evidence of the contradictory nature of the British policy towards the Mughal House and the apparent lack of clarity in its implementation. Both the Resident and the Governor-General were in principle opposed to the prosecution of the mission and were convinced about its futility and impracticability. Still Seton seemed to be in a dilemma. He was not sure as to whether the instructions from the Supreme Government authorized him to prevent the Emperor from sending the mission in case he refused to accept his advice. It was because of this that he solicited a postponement of the mission till another reference to Calcutta was made,[69] even though he had known the sentiments of the Governor-General. Normally, he could have positively told the Emperor to abandon the project, as the Government was decidedly aganist it. But instead of doing so, his representations created an impression that the Government was duty-bound to comply with the wishes of the Emperor. the origin of this contradiction, which is to be sought not at Delhi but at Calcutta, was inherent in the policy itself. To attribute it to the extreme delicacy of Seton's character and his veneration for the Emperor would only be a superficial explanation. It may, however, be added that the outward tenderness towards the Mughal family was warranted by considerations not merely of humanity but also of policy. It was desirable to continue humouring the Emperor without, of course, sacrificing the principles till the British Government was unquestionably the sovereign power.

It had become clear beyond doubt that the British Government would not accept Mirza Jahangir as the heir-apparent in preference to his elder brothers. This opposition, however, did not dissuade Mumtaz Mahal and her adherents from their aims. When direct methods of request and representations failed, they decided to adopt indirect ones for attaining their ambition. They now directed their endeavours to make the appointment of Jahangir a *fait accompli* by providing him a rank and status higher than that of his brothers. The Mirza was given huge amounts of money from the private coffers of Mumtaz

[68] Monckton to Seton, March 8, 1809: *pol. cons.*, March 13, 1809, No. 103.
[69] Seton to H.M., October 25, 1807: *pol. cons.*, November 16, 1807, No. 2.

APPOINTMENT OF THE HEIR-APPARENT

Mahal. He used it for great advantage, employed a considerable number of troops as his personal guards and masquraded with them inside the palace and outside humiliating his elder relations and terrorizing the women and servants. Abu Zafar had no source of income and could hardly eke out a decent livelihood. He had practically no followers and his existence went almost unnoticed in the palace. This naturally helped to enhance the importance of Jahangir as compared to that of his brothers.

At the same time the adoption of Seton as the son of Mumtaz Mahal and the details of the ceremony observed on that occasion were intended to achieve the same end. In May, 1807 Seton was informed through Shah Haji about the desire of Mumtaz Mahal to adopt him as her son.[70] The adoption by the Begam, according to the prevailing custom, was thought to be a great favour and Seton expressed deep gratitude and sincere happiness over the generosity of the Princess. Nevertheless, he urged the postponement of the ceremony as he could not accept the honour without the sanction of the Governor-General. He was, in fact, apprehensive about the intentions of the Begam. He feared that she might employ Mirza Jahangir to place the turban of investiture on his head, which would naturally be construed as an open acknowledgement of his superior rank over his brothers. On clarification, the Resident was assured that the ceremony would be conducted by the Emperor himself.

On June 4, 1807, the birthday of the Emperor, while the Durbar was in session, the Resident was peremptorily informed by Shah Haji about the decision of Mumtaz Mahal to perform the investiture of adoption on that day. All the necessary preparations for the ceremony were complete. He was required to retire to the private apartments of the Begam for the investiture as soon as the Durbar broke up. The Resident was evidently put in a delicate situation. It was undoubtedly embarrassing to refuse the offer in view of the kind sentiment and honour attached to it. At the same time he had not received the concurrence of the Governor-General. He decided to accept the honour to avoid embarrassment and pain to the Begam Consequently, Mirza Jahangir as the representative of the Princess placed

---

[70] Seton to Edmonstone, June 1, 1807: *pol. cons.*, June 19, 1807, No. 28.

upon his head the turban of adoption. The Resident objected to Mirza Jahangir conducting the ceremony so as to avoid an erroneous impression about his status in comparison with his brothers. He was, however, assured that this matter was totally unconnected with the *walli ahdi*.[71]

The Governor-General was posted with this intelligence through the newspapers of Lucknow and Delhi much before the Resident officially informed him about this development.[72] He did not regard it objectionable in case the investiture was performed by the Emperor himself. But he was suspicious of the sincerity and intentions of the Begam owing to the publicity of the investiture in ordinary newspapers and, consequently, in all the courts of India. He believed that Mumtaz Mahal had projected the scheme to accomplish the very object against which the Resident properly endeavoured to guard. The explanation of the Resident about the innocent professions of the Begam did not however satisfy the Governor-General. There is little doubt that in using Mirza Jahangir as her representative at the ceremony, the Princess had evidently establishad his superiority over his brothers. It also created an impression that the Resident had been vested with the *khilat* as deputy to Mirza Jahangir.[73]

This successful attempt to place Mirza Jahangir on a higher pedestal in comparison with the status of his brothers, was then vigorously followed up by the Emperor. On December 1, 1807, the day of the festival of *Ed-ul-Fiter*, the honours of *aftabee*[74] were accorded to Jahangir in the open Court[75] amidst the compliments and congratulations of his immediate dependents and the devoted servants of his mother. The Resident, however, refrained from paying any compliments as he believed that the entire business was out of conformity with the declared desire of the British Government on the subject of *walli ahdi*.[76] It was evident that this particular day was chosen by the Emperor to

---

[71] Seton to Edmonstone, June 7, 1807: *pol. cons.*, June 25, 1807, No. 39.
[72] Edmonstone to Seton, June 19, 1807: *pol. cons.*, June 19, 1807, No. 29.
[73] Edmonstone to Seton, June 25, 1807: *pol. cons.*, June 25, 1807, No. 40.
[74] The *aftabee* is a portable screen or guard against the sun. Its form resembles that of a large leaf affixed to the end of a pole.
[75] Seton to Edmonstone, December 5, 1807: *pol. cons.*, December 21, 1807 No. 42, para 3.
[76] *Ibid.*

APPOINTMENT OF THE HEIR-APPARENT

give the utmost publicity to this measure. Immediately after this the honours of *tuppak*[77] and *nalki-sae-bunder*[78] were also granted to Jahangir.[79]

The Emperor had adopted this measure without previous intimation to the Resident. But he endeavoured to associate the British Government with them by bestowing these honours on Jahangir on a public occasion in the presence of the Resident. This was the first instance when the Emperor carried out a scheme without the concurrence as well as against the declared policy of the British Government. The Government viewed this with a "sensation of infinite regret" and thoroughly disapproved the tortuous course adopted by the Emperor to achieve his object.[80] The Resident in a private interview with the Emperor appraised him of the possible implications of his action. He rightly visualized that the bestowal of these honours would foment discord and unhappiness in the royal family as Abu Zafar was bound to feel the mortification.

The Emperor tried to pacify the British Government by promising to instruct Jahangir to restrict the use of *aftabee* to private occasions and to grant *nalki-sae-bunder* and *tuppak* to all other princes as well.[81] This, however, could not satisfy the Resident. Whether the *aftabee* was or was not to be used in public mattered but little. The very fact that this mark of distinction had been granted to Jahangir in public on a solemn celebration created the impression of his superiority over his brothers. In the same way the intention behind the conferring of *tuppak* and *nalki*, first on Jahangir, would be too obvious to escape notice. It was absolutely necessary therefore to nullify the effect on the mind of the people produced by these events.

Two courses were open to achieve that: first, the conferment of similar honours on other princes; and secondly, the with-

---

[77] This was a cushion or cloth covered with velvet or satin placed upon the throne when the king was seated or upon the ground for the heir-apparent and for him only.
[78] This was a state palanquin which was not so far allowed to be used by the royal children.
[79] Seton to Edmonstone, December 5, 1807, *op. cit.*
[80] Edmonstone to Seton, December 26, 1801: *pol. cons.*, December 28, 1807, No. 1-A.
[81] Seton to Edmonstone, December 5, 1807, *op. cit.*

drawal of honour conferred upon Jahangir. The second alternative was not considered expedient by the Resident.[82] The Governor-General, however, thought differently. He believed that the "evil effects of the distinctions conferred on Mirza Jahangir would be most effectively obviated by inducing His Majesty to withdraw the grant of *aftabee*, *tuppak* and *nalki* or at least by withdrawing the former and conferring *tuppak* and *nalki* on the other sons of His Majesty."[83] The Resident, however, was given the liberty to use his discretion in judging the feasibility of the suggestion. If found unsuitable he was to induce the Emperor to grant similar honours to his other sons also.

The Resident immediately acted upon the suggestion of the Governor-General, even though he was not in complete agreement with it. He urged upon the Emperor the necessity of withdrawing the honours conferred upon Mirza Jahagir.[84] The Emperor who was induced to adopt such a line of action by the persuasion of Mumtaz Mahal, agreed to do so after some hesitation.[85] Consequently, the honours were withdrawn without any serious objection from Mirza Jahangir.[86]

This incident was a serious jolt to the palace junta. They were now convinced about the impossibility of a successful culmination to their endeavours. The rebellion of Mirza Jahangir against the occupation of the palace gates by the British troops and his subsequent removal to Allahabad put the palace party completely out of picture. The stern and decided attitude of the British Government conveyed by the Resident in mild and modest but unmistakable language finally prevailed with the

[82] *Ibid.*, para 11.
[83] Edmonstone to Seton, December 26, 1807, *op. cit.*
[84] Seton to Edmonstone, February 13, 1808, *pol. cons.*, April 25, 1808, No. 40.
[85] Seton to Edmonstone, December 5, 1807, *op. cit.* Seton wrote: "I have learned from unquestionable authority that on his (the Emperor's) return to the private apartments he was extremely irritated against Mumtaz Mahal. He told her that upon two occasions he had suffered her advice and entreaty to overcome his own convictions and that in both the issue had been unfortunate, adding these strong words: You will be the ruin of my family."
[86] Seton to Edmonstone, April 4, 1808: *pol. cons.*, April 25, 1808, No. 41.

Emperor and Prince Abu Zafar was elevated to the exalted posititon of the heir-apparent on January 16, 1810.[87]

Seton had more than once unsuspectedly played into the hands of the royal ladies, but his judicious efforts proved successful in the end. Though he was reprimanded in the beginning, he took command of the situation slowly but steadily and won ultimately the unqualified praise of the Governor-General for efficiently handling this delicate problem.[88] The appointment of Abu Zafar as the heir-apparent naturally increased his prestige and influence. It created a strong impression among the palace circles that the authority of the Resident was indomitable. The influence of Mumtaz Mahal virtually became extinct and the Emperor henceforth gave heed to the advice of the Resident more readily and aqreeally than before.

---

[87] Seton to Edmonstone, January 16, 1810, *pol. cons.*, February 6, 1810, No. 4.

[88] Edmonstone to Seton, March 14, 1808: *pol. cons.*, March 14, 1808, No. 2.

4
The States of Rajputana

DURING THE second Anglo-Maratha war the British Government was primarily influenced by its military requirements in the organization of its various agencies. The military and political authorities in Hindustan were therefore combined at the time of war. It was entrusted to Lord Lake, the Commander-in-Chief, for effective co-ordination and efficient functioning He was authorized to conclude treaties and superintend the political relations with all the states in North India. The Political Agencies of the Government in this region were, hence, subordinated to his authority. But on the conclusion of the war in 1806, it became unnecessary to continue the precedence attached to military affairs. A reorganization of the existing arrangement, therefore, became imperative. Consequently, when Lord Lake resigned his political and diplomatic authorities in January 1806[1] the political affairs were separated from military control.

This change was of great consequence for the Residency at Delhi both in respect to its importance and jurisdiction. Between 1803 and 1806 only the management of the relations with the Mughal Emperor was committed to its charge. Now the superintendence of the political relations with the states of Rajputana including the states of Bharatpur and Alwar came under its jurisdiction. This addition largely increased its political importance and with the Cis-Sutlej states also added to its charge, the Delhi Residency became the premier instrument of the British Government for the conduct of its political and diplomatic activities in North India.

Policy Towards the States of Rajputana

Till the arrival of Lord Wellesley, the states of Rajputana

---

[1] Lake resigned due to his difference of opinion with the Governor-General on the dissolution of the alliance with Jaipur state.

did not fall within the political calculations of the British administrators in India. The Marathas were active in this region, exploiting its resources and consolidating their influence. In view of a possible conflict with the Marathas, Wellesley rightly understood the strategic importance of these states as they were contiguous to the Maratha territory. They could, if bound by an efficient system of alliance, push the military frontier of the Company ahead of the political and act as a barrier against the intrusions of the Marathas into the North.[2] The Governor-General, therefore, decided to extend the network of protective alliances to "all the petty states of the southward and westward of the Jumna from Jayanagar to Bundelkhand."[3] In the execution of this policy Wellesley could not achieve complete success. Only Jaipur, Bharatpur, and Alwar accepted British protection.[4] The treaty with Jodhpur, which was negotiated and signed by the vakils of the Raja,[5] had to be abandoned due to the conflicting interests of the contracting parties.[6] Udaipur, Kotah, and Bundi remained beyond the pale of British influence.[7]

On the outbreak of hostilities with the Marathas, Wellesley's grand design proved a dismal failure in practice, though it was well conceived and useful in theory. The Raja of Bharatpur renounced the treaty obligations and aligned himself with the enemies of the Company. The attitude of Jaipur, though not avowedly hostile, was not the least helpful. The conduct of the

[2] Edmonstone to Graeme Mercer, July 22, 1803: Martin (ed.), *op. cit.* iii, p. 228.
[3] Wellesley to Lake, July 27, 1803: Martin (ed.), *op. cit.*, iii, p. 208.
[4] C.U. Aitchison: *A Collection of Treaties, Engagements and Sanads*, iii, pp. 66, 389 and 400.
[5] *Ibid.*, p. 126.
[6] In the beginning it was the Raja of Jodhpur who was recalcitrant. Instead of ratifying the treaty he had suggested certain fresh provisions (*sec. cons.*, June 14, 1804, No. 56-A). But later on finding the growing power of the British, he had ratified the original treaty (Lake to Wellesley, May 1, 1804: *sec. cons.*, September 6, 1804, No. 4-A). But by then the British Government had already dissolved the treaty. It was not thought desirable to reconsider the decision in view of the understanding arrived at with Sindhia (Wellesley to Lake, May 26, 1804: *sec. cons.*, September 6, 1804, No. 5).
[7] Mercer to Edmonstone, March 5, 1804: *sec. cons.*, April 12, 1804, No. 110.

Raja during the war was so contrary to Wellesley's expectations that he entertained doubts about the claims of Jaipur to British protection.[8]

In the light of this experience, to the successors of Wellesley, this system stood discredited. They considered its reversal expedient and advantageous to the British Government. Cornwallis, who was sent to India for the express purpose of establishing peace, decided to dissolve the alliance with the state of Jaipur.[9] The military exigencies and assurances given by Lake to the Raja about the continuance of British protection then stood in the way of the execution of this resolution.[10] Subsequently Barlow carried this into effect,[11] and bore the odium of making the faith of the Government "subservient to its convenience".[12] Cornwallis had contemplated the dissolution of the alliance with Bharatpur and Alwar as well.[13] This was not effected due to want of plausible reasons.[14] The opposition of Lord Lake and the reluctance of these states to forgo their connexion with the British Government prevented a precipitate action in this respect.[15] Thus in 1806 when the states of Rajputana came under the jurisdiction of Delhi Residency only Alwar and Bharatpur had treaty relations with the British Government.

The reversal of Wellesley's policy had devastating effects on the states of Rajputana. The settlement with Sindhia and Holkar on the conclusion of the second Anglo-Maratha war

[8] Cornwallis to Lake, September 1, 1805: Charles Ross, (ed.): *Correspondence of Charles, First Marquis Cornwallis*, iii, p. 547.

[9] Cornwallis to Castlreagh, August 9, 1805: Ross, *op. cit.*, iii, p. 539.

[10] Mill & Wilson, *op. cit.*, vi, p. 666.

[11] Barlow to Raja of Jaipur, December 4, 1805: *sec. cons.*, December 26, 1805, No. 31.

[12] John Malcolm: *The Political History of India*, i, p. 373. This was a statement by the Agent of the Raja of Jaipur.

[13] Cornwallis to Lake, September 19, 1805: Ross, *op. cit.*, iii, p. 547.

[14] Governor-General's minute, August 7, 1806: *sec. cons.*, August 7, 1806, No. 93. Later on when a coalition of Bharatpur with Holkar and Sindhia was apprehended, Seton suggested that in case it was proved beyond doubt, it could be used as an opportunity for dissolving the alliance with Bharatpur. Seton to Edmonstone, September 30, 1806: *sec. cons.*, October 23, 1806, No. 97.

[15] Malcolm to Hastings, July 17, 1817: Malcolm, *op. cit.*, ii, Appendix IV.

virtually partitioned these states into spheres of influence among these two chieftains. The British Government agreed to refrain from concluding any treaty with Udaipur, Jodhpur, and Kotah and also from interfering in the arrangements which Sindhia might make with them.[16] The cancellation of the treaty with Jaipur amounted to its virtual abandonment to the depredations of Holkar as he had always maintained a claim of tribute on that state. The result of this policy was that the whole of Rajputana "became a source of fearful strife, lawless plunder and frightful desolation for many succeeding years."[17]

The withdrawal of British influence from this area created a political vacuum and this provided unhampered opportunities for the Marathas and the Pathans. The rulers of these states were neither strong enough to tone up the administration and maintain peace and tranquillity, nor were they united enough to offer opposition to the external enemies due to their mutual suspicion and bickerings. The Rao Raja of Alwar was always eager to subvert[18] a contemplated alliance of Jaipur, Sindhia, and Holkar.[19] Alwar and Jaipur were at loggerheads on the question of Dubi and Sikrawa.[20] The rulers of Jaipur and Jodhpur came to grips for the hand of Krishna Kumari, the fair princess of Udaipur. The Raja of Jaipur also espoused the cause of Dhonkal Singh,[21] a pretender to the throne of Jodhpur, against the reigning prince, Man Singh.

The result of these rivalries was the ruinous interference of the Marathas and of Amir Khan, the Pathan chief, in the internal

[16] Aitchison, *op. cit.*, v., p. 402.
[17] Mill & Wilson, *op. cit.*, vi, p. 669.
[18] The Rao Raja of Alwar to Seton, received on March 8, 1807, *sec. cons.*, March 26, 1807, No. 2-A.
[19] Seton to Edmonstone, February 25, 1807: *sec. cons.*, March 12, 1807, No. 2.
[20] Dubi and Sikrawa were two fortresses in Jaipur territory which were captured by the Rao Raja of Alwar in 1812, but later returned to Jaipur at the instance of the Delhi Resident.
[21] Dhonkal Singh was the posthumous child of Vijay Singh, the late Raja of Jodhpur. Man Singh on the occasion of his accession had promised to abdicate, in case the then pregnant Rani gave birth to a male child. When the son was born, Man Singh refused to recognize him on the plea of the birth having taken place under suspicious circumstances. G.H. Ojha: *History of Rajputana*, v, Part II, p. 779.

affairs of these states. In the Jodhpur-Jaipur rivalry, Holkar, Sindhia, and Amir Khan were involved in a manner that sapped the very vitality of these two states. In the beginning of the contest Holkar appeared in the guise of a benevolent mediator.[22] But after exacting a huge amount from the Raja of Jaipur he became indifferent. Sindhia also charged a large sum from the Jaipur Raja for helping him.[23] Amir Khan's role was the most dubious and disastrous. It was characterized by breach of faith, cupidity, and inconsistency. He joined the struggle on the side of Jaipur after exacting one lakh of rupees from the Raja.[24] But soon he showed his true colours and started plunder and pillage in Jaipur territory with inhuman cruelty. He defeated a small force of Jaipur and seriously threatened the very existence of the state.[25] He then joined the Jodhpur camp and managed the murder of Sawai Singh, the chief of the *thakurs* who were opposed to Raja Man Singh.[26] Thereafter he established strong influence in the government which was largely responsible for the insecurity and anarchy that prevailed in Jodhpur. His interference and nefarious manoeuvres in Udaipur culminated in the tragic death of Princess Krishna Kumari.[27]

These, however, were not isolated incidents. All other states of Rajputana were suffering from the same malady of the Maratha, Pathan, and Pindari depredations and pillage. Holkar was exacting huge amounts of money from the Rajas of Kotah and Bundi.[28] The Rana of Udaipur had either to pay unjust and excessive tribute to the Marathas or to submit to the pain-

[22] Roy Ram Singh, vakil of Jaipur, to Seton, February 9, 1807: *pol. cons.*, February 12, 1807, No. 97.
[23] Seton to Edmonstone, July 6, 1807: *pol. cons.*, July 23, 1807, No. 30.
[24] *Ibid.*, No. 31.
[25] Rao Raja of Alwar to Seton, received on August 23, 1807: *pol. cons.*, September 15, 1807 No, 4. The Ranis of Jaipur solicited the help of the Rao Raja. He was forbidden from giving any assistance by the Resident. Seton to the Rao Raja, August 23, 1807: *pol. cons.*, September 15, 1807, No. 5.
[26] Translation of an extract from newspaper: April 12, 1807, *pol. cons.*, No. 68.
[27] James Tod: *Annals and Antiquities of Rajasthan*, p. 369. Amir Khan's advice that the Princess take poison and bring the conflict between Jaipur and Jodhpur for her hand to a close was accepted.
[28] Seton to Edmonstome, May 24, 1807: *pol. con.*, June 11, 1807, No. 16.

ful alternative of seeing his country laid waste.[29] A large force of Amir Khan, of the Marathas and of the Pindaris were sweeping through these states committing wanton aggression and plunder, leaving in their trail misery, chaos, and insecurity. Anarchy was the order of the day. Trade, industry, and agriculture considerably deteriorated. As a result political and administrative institutions broke down and large sections of the population were compelled to migrate to more peaceful regions. The whole of Rajputana, it would seem, was in the grip of Nemesis.

On the contrary, the states of Alwar and Bharatpur which were under the protection of the British Government enjoyed comparative peace and tranquillity, and were safe from the predatory hordes. Moreover, the British Government was exerting a restraining influence on them. In the Jaipur-Jodhpur rivalry, Alwar[30] and Bharatpur had observed strict neutrality at the instance of the British Government.[31] When the Rao Raja of Alwar sent a force for the help of Bohra Raja Kushali Ram, who had rebelled against the Raja of Jaipur, it had to be recalled due to the intervention of the British Government.[32] The case of Dubi and Sikrawa was another instance. In 1812 the Rao Raja invaded the Jaipur territory and captured the fortresses of Dubi and Sikrawa. The Resident at Delhi disapproved of this aggression and compelled the Raja to restore them to Jaipur.[33]

This difference in the condition of the protected and unprotected states could not escape the notice of the latter. For rescuing themselves from the external menace, assistance was immediately needed. Under the existing conditions none other than the British Government, on whom devolved the insignia of paramountcy once held by the Mughals, could provide that. The dread and detestation of the Marathas, the Pathans, and

[29] Seton to Edmonstone, April 26, 1808: *pol. cons.*, May 16, 1808, No. 51.
[30] Seton to Edmonstone, December 28, 1806: *pol. cons.*, January 15, 1807, No. 6.
[31] Seton to Edmonstone, January 15, 1807: *pol. cons.*, January 15, 1807, No. 7.
[32] Seton to Edmonstone, January 16, 1810: *pol. cons.*, February 6, 1810, No. 2.
[33] Metcalfe to Adam, November 19, 1813: *sec. cons.*, December 10, 1813, No. 10.

the Pindaris obliged every Rajput state to seek the protection of the British Government.[34]

The reaction of the British Government to the appeals for protection was not favourable since it was then pursuing a policy of non-intervention in the affairs of Indian states. Even mediation was declined as it could impinge upon the independence of these states.[35] Seton, the main adviser of the British Government regarding the affairs of Rajputana, was a staunch adherent of the policy of non-intervention. He argued that any departure from this policy in respect to these states would create suspicion and distrust in the minds of other Indian rulers who had interests in this region.[36] He also believed that the political instability and anarchy that prevailed in Rajputana as a result of the plunder and pillage by the predatory hordes would not endanger the tranquillity of the British dominions.[37] The first assertion of the Resident was true, as interference in the affairs of the Rajput states would conflict with the treaty obligations with the Maratha powers. But the latter was a misconception. The anarchy and insecurity that prevailed in Rajputana was definitely a threat to the peace and security of the neighbouring British territories.[38] Moreover, the opportunity provided by the weak and unprotected Rajput states to the Marathas to recover their strength had dangerous implications for British imperial interests in India. From the British point of view, political sagacity and acumen demanded the denial of all opportunities to

[34] Seton to Edmonstone, April 26, 1808: *pol. cons.*, May 16, 1808, No. 51, para 5.
[35] Seton to Edmonstone, February 20, 1807: *pol. cons.*, March 12, 1807, No. 26, and Seton to Edmonstone, August 17, 1808, *pol. cons.*, September 12, 1808, No. 28.
[36] Seton to Rao Chathur Bhuj, Vakil of the Raja of Jaipur, August 17, 1808: *pol. cons.*, September 12, 1807, No. 29.C.
[37] Seton to Edmonstone, September 1, 1810: *pol. cons.*, September 25, 1810, No. 107.
[38] Malcolm to Hastings, July 17, 1811: Malcolm, *op. cit.*, ii, Appendix IV. The immediate successors of Wellesley had believed that the policy of non-intervention would secure the British territories from all depredations from Indian powers. On the withdrawl of British protection Barlow argued, they would be inclined to indulge in mutual aggrandizement rather than directing their energy against the British. See Malcolm, *op. cit.*, i, pp. 341-42.

THE STATES OF RAJPUTANA

the Marathas which could make them financially and militarily strong. The policy of non-intervention, in fact, served the opposite purpose. Surprisingly enough, Seton though he was aware of this danger.[39] adhered to the policy without suggesting changes or deviations.

Metcalfe and the British Policy

Charles Theophilus Metcalfe, when he became the Resident at Delhi in 1811, looked on the states of Rajputana from a new perspective. An ardent admirer and a close disciple of "the glorious little man",[40] Metcalfe like Lord Lake Malcolm and Elphinstone, was a severe critic of the policy of non-intervention adopted by the successors of Wellesley. To his mind it was impolitic, inexpedient, and unjust.[41] When the states of Rajputana renewed their appeals for protection[42] immediately after his assumption of office, the policy in force forbade him from returning anything but a negative reply.[43] But he contested the very wisdom behind this policy. To the "Wellesleyian School" the peace and tranquillity of the country did not mean merely the peace and tranquillity of the British territories but that of the whole of India. For effecting that, "the receding policy"[44] of the Government, as Malcolm termed it, was no solution. According to Metcalfe, there could be no policy that did not admit of deviations. The policy of non-intervention undoubtedly was not one.[45] The Government had already deviated in the case of the Cis-Sutlej states and again in favour of Nagpur against Amir Khan. The condition of Rajputana undoubtedly provided stronger reasons than these

---
[39] Seton to Edmonstone, January 15, 1807: *pol. cons.*, January 29, 1807, No. 32.
[40] Lord Wellesley. His subordinates and Colleagues affectionately called him so.
[41] Metcalfe to Edmonstone, June 20, 1811: *pol. cons.*, July 12, 1811, No. 1; and Metcalfe to Jenkings: Kaye, *op. cit.*, i, p. 289.
[42] Metcalfe to Edmonstone, June 22, 1811: *pol. cons.*, July 12, 1811, No. 25.
[43] Metcalfe to Edmonstone, November 29, 1811: *pol. cons.*, December 21, 1811, No. 60.
[44] Malcolm to Hastings, July 17, 1817: Malcolm, *op. cit.*, ii, Appendix IV.
[45] Kaye, *op. cit.*, i, p. 289.

instances. All the states of this area had to be rescued from chaos and political instability. Even if the policy of non-intervention was not renounced, a deviation from it in respect of Rajputana was justified. So thought Metcalfe. To put it in his own words: "It is impossible to live in this part of India and to see the scenes which pass before our eyes, without regretting that the Rajput states are not under our protection. A confederation of Rajput states under the protection of the British Government must be a favourite object with every man who has any charge of the political duties in this quarter. Perhaps no event could take place in India that would be attended with so many advantages."[46]

The advantages referred to by Metcalfe were manifold. An alliance with the states of Rajputana could connect the Bengal and Bombay Presidencies. It could deprive the predatory hordes of their principal targets of ravage and plunder, thereby facilitating the establishment of permanent peace in the country. In the event of a war in the North it could prevent any co-operation between the Southern and Northern powers as the friendly states of Rajputana would interpose between them as an effective check.[47] It could also secure the Southern frontier from the Marathas, thus making it possible to concentrate the whole army in the North.[48]

To Metcalfe the difficulties attending a deviation from the old policy appeared trivial. The foremost of these concerned the existing treaty relations with the Maratha chiefs, the renunciation of which might even involve extensive military operations.[49] Metcalfe considered it prudent to welcome the risk. Lord Minto, who was then the Governor-General, thought otherwise. He was not prepared to depart from the existing treaties and obligations, however alluring be the advantages.[50] But the assumption of the office of the Governor-General by the Earl of Moira (later the Marquess of Hastings) on October 4, 1813, marked the

[46] Metcalfe to Edmonstone, June 20, 1811: *sec. cons.*, July 12, 1811, No. 1, para 9.
[47] *Ibid.*, paras 9, 10 and 11.
[48] *Ibid.*, para 12.
[49] Metcalfe to Edmonstone, June 20, 1811, *op. cit.*, para 16.
[50] Edmonstone to Metcalfe, July 12, 1811: *sec. cons.*, July 12, 1811, No. 2.

beginning of a significant change in the attitude of the British Government towards Indian states. Metcalfe found in him, a statesman who shared his opinion about the political situation of India and was prepared to deviate from the beaten track if the circumstances so warranted. The reversal of Wellesley's policy was equally odious to Moira as it was to Metcalfe. He considered that the existing political relationship with the various states was embarrassing both to the British Government and Indian powers, as the mutually contradictory engagements kept them "constantly on the brink of rupture due to the indefinite nature of the relationship."[51] A confederacy of all Indian states with the British Government as the head could provide a solution to these difficulties. The Governor-General preferred a confederacy as any suggestion of vassalage was bound to be revolting to the pride of the Indian chiefs and might create apprehensions about the intentions of the British Government.[52] According to his plan, "the members of the league shall not make war on each other but shall refer the differences to the arbitration of the head of the confederacy and that the head of the confederacy shall have the right of calling forth the forces of all or any of the members of the league as exigency shall require."[53] This would make "the British Government paramount, in effect, if not declaratory so."[54] As early as 1811 Metcalfe had propounded a similar plan for the states of Rajputana.[55]

The Governor-General's tour of the Upper Provinces in 1814 provided an opportunity to Metcalfe to expound his plan for the settlement of Central India. Lord Moira, already acquainted with his political views,[56] invited him to his camp at Moradabad. Metcalfe joined him there towards the end of

---

[51] Governor-General's minute, April 3, 1814: *sec. cons.*, June 21, 1814, No. 4.
[52] Governor-General's minute, April 3, 1814, *op. cit.*
[53] *Ibid.*
[54] The Marchioness of Bute (ed.): *The Private Journal of the Marquess of Hastings*, i, p. 54.
[55] Metcalfe to Edmonstone, June 20, 1811, *op. cit.*, para 9.
[56] John Adam, the then Political Secretary, had confidentially communicated the letters of Metcalfe on the case of Dubi and Sikrawa to the Governor-General John Adam to Metcalfe, November 15, 1813, Kaye, *op. cit.*, i, p. 279.

November 1814.⁵⁷ It was then that he prepared and submitted to the Governor-General his famous memorandum on Central India.⁵⁸

Metcalfe divided the states of Central India into three distinct categories: the substantive, the military, and the petty. Sindhia, Holkar, and the Raja of Nagpur belonged to the first, the Pindaris, Amir Khan, and Mohammad Shah Khan to the second, while the states of Rajputana were the third.⁵⁹ The absolute extermination of the Pindaris was to be the first and most important step of the settlement. For implementing this plan a confederacy of the substantive powers with the British Government as the acknowledged head was to be established. This could later on provide the foundation of a general confederacy of all the established states of India.⁶⁰ If this were not found feasible, at least their neutrality with right of free passage for the British army through their territories was essential. In case they proved recalcitrant, Metcalfe recommended use of force to bring them under control. This was intended to deprive the predatory hordes of any external assistance.

The states of Rajputana were to be immediately taken under British protection.⁶¹ For this Metcalfe had been pressing the Government for a considerably long time. Apart from depriving the predatory hordes of their main source of income, it would prove to be of great financial advantage to the British Government.

In the event of a war with the Marathas, which Metcalfe thought would inevitably follow the annihilation of the Pindaries, the states of Rajputana could provide considerable money for defraying the expenses of the war. Moreover, humanitarian considerations had always prompted Metcalfe to save these states from the misery inflicted on them by the Marathas, the Pathans, and the Pindaris.⁶²

⁵⁷ Kaye, *op. cit.*, i, p. 292.
⁵⁸ This document was the first on the subject. Malcolm and Jenkins expressed their opinions after him.
⁵⁹ Metcalfe's memorandum on Central India, Kaye, *op. cit.*, i, p. 314.
⁶⁰ *Ibid.*, p. 317.
⁶¹ *Ibid.*, p. 319.
⁶² Metcalfe to Edmonstone, June 20, 1811: *pol. cons.*, July 12, 1811, No. 1, para 14.

Meanwhile, the condition of Rajput states considerably deteriorated. The state of Jaipur was going through one of the most crucial periods of its history. Amir Khan occupied a portion of its territory. Jaipur army was plundering that area as a reprisal against him. The Pathan Chief replied by laying waste the entire countryside of Jaipur. The invasion of Bapuji Sindhia, who practically impoverished the country, further aggravated the situation.[63] Miser Shiv Narain, the Prime Minister of Jaipur, committed suicide by swallowing a pounded diamond as he could not save his country from ruin.[64] Factions and intrigues among the Rajput nobility completely paralyzed the administration.[65] Jaipur's capacity to resist these dangers had reached the point of collapse. It had almost become certain that if no aid was forthcoming from the British Government, the Raja would seek it elsewhere for saving the country from ruin. Actually he had started negotiations with Sindhia for an alliance.[66] In Jodhpur, Amir Khan was endeavouring to exact a huge sum of money amounting to eighteen lakhs of rupees from the Raja.[67] In order to facilitate this payment he contrived the murder of Indraj Singhi, the minister, and Dev Nath, the Maharaja's guru.[68] The states of Udaipur, Bundi, and Kotah were also labouring under miserable conditions.

This situation afforded the best opportunity for bringing these states under British protection. If the general plan could not be put into force, Metcalfe in his memorandum had suggested its execution by degrees. An alliance could be concluded with the state of Jaipur as the first step. Metcalfe rightly foresaw that in case protection was not afforded when it was solicited, it might not be accepted when offered.[69] It was due to the menace of the predatory hordes that the states of Rajputana were eager

[63] Maharaja Jagat Singh to G.G. received on March 28, 1814: *pol. cons.*, July 12, 1815, No. 14-A.
[64] Metcalfe to Adam, September 9, 1815: *pol. cons.*, September 27, 1815, No. 29.
[65] Metcalfe to Adam, October 16, 1815: *pol. cons.*, November 10, 1815, No. 13.
[66] Metcalfe to Adam, September 23, 1815: *pol. cons.*, October 20, 1815, No. 45.
[67] Metcalfe to Adam, October 16, 1815, *op. cit.*
[68] Metcalfe to Adam, November 7, 1815: *pol. cons.*, December 8, 1815, No. 15.
[69] Kaye, *op. cit.*, i, p. 320.

for British protection. Once they had been suppressed, as suggested in Metcalfe's plan, these states were not likely to entertain proposals for alliances with the British Government.

The views of Metcalfe were accepted by the Governor-General without reservations. Moira found in him a person with deep understanding of Indian affairs. Besides Metcalfe's political views were similar to his own. The assistance and advice of so spirited and experienced an officer were considered of great importance, especially because of the opposition of the members of the Council to his plans.[70] He even desired Metcalfe to join the secretariat in the capacity of a secretary[71] but Metcalfe was not enthusiastic about it as he believed that he could do more useful work at Delhi.

The memorandum of Metcalfe provided the basis for the elaborate minute presented by the Governor-General to the Council on December 1, 1815 for the settlement of Central India.[72] "The policy it inculcated was indeed emphatically Metcalfe's policy."[73] This political document which sought a permanent solution for the difficulties of Central India was, in its form and content, the creation of the Delhi Resident.

Implementation of the Policy

Hastings now decided to implement this plan by stages. A fresh appeal from the Raja of Jaipur in March 1816 for an

[70] Edmonstone's minute, March 31, 1814: *sec. cons.*, June 21, 1814, No. 1.

[71] Kaye, *op. cit.*, i, p. 300.

[72] Governor-General's minute, December 1, 1815: *pol. cons.*, June 16, 1816, No. 5.

[73] Ricketts, Private Secretary to the Governor-General, wrote to Metcalfe: "By this dawk I have forwarded to you the outline of a proposed minute to be laid before the Council by his lordship on his arrival in Calcutta. It has been seen by Lord Moira, by Adam and by Fagan, and will meet your approbation generally as the sentiments and plan are your own—nay, the wordings yours in many parts, as taken from the admirable notes with which you furnished his lordship. Still, the whole will require correction, and which I beg of you to undertake without any scruples. You know the value which Lord Moira attaches to your suggestions. As a friend of his lordship, you will feel every anxiety to aid in so good a cause, and I cannot prove my friendship better than by entrusting the labouring oar in the struggle to your able management." Kaye, *op. cit.*, i, p. 326.

THE STATES OF RAJPUTANA

alliance on conditions agreeable to the British Government provided the opportunity.[74] In 1813 the Court of Directors had authorized the Governor-General to renew the alliance with Jaipur state.[75] It was then postponed due to the exigencies of the Nepal war[76] and the strong opposition evinced by the members of the Governor-General's Council.[77] These two impediments were no more in existence. Edmonstone, the senior member in the Council, still opposed the measure.[78] But Seton, another Councillor, had by now changed his opinion and supported the Governor-General.[79] Hastings was, therefore, able to get the sanction of the Council for the proposed measure. Consequently, the Resident at Delhi was instructed to conclude a treaty with Jaipur as the first step in the implementation of the general policy.[80]

The proposed treaty stipulated the establishment of a British subsidiary force in Jaipur; control over the external relations; exclusion from Jaipur territory of all foreign influence and power; the disposal of the military power and resources of Jaipur for purposes connected with the interests of the alliance and the general welfare of the two states.[81]

These provisions were to give the treaty a subsidiary character. The Jaipur vakils were highly apprehensive about the huge British force to be stationed in their territory.[82] Metcalfe, therefore, got their consent for fixing the amount payable by Jaipur without reference to the subsidiary force.[83] The Jaipur vakils agreed to this stipulation as they believed that it could help to

[74] Metcalfe to Adam, March 26, 1816: *sec. cons.*, March 15, 1816, No. 45.
[75] *Letters from the Court of Directors (Pol.)*, December 23, 1813.
[76] Governor-General's minute, April 13, 1816: *sec. cons.*, April 20, 1816, No. 1.
[77] Edmonstone's minute, June 15, 1814: *sec. cons.*, June 23, 1814, No. 1.
[78] Edmonstone's minute, April 16, 1816: *sec. cons.*, April 20, 1816, No. 2.
[79] Seton's minute, April 17, 1816: *sec. cons.*, April 20, 1816, No. 3.
[80] Adam to Metcalfe, April 20, 1816: *sec. cons.*, April 20, 1816, No. 6. Hastings had tried to revise the existing system of political alliances by negotiating treaties with Bhopal, Berar and Sagar. See M.S. Mehta: *Lord Hastings and Indian States*, pp. 36-46.
[81] Adam to Metcalfe, April 20, 1816, *op. cit.*, para 5.
[82] The strength of the force to be kept in Jaipur was not to be less than six battalions of native infantry, two regiments of cavalry, with a field train and a suitable portion of artillerymen and pioneers.
[83] Metcalfe to Adam, August 7, 1816: *sec. cons.*, September 7, 1816, No. 5.

reduce the strength of the British force to be stationed in Jaipur. But they failed to realize that it would transform the nature of the treaty from that of a subsidiary to a tributary one. By this arrangement Metcalfe actually anticipated the treaties of 1817-18 with the states of Rajputana.

The Resident also deviated from the general instructions on the question of British arbitration. He was specifically instructed to provide "for the arbitration and award of the British Government of all questions arising between the Raja of Jaipur and other states."[84] During the course of negotiations this was omitted as the Jaipur vakils strongly objected to its inclusion.[85] This omission was resented by the Governor-General.[86] Metcalfe, however, considered its inclusion redundant because the power of protection implied the power of arbitration as well.[87]

Once the negotiations had started, the Raja of Jaipur began to indulge in procrastinations.[88] Metcalfe himself felt exasperated about the attitude of Jaipur.[89] Modifications after modifications were suggested and incapacity to payment was urged time and again. In this way innumerable excuses were invented by the vakils. The intention of the Jaipur court, so it seemed, was to protract the negotiations as long as possible.[9] The opposition of a faction of the *thakurs* hostile to the British Government,[91] the incapacity of the state to pay the stipulated amount,[92] and pressure from Holkar, Sindhia, and Amir Khan[93] ultimately led to the abandonment of the negotiations.[94]

[84] Adam to Metcalfe, April 20, 1816, *op. cit.*

[85] Metcalfe to Adam, October 10, 1816: *sec. cons.*, November 2, 1816, No. 1.

[86] Adam to Metcalfe, September 7, 1816: *sec. cons.*, September 7, 1816, No. 8.

[87] Metcalfe to Adam, October 10, 1816, *op. cit.*

[89] Metcalfe to Adam, August 7, 1816, *op. cit.*

[89] Metcalfe to Close, Resident with Daulat Rao Sindhia, May 26, 1816: *sec. cons.*, June 15, 1816, No. 16.

[90] Metcalfe to Adam, August 19, 1816: *sec. cons.*, September 7, 1816, No. 7.

[91] Metcalfe to Adam, July 3, 1816, *sec. cons.*, August 3, 1816, No. 3.

[92] Raja of Jaipur to G.G., received on October 7, 1816, *op. cit.*

[93] Metcalfe to Adam, August 11, 1816: *sec. cons.*, September 7, 1816, No. 6.

[94] Metcalfe to Adam, November 27, 1816, *op. cit.*

The attitude of Jaipur undoubtedly was a great disappointment to Metcalfe since he was the most vociferous advocate of a treaty with that state. He had anticipated, as any one would in the existing political conditions, that the states of Rajputana would eagerly grasp any opportunity for a protective alliance with the British Government. Even when the vakils were protracting the negotiations, he was optimistic about the final outcome.[95] He was inclined to dismiss all impediments in the conclusion of the treaty as trivial and momentary. Though he could not achieve success in his first attempt, the truth of his contention that "the distresses of Jaipur government are of permanent nature and nothing in the present state of India can alienate them but the protection of the British Government"[96] stood the test of time. The failure of the negotiations, however, was a useful experience as it gave him an object lesson of the ways and means of the Rajput chiefs.

Meanwhile the Pindari menace was on the increase. For the tranquillity of the country the eradication of the Pindari desperados could not be postponed anymore. The Governor-General-in-Council unanimously decided to take action to this effect.[97] The Court of Directors, though they agreed to this measure,[98] were against a revision of the political relations with Indian states and any further extension of British influence in India. The fallacy inherent in this policy was too apparent to escape the notice of the Governor-General. Hastings held that any action taken against the Pindaris without depriving them of all possible sources of sustenance would not accomplish a final solution of the problem. At best, it could suppress but not exterminate them. The Governor-General, therefore, decided to deviate from the orders of the Court of Directors and execute his general plan, assuming for himself the "unparticipated responsibility" for this measure.[99]

For the complete extermination of the Pindaris, the inclu-

---

[95] Metcalfe to Adam, August 7, 1816, *op. cit.*
[96] Metcalfe to Adam, August 17, 1816: *sec. cons.*, September 7, 1816, No. 17.
[97] Resolution following the *sec. cons.*, December 21, 1816, No. 16.
[98] *Letters from the Court of Directors (Pol.)*, September 26, 1816.
[99] G.G.,'s minute, October 10, 1817, *sec. cons.*, October 28, 1817, No. 1.

sion of the states of Rajputana in a system of protective alliance was inevitable since it was primarily on the riches of these states that the predatory hordes throve. The treaty commitments with the Maratha powers stood in the way of the accomplishment of this system. But, according to Hastings, the failure of the Maratha powers to control the Pindaris, which necessitated British exertions,[100] justified the repudiation of these commitments.[101] The Resident at Delhi was, therefore, instructed to conclude alliances with the states of Rajputana in order to establish a "barrier against the revival of the predatory system and to restrict the extension of the power of the Marathas."[102]

This was to be accomplished by combining at least three principal Rajput states viz., Jaipur, Jodhpur, and Udaipur in a common league under the authority of the British Government or by concluding separate engagements with each.[103] The latter proposition was preferred both by the Government and the Resident.[104] This was not because the Government abandoned the idea of a confederacy, but that the Governor-General and the Resident realized that it could come into conflict with the feelings of pride and independence of these states. Mutual jealousy also could jeopardize such a project. The treaties were to be concluded on the lines suggested for the treaty with Jaipur in 1816.[105] On receiving of these instructions, Metcalfe, immediately started negotiations with the states of Jaipur, Jodhpur, Udaipur, Kotah, Bikaner, Bundi, Karoli, and Banswara. Jaisalmer was initially left out as "that state was remote and was not likely to be affected by the contemplated action against the Pindaris."[106] He did not face much difficulty in concluding treaties with these states except Jaipur.[107]

[100] *Letters to the Court of Directors* (*Pol.*), May 19, 1818.
[101] Adam to Close, September 29, 1817: *sec. cons.*, October 28, 1817, No. 415.
[102] Adam to Metcalfe, October 8, 1817: *sec. cons.*, October 28, 1817, No. 26.
[103] *Ibid.*
[104] Metcalfe to Adam, October 18, 1817: *sec cons.*, November 14, 1817, No. 50.
[105] Adam to Metcalfe, October 8, 1817, *op. cit.*
[106] Metcalfe to Adam, October 18, 1817, *op. cit.*
[107] For the text of the treaties, see Aitchison, *op. cit.*, iii. Jaipur pp. 68-69; Jodhpur pp. 128-29; Udaipur p. 22; Kotah pp. 357-58; Bikaner pp. 288-89; Bundi p. 229; Karoli pp. 384-85; Dungarpur pp. 450-51; Banswara p. 466; Jaisalmer pp. 212-13.

THE STATES OF RAJPUTANA

Metcalfe's Role

The discretionary powers granted to the Resident for negotiations[108] were used to good purpose by Metcalfe. When negotiations were commenced, the Jaipur government again indulged in interminable procrastination and evasion. The alliance with Jaipur was conceived as "a grand, if not a preliminary measure"[109] to the general plan. It was not possible to leave that state alone as independent when all other states of Rajputana accepted the status of tributary dependence. Metcalfe was prepared to make all possible concessions. He even agreed to reduce the tribute from the proposed amount of fifteen lakhs of rupees.[110]

The vacillation of Jaipur called for immediate action. Metcalfe could afford to be complacent and drop the negotiations in 1816. But he could not do so in the present endeavour. In case the normal ways were not helpful, he was even prepared to use coercion. Ochterlony was instructed to advance into the Jaipur territory in order "to bring the procrastinating counsels of the Raja to a decision in favour of the immediate conclusion of the alliance."[111] Amir Khan was allowed to remain in Jaipur territory,[112] although the British Government had a right to demand his evacuation according to the treaty concluded with him.[113] But Metcalfe rightly foresaw that the withdrawal of Amir Khan would adversely affect the prospects of the negotiation.[114] These measures produced immediate results. The advance of Ochterlony's force highly alarmed the Jaipur court. Consequently, a new mission consisting of Shiv Chand Bhandari and Rawal Bhairisal[115] was sent to Delhi to negotiate the alliance.

---

[108] Adam to Metcalfe, October 8, 1817, *op. cit.*
[109] Ochterlony to Adam, August 25, 1817: *For & Mis.* Vol. No. 136.
[110] Metcalfe to Adam, January 29, 1818: *sec. cons.*, February 26, 1818, No. 26
[111] Metcalfe to Ochterlony, November 21, 1817: *sec. cons.*, December 19, 1817, No. 112.
[112] *Ibid.*
[113] Aitchison, *op. cit.*, iii p. 244.
[114] Metcalfe to Ochterlony, November 21, 1817, *op, cit.*
[115] Two very influential *thakurs* of the Jaipur court.

But this mission did not reach Delhi even after a month of its departure.[116]

The next step of Metcalfe which was more decisive was the conclusion of separate alliances with the dependent chiefs of Jaipur state.[117] When Kunwar Bakhtawar Singh, the son of Raja Abhay Singh of Khetri, a dependency of Jaipur, expressed a desire to visit Delhi, Metcalfe immediately extended him a warm invitation in order to alarm "the Jaipur court and expedite the conclusion of the treaty."[118] An alliance was then finalized with that chief according to which the allegiance and dependence of Khetri was transferred from Jaipur state to the British Government. [119] All the formalities were over except the ratification by Raja Abhay Singh. A similar engagement was negotiated with the Raja of Uniara, another dependency of Jaipur state.[120] Metcalfe also intended to conclude similar treaties with all dependent chiefs of Jaipur, if necessary. He justified these measures on the ground that they were only dependents and tributaries of Jaipur and not subjects. They were free to transfer their allegiance to any other power if circumstances so warranted.

In pursuing such a course, Metcalfe's intentions were twofold. He wanted to suggest that the British Government was not entirely dependent on the will of the Jaipur state, but was able and willing to establish order without their concurrence.[121] He believed that this would induce Jaipur to conclude an alliance without any further procrastination. He also wanted to demonstrate the authority of the British Government to dispense with the power of Jaipur over her dependencies, thereby crippling her financial and military resources. These possibilities were not lost on the Jaipur representatives. They entertained serious alarm and repeatedly implored the Resident to suspend the negotiations with the chiefs till the arrival of another

---

[116] Metcalfe to Adam, January 29, 1818: *sec. cons.*, February 20, 1818, No. 26.
[117] Metcalfe to Ochterlony, November 21, 1817, *op. cit.*
[118] Metcalfe to Adam, January 29, 1818, *op. cit.*
[119] *Ibid.*
[120] *Ibid.*
[121] *Ibid.*

THE STATES OF RAJPUTANA

ambassador from Jaipur.[122] But Metcalfe continued the negotiations.[123] The Jaipur court now made no mistake about the intentions of the Resident and ultimately concluded the treaty on April 2, 1818.[124]

Metcalfe's role in finalizing the form and content of the treaties was equally important. Instances of his departure from the general instructions of the Governor-General are numerous. The case of Bundi provides a classic example. The treaty with Bundi was concluded by Captain Tod who was on a special mission to Kotah and Bundi for eliciting the co-operation of these states for the suppression of the Pindaris.[125] The Governor-General had decided to renounce the tribute from Bundi as its resources were very inconsiderable.[126] He believed that the amount payable by Bundi to Sindhia, the payment of which consequently devolved upon the British Government, was only Rs. 10,000. Metcalfe, however, instructed Tod to ascertain this and specify it in the treaty as tribute from Bundi.[127] Sindhia's claims, as worked out by Tod, amounted to Rs. 80,000. Metcalfe's suggestion was accepted by the Governor-General[128] and this stipulation was included in the treaty.[129] The initiative of the Resident saved the British Government from a great financial commitment.

Hastings was strongly opposed to British interference in the internal affairs of Indian states,[130] and wanted to apply this principle to the Rajput states as well.[131] But prompted by considerations of advantage and expediency Metcalfe introduced some clauses in certain treaties, which actually implied interference

[122] *Ibid.*
[123] Metcalfe to Adam, February 27, 1818: *sec. cons.*, March 21, 1818, No. 21.
[124] Aitchison, *op, cit.*, iii, pp. 68-69.
[125] Adam to Close, November 7, 1817: *sec. cons.*, November 7, 1817, No. 3.
[126] Adam to Metcalfe, October 8, 1817, *op. cit.*, para 12.
[127] Metcalfe to Tod, November 25, 1817: *sec. cons.*, December 19, 1817, No. 103.
[128] Adam to Metcalfe, November 28, 1817: *sec. cons.*, December 19, 1817, No. 104.
[129] Aitchison, *op. cit.*, iii, p. 229, art. 5.
[130] *Hastings' Private Journal*, i, p. 48.
[131] Adam to Metcalfe, October 8, 1817, *op. cit.*, para 2.

in the internal affairs of those states. The treaties with Bikaner, Banswara, and Kotah may be cited as examples.

In the case of Bikaner, the Governor-General was not very anxious to have intimate connexion with that state.[132] But Metcalfe thought otherwise. During this time some of the important nobles of Bikaner had rebelled against the authority of the Raja. They also threatened the security of the adjoining British territories.[133] The Raja was not powerful enough to control them. The British Government, according to the treaty, pledged itself to assist him in reducing "to subjection the *taukoors* and other inhabitants of his principality who have revolted and thrown off his authority."[134] This commitment of the British Government in favour of the ruling prince was justified by Metcalfe as it was necessary for the establishment of internal tranquillity.[135] The Governor-General agreed with this contention.[136] In the case of Banswara, the Raja was bound to conduct the state affairs according to the advice of the British Government.[137] This was intended to help the Raja to quell the disturbances that prevailed in that state.[138] It was the commercial interests of the Company that prompted Metcalfe to stipulate these provisions. Both Bikaner and Banswara lay on important trade routes; Bikaner on the route to the North-Western, countries, and Banswara on the route to Gujarat and Malwa. It was essential therefore to have complete peace in these states for the expansion of British trade.[139]

In the treaty with Kotah a supplementary article was introduced which vested the administration of the state in "Rajrana Zalim Singh and after him in his eldest son, Kunwar Madho Singh and his heirs, in regular succession and perpetuity".[140] Zalim Singh was the prime minister of Kotah who

[132] Adam to Metcalfe, October 8, 1817, *op. cit.*, para 19.
[133] Metcalfe to Adam, April 4, 1818: *sec. cons.*, April 10, 1818, No. 23.
[134] Aitchison, *op. cit.*, iii, p. 287, article 7.
[135] Metcalfe to Adam, March 20, 1818: *sec. cons.*, April 10, 1818, No. 23.
[136] Adam to Metcalfe, April 4, 1818: *sec. cons.*, May 17, 1818, No. 16.
[137] Aitchison, *op. cit.*, iii, p. 466, article 5.
[138] Metcalfe to Adam, September 22, 1818: *sec. cons.*, October 10, 1818, No. 4.
[139] *Ibid.*
[140] Aitchison, *op. cit.*, iii, p. 361.

had saved the country from the depredations of the Marathas, the Pindaris, and the Pathans. He completely overhauled the administration and placed it on a sound footing. He had acquired great prestige and authority. He was, in fact, the ruler; Maharao Umed Singh, the Raja, only exercising nominal authority. During his negotiations Metcalfe had anticipated that Zalim Singh would "wish to stipulate for the continuation of the administration in his own person and his descendants".[141] When such a stipulation was desired subsequently he agreed to it at once. The Governor-General gave the Resident unconditional discretion to make any alteration in the treaty.[142]

These provisions in the treaties of Bikaner, Banswara, and Kotah were tantamount to interference in their internal affairs. In Kotah, it even meant an infringement of the sovereignty of that state. The British Government committed itself to secure the office of the prime minister to Zalim Singh and his heirs and successors in perpetuity. This means that the British Government took over from the Raja the authority to appoint his prime minister. The British Government was thereby creating a dual authority in the state.

It is rather odd that Metcalfe, a strong advocate of the policy of non-interference in the internal affairs of Indian states, should be instrumental for these deviations. His attitude towards Indian states was characterized by benevolent paternalism,[143] for he wanted to promote internal peace and security of the states in particular and India in general. The basic aim of these treaties, according to Metcalfe, was the establishment of peace, tranquillity and good government. If this could not be achieved, the treaties, to his mind, stood discredited and defeated. He realized that in Bikaner and Banswara this aim could not be achieved without the interposition of British authority. In Kotah, the Resident believed that the administration had already been guaranteed to Zalim Singh and his heirs without any formal stipulation.[144] He did not, therefore, find any objection in

[141] Metcalfe to Adam, January 8, 1818: *sec. cons.*, January 30, 1818.
[142] Adam to Metcalfe, January 19, 1818: *sec. cons.*, February 6, 1818, No. 19.
[143] Eric Stokes: *The English Utilitarians and India*, p. 18.
[144] Metcalfe to Adam, January 8, 1818: *pol. cons.*, January 30, 1818, No. 69.

introducing such a provision.

Metcalfe tried to deviate from the general instructions in respect of military articles of these treaties also. According to the general instructions, the treaties were to provide for the whole military resources of the tributary states to be placed at the service of the British Government when so demanded.[145] Apart from the general assistance, a specification of exact troops was to be made only in the case of Jodhpur.[146] During the negotiations, Metcalfe endeavoured to obtain the services of a specified number of troops.[147] But the states, in general, were not prepared to stipulate for a contingent considered sufficient by Metcalfe.[148] Hence he preferred to have a general engagement to a "precise and inadequate stipulation."[149]

By 1818 the British Government concluded treaties with all the states of Rajputana. In the evolution of this policy and the execution of the treaties, the Delhi Resident had a stellar role. The imprint of his influence is clearly discernible in the contents of the treaties. Kaye is very right in asserting that both the policy and its execution were emphatically the work of Metcalfe.[150]

---

[145] Adam to Metcalfe, April 20, 1816, *op. cit.*
[146] Adam to Metcalfe, October 8, 1817, *op. cit.*
[147] For example Karoli and Kotah. Metcalfe to Adam, November 12, 1817, *sec. cons.*, December 5, 1817, No. 24.
[148] Metcalfe to Adam, April 27, 1818: *sec. cons.*, May 29, 1818, No. 31.
[149] Metcalfe to Adam, January 8, 1818: *sec. cons.*, January 30, 1818, No. 69.
[150] Kaye, *op. cit.*, i, p. 326.

5
Implementation of British Policy in Rajputana

THE EXTENSION of protective alliances to the states of Central India and Rajputana was a significant advance in the evolution of British imperialism in India. By the settlement of 1817-18 about one hundred and sixty-five principalities of these two regions were written into the treaty map of the Company. Unlike the earlier engagements, the new treaties emphasized the subordinate co-operation and isolation of the protected states with strict vigilance over their external relations.[1] The British Government, in fact, was assuming the role of the paramount power in practice, though not in theory. The duties, rights, and responsibilities emerging out of this changed situation necessitated a rearrangement in the set-up of the Political Agencies in these regions. Anticipating difficulties in the settlement of the political and financial problems resulting from the treaties, the Government decided to entrust the superintendence of its relations with the states of Rajputana to an officer with a military command. These states were, therefore, removed from the jurisdiction of the Delhi Residency and a separate Agency was created in March 1818 under the charge of David Ochterlony.[2] But this arrangement was reversed in December when Metcalfe left Delhi to assume the office of the Secretary in the Secret and Political Department at Calcutta. David Ochterlony was selected to succeed him at Delhi and as a result the states of Rajputana came again under the control of the Delhi Residency.[3]

[1] See William Lee-Warner: *The Native States of India*, pp. 124-25 for a comparison of the nature of the treaties concluded by Lord Wellesley and Lord Hastings.
[2] Adam to Metcalfe, March 27, 1818: *pol. cons.*, April 24, 1818, No. 16.
[3] The management of the relations with the states of Udaipur, Kotah, Bundi, and Jodhpur were entrusted to a new Agency—Western Rajputana States Agency, under the control of Captain Tod.

Ochterlony was "in a tumult of joy and exultation."[4] He regarded his reappointment as a vindication of his merit and reputation which had suffered by his removal from that office in 1806.[5]

The British interests in the states of Rajputana which resulted from the new treaties can be broadly categorized under two heads—economic and political. Metcalfe had underlined in his general plan for the settlement of the financial advantages that might accrue from a close alliance with these states. The treaties concluded by him, barring a few exceptions, stipulated the payment of tributes to the Company. The tribute was in principle intended to meet the expenses that the British Government might incur for proffering protection against external enemies.[6] The amount of the tribute, however, was fixed in most cases, but certain states, such as Udaipur and Jaipur, were charged a portion of their total revenue.[7] Since threat to the security of these states was eliminated once for all by the subjugation of the Marathas and by the pacification of Central India, and consequently no military exertions were required for their defence. The tributes realized from them were a definite financial gain to the Company.[8]

The political interest of the British in this region was primarily the preservation of peace and tranquillity because many of these states had common boundaries with the Company's territories. Any serious disturbance in this area could naturally

[4] Kaye, *op. cit.*, p. 337.
[5] Ochterlony wrote to Metcalfe: "All that I have since gained appears no recompense for a removal which stamped me with those who knew me best and loved me most, as ignorant and incompetent, and with the world in general, venial and culpable. I would not care where; the name alone (the Resident) seems as if it would wash out a stain." Kaye *op. cit.*, i, p. 326.
[6] See M.S. Mehta, *op. cit.*, pp. 157-59.
[7] Udaipur was to pay 1/4th of the total revenue as tribute to the British Government for the first five years. After this term 3/8th of the total revenue in perpetuity. In Jaipur, if the revenues exceeded forty lakhs of rupees, 5/6th of the excess was to be paid to the British Government, over and above the fixed tribute of eight lakhs of rupees. Aitchison, *op. cit.*, iii, pp. 22 and 69.
[8] The British Government had agreed to pay to the Maratha chiefs the tribute which they had been exacting from the Rajput states. This, however, was not the basis on which the tribute was stipulated and therefore, need not be interlinked.

endanger the security of its possessions and also help the resuscitation of the Maratha and the Pindari powers who had only recently been worsted by British arms.

The British Government clearly saw that these interests could not be preserved merely by providing protection against external enemies. The internal conditions of these states almost verged on anarchy, the administrative machinery was in disorder, and the feudal chiefs were up in arms against the ruling authority. Unless these states were restored to a condition of peace and prosperity, the British could not evidently attain the benefits of the new system. This, among other things, involved the task of administrative reorganization and the suppression of the recalcitarant feudal chiefs, which the princes were incapable of achieving without external assistance. But the British had, according to the treaties, promised to refrain from interference in the internal affairs of these states. Be that as it might, they could not remain passive spectators while their principal interests were at jeopardy and, hence, the Governor-General decided to deviate from the general principles of the engagements and sanctioned "some degree of interference to the extent of advice and partial assistance."[9] This deviation in course of time seriously infringed the sovereignty of the states since "the advice and partial assistance" suggested by the Governor-General took the form of active interference and vigorous collaboration in their internal affairs. This gave rise to pro-British factions in almost all courts and, to a great extent, the people, the nobles, and even the ministers looked upon the Resident rather than their master as the source of power and authority. The Residents, who were not infrequently influenced by personal predilictions, betrayed in most cases woeful ignorance of the local traditions, customs and manners. Many of them were fired by exaggerated notions of their rights and duties as the representatives of the paramount power. The developments in Jaipur and Bharatpur and the British attitude towards them clearly manifest these tendencies. In Jaipur the British Government interfered to safeguard its economic interests while at Bharatpur for the sake of peace and tranquillity.

[9] Adam to Ochterlony, March 27, 1818: *pol. cons.*, April 24, 1818, No. 13.

The Affairs of Jaipur

Immediately after the assumption of office, Ochterlony turned his attention to the affairs of Jaipur state which was then facing serious difficulties. The Maratha and Pindari incursions had almost put its administrative machinery out of order. Its financial resources, and its social life were crippled and mangled. The feudal chiefs were rebellious, and the authority of its ruler, Maharaja Jagat Singh, was seriously undermined. Ochterlony took it as his duty, to save the state from this impasse. He applied himself to this task with great zeal and enthusiasm as he was eager to establish himself as an effective diplomat and efficient administrator. At the very outset he exerted himself to reorganize the administration by establishing the authority of the Raja. Under his persuasion, the Raja appointed a new ministry with Mohan Ram Nazir as the chief minister, Thakur Megh Singh as the commander of the state forces, and Rao Chathur Bhuj Huldia as the counsellor.[10] He then paid attention to the resumption of lands and fortresses from the rebellious chiefs and effecting their subordination to the Raja.[11] But the death, on December 21, 1818, of Maharaja Jagat Singh rudely interrupted his endeavours.

As Maharaja Jagat Singh had no son to succeed him, Mohan Ram Nazir installed Mohan Singh, a Narwar[12] prince, as the Raja. According to the Nazir, Mohan Singh was adopted by the late Maharaja as his son and successor. The British recognition was immediately solicited, but the Resident did not promptly accord his approval, since he felt that the legality of the succession had not been established beyond reproach. Rumours were afloat that the young Raja was foisted by the Nazir to perpetuate his authority. Ochterlony called for a report of the prevailing customs and usages in Rajput states and sought the opinion of the eminent *thakurs* of Jaipur. During the enquiry certain important *thakurs* like the Rao Raja of Uniara unequivocally supported the claims of Mohan Singh and no objection

---

[10] Ochterlony to Adam, May 21, 1818: *sec. cons.*, June 19, 1818, No. 22.
[11] Ochterlony to Adam, June 22, 1818: *pol. cons.*, July 17, 1818, No. 42.
[12] A branch of the Jaipur family.

was publicly expressed to his succession.[13] This apparently satisfied Ochterlony about the legitimacy of the Mohan Singh and honesty and probity of the Nazir in effecting the succession. He, therefore, addressed a *kharita* to the young Raja[14] which implied recognition by the British Government. He believed that the succession of Mohan Singh would facilitate friendly intercourse between the British Government and the state of Jaipur.[15]

However, Mohan Singh was not unanimously supported by the *thakurs* as Ochterlony had believed. A section of the nobles who had earlier opposed the alliance with the British Government did not accept the Narwar prince as the rightful claimant to the throne. Mohan Singh was looked upon as a protege of the Nazir who was disliked by them because of his active participation in the resumption of Khalsa lands and close collaboration with the Resident in administrative reorganization. He was considered a friend of Ochterlony and a stooge of the British Government, and was often accused of "giving up everything to the English". In the succession of Mohan Singh this party saw the perpetuation of the Nazir's authority and through him the influence of the British Government. They put forward Thakur Bahadur Singh of Jhallye as an alternate candidate whose claims, according to them, were superior to those of the Narwar prince and they therefore directly approached the Government for its intervention in his favour.[16] The Governor-General promptly instructed the Resident to procure "more satisfactory proofs of the actual succession either in the way of hereditary right or by indubitable act of adoption" before a final declaration could be made in favour of Mohan Singh.[17]

Ochterlony once confessed that he was "not bred in a

---

[13] Ochterlony to Adam, February 1, 1819: *pol. cons.*, March 6, 1819, No. 83.
[14] Ochterlony to Metcalfe, February 25, 1819: *pol. cons.*, February 25, 1819, No. 15.
[15] Ochterlony to Adam, January 20, 1819: *pol. cons.*, February 6, 1819, No. 44.
[16] Lachman Rao to Metcalfe, Received on February 14, 1819: *pol. cons.*, February 20, 1819, No. 44.
[17] Metcalfe to Ochterlony, February 20, 1819: *pol. cons.*, February 20, 1819, No. 45.

school which teaches a proper degree of caution."[18] When he was sounded about the impropriety of the succession, instead of viewing it objectively and examining all available evidence before coming to a conclusion, he clung tenaciously to his former decision. He regarded the objection of the *thakurs* to the succession as an injury to his personal prestige. He believed that the opposition was animated by selfish motives, the sole aim of which was to create anarchy, to weaken the hands of the government, and thus to evade the payment of money due from them.[19] Though Ochterlony left for Jaipur to guage the sentiments of the dissenting *thakurs*, according to the instructions of the Governor-General, he was strongly prejudiced against them.[20] He was not prepared to grant any possibility of truth in their contention.[21]

Meanwhile the birth of a posthumous son to Maharaja Jagat Singh on April 25, 1819, changed the situation radically. He was proclaimed the Raja under the title of Sawai Jai Singh.[22] Rani Bhattianiji, the queen-dowager, immediately took up the issue of the appointment of a ministry to manage the administration during the minority of the Raja. The new administration, as contemplated by her, was to consist of Rathori Rani[23] as the regent, Rawal Bhairisal as the *mukhtiar*, and Fouji Ram as one of the counsellors. Ochterlony, to his dismay, understood that in the new set-up Mohan Ram Nazir would have no place. The Nazir had made himself odious to the Rani and a large section of the *thakurs* by his insolent behaviour.[24] But according to

[18] Ochterlony to Metcalfe, March 21, 1819: *pol. cons.*, April 17, 1819, No. 30.
[19] Ochterlony to Metcalfe, March 15, 1819: *pol. cons.*, April 3, 1819, No. 21.
[20] Ochterlony to Metcalfe, March 21, 1819, *op. cit.*
[21] Ochterlony to Metcalfe, March 15, 1819, *op. cit.*
[22] Ochterlony to Metcalfe, April 25, 1819: *pol. cons.*, May 14, 1819, No. 29.
[23] Rathori Rani was the senior Rani of Raja Jagat Singh and so enjoyed greater prestige and authority. She adopted Jai Singh as her son and, therefore, could claim the situation of the regent.
[24] It was openly talked in the court that the Nazir had secretly plotted the death of Maharaja Jagat Singh. The Rani even believed that he had tried to effect a miscarriage of her pregnancy by use of charms. Rani Bhattaini to Ochterlony, May 2, 1819: *pol. cons.*, June 3, 1819, No. 20.

the Resident's estimate, he was the best person in Jaipur to head the administration. During his tenure of office the revenues of the state had shown considerable improvement. He was honest and efficient and, above all, amenable to the influence and advice of the British Government.[25] In his removal the Resident saw the end of his personal influence as well as the ruin of the state. Ochterlony therefore decided to resist all attempts to keep away the Nazir from office by the Rani. The first step in this direction was his endeavour to establish the legality and propriety of the adoption of Mohan Singh in order to absolve the Nazir from the charges of selfish motives brought against him by the *thakurs*. Much against the wishes of the *thakurs*, Ochterlony raised the question of the adoption in their assembly and the Nazir was thus given an opportunity to explain his conduct.[26] The *thakurs* then agreed that the adoption was in keeping with the regular practice and unanimously declared that they would have undoubtedly acknowledged the adopted son, if Maharaja Jai Singh had not been born.[27] This was tantamount to a vindication of the Nazir's action, which precisely was the purpose of Ochterlony in bringing up this issue at that stage. He then tried to secure the post of *mukhtiar* for the Nazir by influencing Rani Bhattianiji. He advised her against the appointment of Rathori Rani as the regent for by doing so she would be dispensing with the powers and previleges of sovereignty which by right belonged to her.[28] Ochterlony knew that Rathori Rani would be more unmanageable than Rani Bhattianiji as she was considered to be more efficient and more conscious of the rights and independence of the state. He pursuaded the Rani to place complete confidence in the Nazir and employ him for the welfare of the state. If this were not acceptable to the Rani, he informed her that the Nazir could not be dismissed without the express order of the Governor-General. He also made the Rani responsible for the "life, honour,

[25] Ochterlony to Metcalfe, April 25, 1819: *pol. cons.*. May 22, 1819, No. 27.
[26] Ochterlony to Metcalfe, April 29, 1819, *op. cit.*
[27] *Ibid.*
[28] Ochterlony to Rani Bhattiani April 30, 1819: *pol. cons.*, June 3, 1819, No. 20.

and reputation" of the Nazir.[29]

In these demands of the Resident, the Rani saw the violation of the treaty stipulations and infringement of the sovereignty of the state.[30] The appointment of *mukhtiar* was a question of internal arrangement and the British Government, she thought, had no right to interfere. To Ochterlony, however, matters stood on a different footing. He considered a strict adherence to the letter of the treaty as delusive, unimaginable, and inexpedient. He contented that the right of interference, though not provided in the treaty, was implicit in the role of a protector.[81] If circumstances so warranted he did not rule out active interference as he believed that he was "not fighting the battle of Mohan Ram Nazir, so much as the prosperity of the state and the interest of the infant Raja."[32] The Government did not share the Resident's viewpoint. The Governor-General was concerned only with the preservation of the rights and interests of the British Government as well as those of the minor Raja, without the least consideration for the individuals who managed the administration. Interference was to be resorted to only when those interests were in any way injured but not for the selection of personnel and other minor details of administration.[33] But in view of the long minority of the Raja the Government foresaw the possibility of interference in future, from which the Governor-General wanted to abstain as long as possible. In the present circumstance the Resident was instructed to offer only advice and assistance.

Meanwhile, opposition to the Nazir was increasing every day. Some important nobles like Megh Singh of Diggi who had formerly stood by the cause of the Nazir now withdrew their support.[34] The Rani and the *thakurs* headed by Bhairisal had also become very stiff in their opposition. Ochterlony realized the futility of upholding the Nazir in the office and ultimately

---

[29] Ochterlony to Rani Bhattiani April 30, 1819, *op. cit.*
[30] Rani Bhattiani to Ochterlony, May 5, 1819: *pol. cons.*, June 3, 1819, No. 20.
[31] Ochterlony to Metcalfe, May 7, 1819: *pol. cons.*, June, 3, 1819, No. 19.
[32] *Ibid.*
[33] Metcalfe, to Ochterlony, June 3, 1819: *pol. cons.*, June 3, 1819, No. 24.
[34] Ochterlony to Metcalfe, May 9, 1819: *pol. cons.*, June 3, 1819, No. 22.

IMPLEMENTATION OF BRITISH POLICY IN RAJPUTANA

agreed to his dismissal.[35] He, however, extracted a guarantee from the Jaipur government in respect of the "life, honour, and subsistence" of the Nazir.[36]

The opposition of the Rani and her adherents to his attempt to foist his nominee in the office of the *mukhtiar* highly embittered the Resident. The Rani had unfavourably reacted to his advice regarding the formation of the ministry and had selected the personnel of the government without consulting him. The influence of the Resident was clearly at an end. This discomfiture naturally coloured the attitude of Ochterlony towards the new administration. He became unsympathetic, if not hostile, to the Rani and her ministers. He believed that they were corrupt and insincere and lacked vigour and boldness for tackling the host of problems that faced the state. The result of their management, according to him, was most disappointing. The collection of revenue considerably diminished, people were oppressed by the government officials, the peasantry were impoverished and discontented, the troops dissatisfied and mutinous and even the battalion stationed at the palace some time went without food.[37] He pointed out that a minister of real integrity, knowledge, and discernment would be able to revitalize the administration and set the state on the path of prosperity. As the Governor-General, was not prone to sanction any interference in the selection of the personnel of the administration, Ochterlony solicited the appointment of a Political Agent authorized to interfere in the internal arrangements of the state it was the only possible panacea for the evils engulfing the state, according to him.[38] Though the Government was in agreement with the basic assumptions of the Resident in respect of the rights and duties of the paramount power, particularly the prevention of the defalcation of the revenue during the minority of a ruler, it was not inclined to accept the remedy suggested by him. The recommendation of Ochterlony for the appointment of an Agent was,

---

[35] Ochterlony to Metcalfe, May 25, 1819: *pol. cons.*, September 11, 1819, No. 19.
[36] Ochterlony to Bhairisal, May 6, 1819: *pol. cons.*, June 3, 1819, No. 20.
[37] Ibid.
[38] Ochterlony to Metcalfe, October 10, 1820: *pol. cons.* October 28, 1820, No. 18.

hence, turned down. The Governor-General, however, foresaw the necessity of direct interference in the internal administration, if the condition further deteriorated. But the Government decided to wait and watch instead of taking a precipitate action. Ochterlony was highly critical of this attitude, especially as interference had already been sanctioned in Kotah and Udaipur. He lamented the "coquetry of the British proceedings, advancing at one moment and retiring at another," thereby losing power, prestige, and popularity.[39] He was convinced that nothing but a direct and decided interference in the administration could save the state from ruin. And the earlier it was resorted to the better.

A scuffle between Fauji Ram[40] and Hanumant Chela,[41] resulting in the death of both, provided Ochterlony with an opportunity to enlarge upon the ineptness of the administration.[42] The Governor-General now decided to depute a European officer to Jaipur to assist the state government to establish a clean and efficient administration, but he was not authorized to interfere in its working. Captain Stewart was consequently appointed the Agent to the Governor-General under the direct control of the Resident at Delhi.[43]

The intention of Ochterlony in seeking the appointment of an Agent was to prove his case in favour of an extensive interference in Jaipur. "A full and partial report" from the local Agent, he believed, would favourably influence the Governor-General. He told Stewart in unmistakable terms: "It is only imperious necessity which perhaps will warrant or induce the authorities to exercise a more positive and direct interference. When that necessity is proved and the happiness of the people, the welfare of the state and the interests of the infant Raja are shown to be involved or benignant, the Government will no

---

[39] Ochterlony to Stewart, April, 13, 1821: *pol. cons.*, May 26, 1821, No. 6.
[40] Fauji Ram was a close associate of Rathori Rani. He wielded great influence in the palace circles.
[41] Hanumant Chela was the guru of Rani Bhattiani. He also held the command of the palace guards.
[42] Ochterlony to Swinton, Secretary to Government, January 19, 1821: *pol. cons.*, February 10, 1821, No. 7.
[43] Swinton to Stewart, February 10, 1821: *pol. cons.*, February 10, 1821, No. 11.

longer hesitate."⁴⁴ It implied that Stewart should prove that imperious necessity, which he did admirably well.

A few days after his assumption of office, Stewart bitterly complained about his inability to check the prevailing malpractices without authority to interfere in the administration. His position in Jaipur was that of a passive spectator.⁴⁵ The Rani purposely kept the Agent aloof from all important state functionaries.⁴⁶ Even Rawal Bhairisal had to seek the pretence of a hunting excursion to convey his sentiments to the Agent.

The malpractices as detailed by Stewart were gross speculation of revenue, mismanagement in revenue collection, wasteful expenditure and all other evils connected with them. To prevent them he suggested the direct interference of the British Government, particularly in the revenue settlement.⁴⁷ Supported by the local Agent, Ochterlony now seized this opportunity to press his demand for active interference.⁴⁸ In these circumstances, the Governor-General realized that British interference was the only effective means to prevent the diminution and defalcation of revenue. It alone could enable the Jaipur government to fulfil the tributary obligations and avert the apparently inevitable ruin of the state. The Governor-General, therefore, authorized the Resident to interfere in the internal administration of Jaipur.⁴⁹ The interference, it was pointed out, was to be limited "to the improvement of revenue by the adoption of a fair and judicious settlement" and was not to include the details of the disbursements of the government.⁵⁰ The Agent was also not to meddle with the choice of the executive officers of the state. The failure of the Jaipur government to fulfil the payment of the fixed tribute, not to say about the failure to provide the benefit beyond the stipulated fixed tribute was, according to the Governor-General, the *raison d'etre* of this measure.⁵¹

⁴⁴ Ochterlony to Stewart, April 13, 1821, *op. cit.*
⁴⁵ Stewart to Swinton, June 7, 1821: *pol. cons.*, June 30, 1821, No. 7.
⁴⁶ *Ibid.*
⁴⁷ Ochterlony to Swinton, May 27, 1821: *pol. cons.*, June 23, 1821, No. 14.
⁴⁸ *Ibid.*
⁴⁹ Swinton to Ochterlony, June 30, 1821: *pol cons.*, June 30, 1821, No. 8.
⁵⁰ *Ibid.*
⁵¹ *Ibid.*

Ochterlony was largely responsible for British interference and consequently for the violation of the treaty stipulations. It must also be emphasized that he was in no small measure responsible for the confusion and corruption in the state. He did not allow the Rani to settle down to the management of the state affairs. His support to Mohan Ram Nazir only helped to aggravate factional rivalries. There was no justification for his feverish attempts to foist the Nazir on her. It clearly suggested that he wanted to perpetuate his influence on the Jaipur court rather than ensure an efficient administration. It is really inconceivable that there was no other efficient man available in the state to head the administration. After Mohan Ram Nazir, ceased to be a power, we must not think, as Ochterlony believed, that there was nothing but chaos in Jaipur. The Governor-General was quite correct in his view that it was not within the rights of the British Government to be interested in the appointments of administrative personnel in the protected states.

Ochterlony also tried to create some sort of a dual authority in Jaipur. Rawal Bhairisal and the Rani were not getting on well. Bhairisal was *mukhtiar* only in name, the actual authority was wielded by the Rani. The Resident coaxed Bhairisal "to avail himself of his rank and influence on all important matters and occasions and the benefit he would derive from his being acknowledged as the *mukhtiar* by the British Government."[52] Instead of effecting a reconciliation between them, Ochterlony only helped to increase their estrangement. With the backing of the Resident, Bhairisal became more and more indifferent to the orders and authority of the Rani, thereby aggravating inefficiency and chaos in the administration. Ochterlony possibly aimed at setting up a strong pro-British party at the court, more so after the dismissal of Mohan Ram Nazir, and this created serious complications. There is little doubt that the Government did not use its discretion and judgment fairly in supporting Ochterlony and in approving of direct interference in the administration of Jaipur.

---

[52] Ochterlony to Metcalfe, October 1, 1820: *pol. cons.*, October 20, 1820, No. 8.

Bharatpur Succession

Succession disputes culminating in internecine strife were the bane of almost all Indian states. The Jat state of Bharatpur, which had in the past very often set aside the legal claimant to the throne was no exception, violating the right of primogeniture and heredity in favour of a vigorous and capable ruler. In February 1825, Baldev Singh, the ruler of Bharatpur, died leaving behind an illegitimate son, Balwant Singh. Before the death of the Raja, Ochterlony had recognized Balwant Singh as the legal heir by conferring a *khilat* on him without obtaining the approval of the Governor-General. On the demise of the Raja, Balwant Singh immediately succeeded to the throne under the guardianship of Rao Ram Ratan, his maternal uncle.[53]

Durjansal, a nephew of Baldev Singh, had put forward his claim to the throne on the occasion of the latter's accession, on the plea that Randhir Singh, the former Raja, had intended to adopt him as his son and successor.[54] He was then set aside as his claim was generally considered to be false. Now he found another opportunity to press his claim, especially because the Raja was a minor. On March 13, 1825, he seized the fort of Bharatpur and the person of the minor Raja by *coup d'etat*.[55]

Ochterlony immediately reacted against the precipitate action of Durjansal. He had already committed the British Government to uphold the claims of Balwant Singh. He therefore proclaimed the determination of the British Government to expel the usurper from Bharatpur[56] and punish him for his "vile acts."[57] In order to crush any possible resistance from Durjansal, he ordered the mobilization of the army, calling for

---

[53] Baijnath, vakil of Bharatpur, to Ochterlony, March 2, 1825: *pol. cons.*, April 5, 1825, No. 37.
[54] Ochterlony to Swinton, January 28, 1824: *pol. cons.*, February 21, 1824, No. 14.
[55] Macsween, Magistrate of Agra, to Ochterlony, March 14, 1825: *pol. cons.*, April 15, 1825, No. 7.
[56] Proclamation of Ochterlony: *pol. cons.*, April 5, 1825, No. 44.
[57] Ochterlony to the Chiefs and people of Bharatpur, March 28, 1825: *pol. cons.*, April 15, 1825, No. 13.

troops from Nasirabad, Agra, and Mathura. But realizing the strength of the opposition, Durjansal disclaimed any intention of usurping the throne[58] and offered himself for the guardianship of the young Raja and the *mukhtiari* during his minority.[59] But Ochterlony was apprehensive about his intentions and sincerity and continued the military preparations.[60] He was prepared to believe him had he executed a written engagement disclaiming all his intentions to usurp the throne[61] and delivered the minor Raja to the British Government personally in his camp.[62]

But the Government, chafing under the reverses of the Burmese War, did not approve of the steps taken by Ochterlony. The Home Government's disapprobation of interference in Nagpur succession, the depleted financial resources, and weak military position in North India, all these influenced their decision. The Governor-General looked upon the problem of succession as a purely internal question in which the British Government was not authorized to interfere according to the treaty stipulations. If at all a deviation became necessary due to political expediency, that decision could be taken by the Government and not by the Resident.[63] Ochterlony was, therefore, instructed to stop the advance of the troops towards Bharatpur and withdraw the proclamation issued by him against Durjansal.[64]

It was indeed a severe rebuff to Ochterlony. He had not anticipated that the Governor-General would disagree with him on a matter concerning the rights and obligations of the British Government as the paramount power. He received the sentiments of the Government with a sense of "surprise, mortification, and regret", and preferred to resign his office rather than accept the

[58] Ochterlony to Swinton, March 30, 1825: *pol. cons.*, April 15, 1825, No. 15.
[59] Ochterlony to Swinton, March 24, 1825: *pol. cons.*, April 5, 1825, No. 45.
[60] Ochterlony to Major General Martindell, March 25, 1825: *pol. cons.*, April 15, 1825, No. 11.
[61] Ochterlony to Lumsden, Department of Commissariat General, March 25, 1825: *pol. cons.*, April 15, 1825, No. 11.
[62] Ochterlony to Swinton, April 5, 1825: *pol. cons.*, July 15, 1825, No. 4.
[63] Swinton to Ochterlony, April 3, 1825: *pol. cons.*, April 5, 1825, No. 46.
[64] *Ibid.*

repudiation of his policy.⁶⁵ The Government welcomed the offer. The Governor-General was, in fact, contemplating the retirement of Ochterlony.⁶⁶ The physical debilities due to old age, for he was then 67 years old, and frequent illness had almost incapacitated him from attending to his duties with promptitude and regularity. Moreover, it was suspected that he was overstepping the limits of independent action authorized to a Resident. His management of Jaipur affairs, the investiture of *khilat* on Balwant Singh,⁶⁷ and the mobilization of troops without the approval of the Government, justified this suspicion. His resignation was, therefore, taken as a convenient opportunity to effect his retirement.⁶⁸

Upon Ochterlony's retirement, Charles Metcalfe was selected to fill the "high diplomatic situation in Upper India," as the Resident and Civil Commissioner of Delhi, with the state of Rajputana annexed to his charge.⁶⁹ Consequently, Metcalfe took charge of the Residency on October 21, 1825.⁷⁰ A liberal in political beliefs, Metcalfe belonged to the "paternalist school" in his attitude towards Indian states. He was,

---

⁶⁵ Ochterlony to Swinton, April 14, 1825: *pol. cons.*, July 15, 1825, No. 12.

⁶⁶ Swinton to Metcalfe, April 16, 1825: Kaye, *op. cit.*, ii, p. 23.

⁶⁷ The Government knew about it only when Balwant Singh addressed a *kharita* to the Governor-General.

⁶⁸ However, this did not become necessary as Ochterlony died on July 15, 1825, with a feeling that he was injured, insulted and dishonoured. There is a general misconception that Oehterlony at the time of his resignation was the Resident at Delhi. Even Kaye mentions him to be so. (Kaye, *op. cit.*, ii, p. 25). He, however, had no connection at this time with the Delhi Residency. He was then the British Resident for Malwa and Rajputana with his headquarters at Delhi.

⁶⁹ In 1821 the states of Rajputana were separated from the jurisdiction of the Delhi Residency and a new Agency, Malwa and Rajputana States Agency, was organized under the charge of David Ochterlony. The Delhi Residency was then relegated to the status of an Agency and H.J. Middleton was appointed as the Agent. Middleton remained in office for about seven months. After that changes took place in quick succession. A Ross who succeeded him left Delhi after one year. Then William Fraser was in charge for a few months. C. Elliot took over from him and remained in office till 1825.

⁷⁰ Metcalfe to Swinton, October 21, 1825: *pol. cons.*, November 11, 1825, No. 5.

in principle, a staunch advocate of the policy of non-interference in the affairs of the protected states. His attitude was mainly conditioned by the revolution that had taken place in the position of the British power in India in the second decade of the nineteenth century. The subjugation of the Marathas removed from the Indian political scene the only possible contending power to the sovereignty of India, and placed the British in the unquestionable, though not unchallenged, position of the paramount power with a vast territory to govern. The problem that faced the British administrators and diplomats now was not the conquest but consolidation of the hard-earned empire in an alien country, which was indeed a more arduous task than conquest.[71]

The consensus of opinion among British statesmen at this time was that the British empire in India was at the threshold of a *siecle d'or*. Metcalfe did not share this view. He was sceptical about the future of the Empire and believed, in fact, that it had that already passed the brilliance and vigour of youth, and that it was destined to be short-lived.[72] In order to forestall its eventual death, he considered the policy of non-interference with a paternalist bias, the most sound and suitable. He was prepared to accept annexation as an alternative.[73] If that was not possible he was inclined to leave the states to themselves to manage their internal affairs, which he believed would help to conciliate both the princes and the people who undoubtedly preferred their own traditions and institutions to those of the West. This awareness is clearly discernible in his advocacy of the policy of non-interference towards the states of Rajputana, Hyderabad, and Nagpur.

In implementing this policy in Rajputana, as Metcalfe himself confessed, there were very many impediments. The fulfilment of the duties and obligations of the paramount power involved in itself interference to a certain extent, especially when these states were to be guarded not only against external enemies but also against a host of internal problems. A strict adherence

[71] Malcolm, *op. cit.*, ii, p. 65.
[72] Metcalfe's minute, October 11, 1829, John William Kaye, (ed.): *Selection from the Private Papers of Lord Metcalfe*, pp. 161-77.
[73] Metcalfe's paper, September 7, 1820, *ibid.*, pp. 151-52.

to non-interference would naturally lead to the abrogation of the responsibilities of paramountcy, thereby allowing forces of dissension and turbulance to thrive freely and this would eventually endanger not only the protected states but their protectors as well. This consideration had often compelled the Home authorities to sanction deviation from the declared policy and in some cases even to direct it.[74] The situation in Bharatpur, according to Metcalfe, warranted vigorous British exertions as it threatened the recurrence of anarchy and disorder in that region from which it was only recently rescned by the British Government. It was, therefore, imperative that the British Government should intervene to safeguard the interests of the lawful succession in Bharatpur.[75]

The views of Metcalfe on this issue were closely akin to those of Ochterlony. Although the Governor-General had reprimanded the old General, he now agreed with Metcalfe.[76] To this change in policy two reasons were attributed. First, Durjansal's intentions of usurping the authority of the Maharaja of Bharatpur had now become quite clear. Secondly, the desertion of Madho Singh,[77] the brother of Durjansal, had created "the most serious internal anarchy, bloodshed and commotion", thereby threatening the tranquillity of the adjoining British territories.[78] But behind this decision of the Government the influence of Metcalfe was too apparent.[79] The Government now decided to

[74] Memorandum of Metcalfe, August 29, 1825: *sec. cons.*, September 16, 1825, No. 21.
[75] *Ibid.*
[76] Resolution of the Governor-General-in-Council, September 16, 1825: *sec. cons.*, September 16, 1825, No. 25.
[77] Madho Singh tried to capture power and failing in this object, he went out of Bharatpur and captured the fort of Deeg. He then solicited the help of the British Government, promising the accession of Maharaja Balwant Singh and demanding for himself the *mukhtiari*. Macsween to Ochterlony, July 1, 1825: *pol. cons.*, July 29, 1825, No. 11; and Baijnath to Ochterlony, July 1, 1825: *pol. cons.*, July 29, 1825, No. 14.
[78] Resolution of the Governor-General-in-Council, September 16, 1825, *op. cit.*
[79] After the fall of Bharatpur, Amherst wrote to Metcalfe: "That in undertaking this great achievement I was principally influenced by your advice, I shall readily acknowledge. You would have shared the disgrace of failure, and must, therefore, be admitted to the honours of the triumph." Amherst to Metcalfe, January 29, 1826: Kaye, *op. cit.*, ii, Appendix, p. 462.

interfere in Bharatpur in favour of the minor Raja in order to forestall the possibility of general commotion in North India, which the disturbances in Bharatpur might otherwise produce.[80] Metcalfe was instructed to uphold the claims of Balwant Singh, if practicable by expostulation and remonstrnace, and should these fail by the use of force."[81]

Metcalfe preferred peaceful methods to solve the tangle to begin with. But the turbulent situation in Bharatpur and the uncompromising attitude of Durjansal soon convinced him that it would be necessary to use force to achieve his aim. The preparations for a field force were, therefore, immediately started under the command of Lord Combermere, the Commander-in-Chief. Durjansal's attempts to protract the negotiations and suspend the advance of the British troops in order to gain time for war preparations were defeated by Metcalfe's insistence on his unqualified submission and personal surrender. The details of the seige of Bharatpur need not detain us here. The fort which had admirably withstood the British onslaughts in 1805 now succumbed before the British might on January 18, 1826. Durjansal was captured and sent to Allahabad as a prisoner. This ensured the succession of Balwant Singh and peace was established.

New Administration in Bharatpur

Metcalfe was now confronted with the problem of establishing an efficient administration in Bharatpur. The disputed succession and the turmoil that followed had completely paralyzed its administration. He realized that the government of Bharatpur could not be put on an efficient footing without external assistance, and that posed the question of the extent to which the British Government should exert itself in that direction. Metcalfe was of the opinion that the paramount power after restoring the legal heir could not abandon the state to its fate and ignore the task of administrative reorganization, even if it amounted to a violation of the principles of non-interference. But while discharg-

[80] Resolution of the Governor-General-in-Council, September 16, 1825, *op. cit.*
[81] *Ibid.*

ing the obligations of the paramount power, he wanted to limit interference to a minimum. He was eager to leave the Bharatpur government to itself without any semblance of British interference, but in the prevailing circumstances he found it almost impossible. The personnel of the administration had, therefore, to be selected with the approval of Metcalfe. It consisted of Rani Amrit Kunwar, the eldest Rani of Baldev Singh, as the regent; Faujdar Churaman, Diwan Jawaharlal as ministers; and Gyani Baijnath, a close confidant of the Rani, as her agent.[82] Major Lockett was appointed the Political Agent on the request of the Rani and the ministers in order to give them "the countenance and support of the British Government."[83] The Governor-General was not in favour of the appointment of an Agent partly for political and partly for economic reasons.[84] Metcalfe, however, considered it an indispensable measure on account of the minority of the Raja and the symptoms of inefficiency visible in the local government.[85] The Governor-General then sanctioned the appointment.[86]

The new administration by its very character was foredoomed to failure. In Bharatpur, Churaman and Jawaharlal were generally looked upon as quislings since they had joined the British camp during the time of the siege. They had earlier supported the claims of Durjansal, which made them obnoxious to the Rani as well. Their appointment as ministers was, unfortunate as they enjoyed neither popularity with the people nor the confidence of the Rani. But Metcalfe had intended them to be the spearhead of the administration, constituting in themselves "an efficient and responsible government" and conducting the business of the state in collaboration with the Rani.[87]

The Rani was an ambitious lady who wanted to concentrate all powers in her hands. With the assistance of Baijnath,

[82] Metcalfe to Swinton, February 10, 1826: *pol. cons.*, February 24, 1826, No. 16.
[83] Metcalfe to Swinton, February 9, 1826: *pol. cons.*, February 24, 1826, No. 17.
[84] Swinton to Metcalfe, February 24, 1826, *op. cit.*
[85] Metcalfe to Swinton, March 14, 1856: *pol. cons.*, April 14, 1826, No. 4.
[86] Swinton to Metcalfe, April 12, 1826: *pol. cons.*, April 14, 1826, No. 7.
[87] Metcalfe to Swinton, February 10, 1826, *op. cit.*

her close confidant and alleged paramour, she endeavoured to attain this end. Her first step was the supersession of Jawaharlal in the revenue department by Govindram, who was a nephew of Churaman.[88] Metcalfe agreed to this change on the plea of "adhering to the sound principle of not interfering in the internal concerns of a foreign state."[89] But he did not realize that by doing so he was virtually transferring the government to the Rani from the hands of the ministers. Elated by this success, the Rani strove to consolidate her power. She was eager to dispense with the services of Churaman because he had disobeyed her commands during the siege of Bharatpur.[90] She completely excluded the ministers from all transactions of the state business. They were even prohibited from meeting the British Agent, except in the presence of Baijnath[91] who had acquired a pernicious ascendancy in the affairs of the state. He was, in fact, the *mukhtiar* and actual administrator all but in name. But he had no insight into the problems of administration. Consequently, chaos and confusion were rampant in the affairs of the state. People generally complained that there was "no government, no administration and no office to hear and redress their grievances."[92] The only corrective to this mismanagement, Lockett believed, could be a direct interference of the British Government. But neither the Resident nor the Governor-General was then inclined to sanction it. Lockett felt helpless and ineffective.[93]

In pursuance of the policy of non-interference, Metcalfe had so far given the Rani a free hand in all the affairs of the state. But the outbreak of a mutiny among the troops of Bharatpur, which further highlighted the inefficiency and mismanagement of Baijnath, compelled the Resident to reconsider his stand.[94] The experiment of conceding unlimited power to the Rani had proved unwise and impractical. He therefore decided

[88] Lockett to Metcalfe, February 28, 1826: *pol. cons.*, April 14, 1826, No. 14.
[89] Metcalfe to Swinton, March 14, 1826: *pol. cons.*, April 14, 1826, No. 4.
[90] Lockett to Metcalfe, May 12, 1826: *pol. cons.*, July 7, 1826, No. 11.
[91] *Ibid.*
[92] *Ibid.*
[93] Lockett to Metcalfe, May 27, 1826: *pol. cons.*, July 7, 1826, No. 15.
[94] Lockett to Metcalfe, May 26, 1828: *pol. cons.*, July 7, 1826, No. 13.

to revert to the initial system and entrust the administration to
Jawaharlal and Churaman, with Govindram as their assistant,
under the nominal regency of the Rani.[95] He, however, did not
want to insist on these individuals, if better qualified persons were
available to manage the administration. But the influence of
Baijnath was to be curbed and he could even be removed from
Bharatpur if the ministers so desired.[96] The Political Agent
was not to have any hand in the administration, except that he
could tender advice whenever necessary.

The proposal for the new set-up caused all round dissatisfaction in Bharatpur. The Rani was not prepared to head any
administration in which Jawaharlal was associated.[97] If it was
imposed on her, she threatened to shut herself up in the palace
with the young Raja and Baijnath.[98] Metcalfe had already
instructed the Agent to inform the Rani that the British
Government might either assume direct control over the affairs
of Bharatpur or desist entirely from affording any protection to
that government, in case any opposition was evinced by her to
the proposed changes.[99] This was intended to be simply a threat
to bring about the submission of the Rani. But she defeated
this move by readily agreeing to the direct control of the
British Government rather than accepting the administration of
Jawaharlal and Churaman.[100]

The ministers also did not consider this arrangement to be
practical, unless the general superintendence of affairs was
assumed by the British Government. It was evident that the
Rani would not co-operate with Jawaharlal and Churaman. A
ministry responsible to itself with no superior authority to
inspect the public accounts and proceedings could not be
effective and popular with the people. As Jawaharlal put it,
"a *malik* was absolutely necessary and that *malik* should be the
British Government."[101] The Agent was also of the view that
the ministers would not be able to discharge their duties without

---

[95] Metcalfe to Lockett, May 28, 1826: *pol. cons.*, July 7, 1826, No. 11.
[96] *Ibid.*
[97] Lockett to Metcalfe, May 26, 1826, *op. cit.*
[98] Lockett to Metcalfe, June 3, 1826: *pol. cons.*, July 7, 1826, No. 19.
[99] Metcalfe to Lockett, May 28, 1826, *op. cit.*
[100] *Ibid.*
[101] *Ibid.*

the direct authority of the British Government.[102]

The refusal of the Rani to associate herself with the new set-up and the hesitation of the ministers to undertake the task without an acknowledged superior authority created a complicated situation. But Metcalfe was not inclined to abandon the policy of non-interference. He was prepared, at the most, to allow the Agent to inspect the accounts and proceedings of the ministers. He thought that the assumption of the role of *malik* as suggested by Jawaharlal, would change the national character of the government at Bharatpur. Therefore he did not want to mix up the authority of the British Government in its administration. His refusal to sanction the proclamation, as suggested by Lockett, was an expression of this intention.[103] The proclamation was to announce to the people of Bharatpur the establishment of the new administration and the determination of the British Government to maintain it, if necessary.[104] The implication of this proclamation was too apparent not to escape the notice of Metcalfe. It would have undoubtedly convinced the people that the administration would be conducted under the immediate superintendence of the British Government. But in view of the fluid state of affairs at Bharatpur he agreed to consider the ministry responsible to the British Government and provide all possible help for the discharge of its public duties. Nevertheless, the ministry was not to act as a part of the British Government, but was to conduct its affairs on behalf of the Raja.[105] In effect, the edges of demarcation between the two poses were not very sharp. But what Metcalfe wanted was to allow the Bharatpur government to remain national in character and to make no other government "ostensibly concerned in its public acts".[106] If this system could not be implemented, he preferred complete assumption of the administration by the British Government or the abandonment of the state "to its fate in the hands of the present objectionable ministry". The Governor-General was in agreement with this view and sanctioned the experiment of a native administration

[102] Lockett to Metcalfe, June 9, 1826: *pol. cons.*, July 7, 1826, No. 21.
[103] Metcalfe to Lockett, June 11, 1826: *pol. cons.*, July 7, 1826, No. 21.
[104] Lockett to Metcalfe, June 9, 1826, *op. cit.*
[105] Metcalfe to Lockett, June 17, 1826: *pol. cons.*, July 7, 1826, No. 23.
[106] Metcalfe to Lockett, Jnue 11, 1826, *op. cit.*

IMPLEMENTATION OF BRITISH POLICY IN RAJPUTANA 87

responsible to the British Government before adopting any other course of action.[107] In case the Rani objected to the minitsry of Jawaharlal and Churaman, the Resident was authorized to deprive her of the position of the regent and entrust the government to a council of regency consisting of the ministers.[108] At last the Rani realized the urgency of the situation and agreed to the suggestions of Metcalfe. Jawaharlal was placed at the head of the revenue department, Churaman with Govindram as his assistant at the head of *faujdari*, while Sriram Poojari was appointed to act as a liaison between the Agent and the Rani.[109] Baijnath was expelled from the city. The responsibility and powers of the government were vested entirely in the ministers, with the Rani as the nominal regent. Yet the ministers were prohibited from doing anything without consulting her.

As earlier foreseen by the ministers and the Political Agent, this arrangement did not work well. The acquiescence of the Rani in this arrangement was only a stratagem to keep the power in her hands as far as possible. Baijnath, though expelled from the city, continued to exert influence on her through his secret agents[110] and also on the administration through his numerous friends and relatives who occupied important administrative posts.[111] These elements completely paralyzed the efficient working of the ministry by their non-co-operation and insubordination. The Rani attempted to exclude the ministers from all business of the state by degrees.[112] She did not allow Churaman to have any control over the newly organized corps, and induced the *jagirdars* not to comply with the orders of the ministers without her consent.[113] She also expressed her intention to assume complete authority over the army and administration, and general control and superintendence of all departments of the state. The ministers were helpless and ineffective and found themselves in a predicament as according to the customs of the

[107] Swinton to Metcalfe, July 7, 1826: *pol. cons.*, July 7, 1826, No. 24.
[108] Ibid.
[109] Lockett to Metcalfe, July 5, 1826: *pol. cons.*, July 27, 1826, No. 33.
[110] Lockett to Metcalfe, August 15, 1826: *pol. cons.*, September 8, 1826, No. 11.
[111] Lockett to Metcalfe, July 10, 1826: *pol. cons.*, August 25, 1826, No. 5.
[112] Lockett to Metcalfe, August 15, 1826. *op. cit.*
[113] Ibid.

state they could not act against the orders of the regent. So they recommended a change in the regency from Rani Amrit Kunwar to Rani Sahib Kunwar, the actual mother of the Raja. They also maintained that no corrective could be applied to the evils menacing the state without the direct interference of the British Government.[114] In the light of this, the Governor-General decided to set aside the Rani and to appoint a council of regency.

The Rani reacted against this decision frantically. She declared her intention to resist this move,[115] vainly attempted to go out of the palace[116], and then shut herself up inside the palace with the young Raja.[117] She even solicited the help of the *thakurs* of the state to maintain her right. However, on receipt of a personal letter from Metcalfe,[118] she complied with the wishes of the British Government.[119] A regency council consisting of the ministers was then established.[120]

After establishing the regency council, which to his mind ensured an efficient administration, Metcalfe wanted to refrain from any further interference in its working and preserve it as a national government. His refusal to sanction the use of British force for the suppression of the refractory zamindars of Biana and Mewat,[121] as suggested by Lockett,[122] was an

[114] Lockett to Metcalfe, July 14, 1826, *pol. cons.*, August 25, 1826, No. 5.
[115] Lockett to Metcalfe, August 28, 1826: *pol. cons.*, October 6, 1826, No. 13.
[116] Lockett to Metcalfe, August 28, 1826: *pol. cons.*, October 6, 1826, No. 14.
[117] Lockett to Metcalfe, August 29, 1826: *pol. cons.*, October 6, 1826, No. 15.
[118] The Rani had expressed her readiness to retire to the Mahal and renounce all her claims if Metcalfe wrote a letter to her to that effect. It was in response to this Metcalfe wrote the letter. It strongly suggests the influence and prestige of Metcalfe.
[119] Lockett to Metcalfe, September 8, 1826: *pol. cons.*, October 6, 1826, No. 27.
[120] Lockett to Metcalfe, September 4, 1826: *pol. cons.*, October 6, 1826, No. 27.
[121] Metcalfe to Lockett, September 18, 1826: *pol. cons.*, October 13, 1826, No. 13.
[122] Lockett to Metcalfe, September 16, 1826: *pol. cons.*, October 13, 1826, No. 13.

expression of this idea. He was also opposed to the use of British force by the Bharatpur government for the realization of revenue, because he thought that it would ultimately degenerate into an instrument of exploitation in their hands.[123] If the British Government in order to prevent such a contingency used its discretion and scrutinized the revenue demand and collection, it would amount to active participation in the administration. Metcalfe contended that the Bharatpur government should act without any aid from the British in the prosecution of its demand for revenue.[124] He also wanted to associate with the regency some respectable chiefs or public officers who were in no way considered British partisans or adherents. This was intended to remove the general impression that the administration was manned by British stooges and to give it a more national character and reputation. His endeavour was to maintain "the government of Bharatpur as Bharatpur government."

Developments in Jaipur

The interference in the revenue administration of Jaipur sanctioned in 1821 led to the progressive entanglement of the British Government in the various aspects of the administration. The year 1823 saw its culmination when the British Government supported Rawal Bhairisal, the *mukhtiar*, against the wishes of the Rani and maintained him in the office with independent authority directly responsible to the British Government.[125] The Rani's duties and authority were confined to the charge of the infant Raja's person and the control of the interior of the palace. Jhota Ram, her favourite and adviser, was expelled from Jaipur.[126]

In adopting such a course of action the British Government was motivated by a feeling that its interference would help to enhance the revenue of the state to a considerable extent. The Agent was of the opinion that within a period of three

[123] Metcalfe to Lockett, October 17, 1826: *pol. cons.*, November 10, 1826, No. 41.
[124] *Ibid.*
[125] Swinton to Ochterlony, March 18, 1823: *pol. cons.*, March 21, 1823, No. 37.
[126] Stewart to Ochterlony, April 5, 1823: *pol. cons.*, May 2, 1823, No. 21.

years the revenue would increase to sixty lakhs of rupees.[127] This, however, proved to be a great misconception created by the exaggerated notions about the resources of the state. The maximum amount ever realized by the Jaipur government was thirty-four lakhs of rupees during the time of Mohan Ram Nazir. Under the management of Bhairisal and with the assistance of the British Government the revenue collection came down as low as two lakhs of rupees a year. The British Government was greatly dismayed at the result of its interference. Moreover, Rawal Bhairisal leaning heavily on British support had become extremely indifferent and insolent to the Rani. The indignant Rani was endeavouring to remove Bhairisal from the office. The opportunity came when the troops stationed at Turrawatti mutinied for realizing their pay, which was in arrears for about a year.[128] Convinced about the bad effects that the interference had produced in Jaipur, the British Government now decided to entrust the administration to the Rani,[129] allowing her complete freedom in the selection and appointment of administrative personnel.[130] Consequently, Rawal Bhairisal was removed from the office and Thakur Megh Singh of Diggi was appointed *mukhtiar* and Misser Ganesh Narain and Govind Narain the chief revenue officers.[131] This, however, was adopted by the Government as an "experimental measure,"[132] as the efficiency of the new set-up was not beyond doubt.

Matters stood on this footing when Metcalfe came to the scene with his pronounced bias towards the policy of non-interference. When the Political Agent lamented the decision of the Government to withdraw the interference even as an "ex-

[127] J.C. Brooke: *Political History of the State of Jeypore*, p. 22.
[128] Raper, Political Agent at Jaipur, to Ochterlony, October 9, 1824: *pol. cons.*, November 12, 1824, No. 10.
[129] Swinton to Ochterlony, November 12, 1824: *pol. cons.*, November 12, 1824, No. 35.
[130] Ochterlony to Raper, December 20, 1824: *pol. cons.*, April 15, 1825, No. 20.
[131] Ochterlony to Swinton, January 6, 1825: *pol. cons.*, April 15, 1825, No. 27.
[132] Swinton to Ochterlony, April 10, 1825: *pol. cons.*, April 15, 1825, No. 38.

IMPLEMEATATION OF BRITISH POLICY IN NORTH INDIA

perimental measure,"[133] Metcalfe considered it unfortunate that it was ever sanctioned in Jaipur.[134] His endeavour was to abstain from interference in the internal affairs of Jaipur, a state in which the British Government "interfered most largely but with least benefit."[135] The Resident, however, did not rule out the right of British Government to interfere, in case the interests of the state and the minor Raja were jeopardized by the maladministration of the ministry.[136] But he wanted to restrict it to the sphere of advice and remonstrance, if possible.[137] A complete abstinence from the details of the revenue administration was also considered essential by him.[138]

But Metcalfe found it difficult to confine the Jaipur question within the framework of the general policy, as the problems of that state were unique and embarrassing. The state of Jaipur was professedly dependent on the British Government, the Raja was a minor, and, above all, the British Government had acquired a direct pecuniary interest in its revenue administration by the treaty of 1818. Captain Low, the Agent at Jaipur, who was in agreement with Metcalfe regarding the general policy of non-interference, believed that this pecuniary interest involved a system of minute interference of the British Government in the revenue administration.[139] To dispense with it he suggested the fixation of permanent tribute without any reference to the revenue of the state. This was originally suggested by Ochterlony with the same purpose[140] and was accepted in

---

[133] Low, Political Agent at Jaipur, to Metcalfe, April 13, 1827: *pol. cons.*, May 7, 1827, No. 17.
[134] Metcalfe to Stirling, Secretary to the Government, May 7, 1827: *pol. cons.*, May 7, 1827, No. 17.
[135] J. Sutherland: *Sketches of the Relations Subsisting between the British Government in India and the Different Native States*, p. 75.
[136] Memorandum of Metcalfe, August 29, 1825: *sec. cons.*, September 16, 1825, No. 21.
[137] Metcalfe to Low, January 10, 1826: *pol. cons.*, February 17, 1826, No. 21.
[138] Metcalfe to Low, January 10, 1826: *pol. cons.*, February 17, 1826, No. 20.
[139] Low to Metcalfe, January 20, 1826: *pol. cons.*, February 17, 1826, No. 26.
[140] Ochterlony to Swinton, February 23, 1824: *pol. cons.*, August 6, 1824, No. 7.

principle by the Government though it was not implemented.[141] Both the Resident and the Governor-General were now in complete agreement with this suggestion, but were sceptical about its successful implementation as the government of Jaipur would not agree to a modification which would involve an immediate increase of the tribute.[142] It was, therefore, decided to reserve the right of interference in order to ascertan the revenue collection of the state and to secure the due share of the British Government, but to waive the "obnoxious interference" founded on that right until it became evident that "some adequate benefit would accrue from a rigid scrutiny."[143] The non-interference in this respect, it is evident, was motivated not by principles, but by considerations of benefit. Metcalfe now instructed Low to abstain from scrutinizing the revenue accounts as was the practice earlier and forbade him from receiving complaints from the people against the Jaipur government.[144]

The withdrawal of British superintendence unleashed forces of disruption resulting in further deterioration of administrative efficiency. On regaining her authority the Rani disregarded the advice of the high functionaries of the state and relied on her sycophants who were mostly of low origin and of questionable repute. Megh Singh, the *mukhtiar*, receded into the background and Rupa Bhandarin, an avaricious slave girl, Hukum Chand, a former clothier of Delhi, and Jhota Ram, a former *gumasta*, came to hold the reins of the state.[145] The influence of this triumvirate on the Rani was so absolute that she often did not know what was goining on in her kingdom. It was reported that Rupa Bhandarin kept the Rani under the influence of intoxicating drugs and then exacted her sanction for attaining the selfish ends of this junta. For safeguarding the interests of the minor Raja and the welfare of the state, it was evident that the

---

[141] Swinton to Ochterlony, August 6, 1824: *pol. cons.*, August 6, 1824, No. 13.

[142] Swinton to Metcalfe, February 17, 1826: *pol. cons.*, February 17, 1826, No. 27.

[143] Ibid.

[144] Metcalfe to Low, January 10, 1826: *pol. cons.*, February 17, 1826, No. 2.

[145] Low to Metcalfe, March 12, 1826: *pol. cons.*, May 19, 1826, No. 12.

IMPLEMENTATION OF BRITISH POLICY IN RAJPUTANA 93

elimination of this pernicious influence from the high echelons of the government was inevitable. Captain Low believed that the public appearance of the Raja, which according to the customs of the state would end the regency of the Rani, would afford an opportunity for its realization. The Raja then ould be placed under the supervision of a *thakur* who could also act as the *mukhtiar*. A section of the nobles led by the Raja of Uniara, Rawal Bhairisal, and Megh Singh who were excluded from the concerns of the state by the ascendancy of the Jhota Ram group, also desired a change in the administration which was construed by the Agent as a universal demand of the *thakurs* for ending the regency of the Rani. They also testified that the public appearance of the Raja and the consequent changes envisaged by the Agent were in conformity with the customs and usages of the state.[146] Moreover, doubts were expressed in Jaipur about the existence of the Raja. It was rumoured that the real Maharaja had died long ago and the present one was spurious, and that he was ushered into the palace by Rupa Bhandarin with the connivance of the Rani.[147] The Agent, therefore, recommended to the Government to demand the public appearance of the Raja and to convene an assembly of the *thakurs* in order to decide the guardianship of the Raja and other related matters.

Though Metcalfe agreed with the Agent on the broad outline of this procedure, he had considerable reservations on the extent of British participation in this affair. He was led to believe the testimony of the dissident nobles that the *thakurs* had the right to decide the character and content of the government after the public appearance of the Raja. He was, therefore, in favour of an assembly of the *thakurs* convened by the Rani or, on her refusal, assembled by themselves, but not in any case at the instance of the British Government.[148] The Rani did not betray any enthusiasm about the assembly of the *thakurs* or the public appearance of the Raja when she was approached by the Agent. She pleaded inability to conduct the ceremony since there was no auspicious day till the Raja attained his ninth year.

[146] *Ibid.*
[147] Low to Metcalfe, March 22, 1826: *pol. cons.*, May 19, 1826, No. 12.
[148] Metcalfe to Low, April 10, 1826: *pol. cons.*, May 19, 1826, No. 12.

She, however, agreed to a change in the personnel of the administration and also consented to produce the Raja in a select gathering of the *thakurs* in order to discredit the rumours regarding the authenticity of the Prince. This proposal, the Agent believed, was nothing but a move of the Rani to keep the Raja under her thumb and enjoy the prerogatives of sovereignty in the capacity of the regent. The British Government, as it was convinced about the constitutionality of the assembly, insisted on its convention and the Rani had to agree to hold it in October 1826. She, however, wanted to exclude Rawal Bhairisal, Thakur Singh, and Bahadur Singh who were all professedly against her. But this suggestion did not find favour with the Resident because he wanted the assembly to be as far as possible representative and not a partisan one.[149]

By September 1826 *thakurs* from the various parts of the state had started gathering in Jaipur for the proposed assembly. Rawal Bhairisal and his followers who were opposed to the Rani pitched their camp near the Agency House, whereas the supporters of the Rani encamped inside the city. This created an impression that the British Government was supporting the faction headed by Bhairisal. The Rani deeply resented it and in reprisal forbade communications between the *thakurs* assembled inside and outside the city.[150] The Resident also deplored this factionalism and was eager to remove the misunderstanding of the Rani about the attitude of the British Government. He, however, disapproved of her reaction and threatened to accept the verdict of the chiefs encamped outside the city, if the Rani obstructed their freedom of expression and communication.[151]

Meanwhile, the orders of the Government had arrived authorizing the Agent to convene the assembly in case the Rani did not do so.[152] After a preliminary meeting of the *thakurs* on October 2, 1826, the assembly was held on October 14 at the

---

[149] Metcalfe to Low, September 13, 1826: *pol. cons.*, October, 6 1826, No. 61.

[150] Low to Metcalfe, September 13, 1826: *pol. cons.*, October 6, 1826, No. 61.

[151] Metcalfe to Low, September 16, 1826: *pol. cons.*, October 6, 1826, No. 61.

[152] Stirling to Metcalfe, September 29, 1826: *pol. cons*, October 13, 1826, No. 14.

residence of the Political Agent. The opinion of the *thakurs* about the continuation of the Rani as the regent after the public appearance of the Raja was recorded by the Agent secretly by conducting individual interviews in a separate room. The verdict was in favour of removing the Rani from the regency with 31 voting for and 23 against.[153] But Low did not execute this decision immediately, in view of the impending visit of Metcalfe to Jaipur.

On his arrival at Jaipur Metcalfe became severely critical of the role that the Political Agent played in the recent developments in the state. In spite of his earlier attempts to discredit the feelings of British partisanship, opinion was current at Jaipur that the British Government was supporting Rawal Bhairisal against the Rani. This belief naturally had shaken the confidence of the Rani's supporters who were not unaware of the implications of the British support to the Rawal. Metcalfe, therefore, had no doubt that the presence of the Agent at the time of the voting would have influenced the result. As a proof, if at all proofs were needed, for the play of an external influence, the *outs* who were opposed to the Rani were "few in number and bore the appearance of a small body."[154]

Metcalfe was so far under the conviction that the laws and customs of the state provided for a change in the regency after the public appearance of the Raja. He believed that the right to decide the regency, was vested with a constitutional assembly of the *thakurs*. Low had given great importance to this idea. The assembly of *thakurs* held in 1819 had also helped to strengthen this belief. But a series of interviews with several *thakurs* now convinced Metcalfe that the state of Jaipur knew no such law or custom.[155] To his dismay he also found that the *thakurs* possessed no constitutional right to decide the form and character of the government. The only other case of minority in Jaipur was that of Maharaja Pratap Singh. Then, of course, the Rani was removed from the regency and the Raja was kept

---

[153] Low to Metcalfe, October 15, 1826: *pol. cons.*, November 24, 1826, No. 11.
[154] Metcalfe to Amherst, November 23, 1826: *pol. cons.*, February 2, 1827, No. 19.
[155] *Ibid.*

under the guardianship of a *thakur*.[156] This was a "single unprecedented event," of which circumstances were basically different. All the *thakurs* were then generally opposed to the Rani. But now an influential section of the *thakurs* evinced a feeling in favour of the continuance of the Rani as the regent. The Resident became convinced that the British Government was so far acting on false notions and wrong assumptions.[157]

In order to rectify the mistakes which were already committed, Metcalfe decided to convene another assembly, although he himself did not consider it constitutional or its decision binding on the Rani. But as the first assembly was held, apparently under the countenance of the British Government, and its decisions were unduly coloured by external influence, he considered it necessary to conduct an impartial voting. This assembly, he believed, could also act as a heralder of constitutional assemblies in all the states of India, furnishing a legitimate control over the government and voicing the opinion of the nation on vital issues.[158] The Governor-General, though not enthusiastic about a second assembly, gave discretionary powers to Metcalfe to act according to his judgment.[159]

The assembly of the *thakurs* was now called for a second time on November 8, 1826.[160] Metcalfe changed the procedure earlier adopted by Low in order to suggest an impartial investigation. Instead of asking the *thakurs* about the rights of the Rani as Low did, he enquired into her legal position after the public appearance of the Raja. The votes were recorded in the presence of two chief of each party in order to prevent any appearance of interference on the part of the British Government. The verdict of this assembly was in favour of the Rani by 28 votes against 22.[161] Metcalfe immediately assured the Rani of her position with full authority to select and appoint the officials without any inter-

[156] Raper to Swinton, May 26, 1825: *pol. cons.*, July 15, 1825, No. 70.
[157] Metcalfe to Amherst, November 23, 1826, *op. cit.*
[158] Metcalfe to Low, October 23, 1826: *pol. cons.*, November 24, 1826, No. 11.
[159] Amherst to Metcalfe, November 7, 1826: *pol. cons.*, November 24, 1826, No. 13.
[160] Low to Metcalfe, November 9, 1826: *pol. cons.*, January 12, 1827, No. 20.
[161] Metcalfe to Amherst, November 23, 1826, *op. cit.*

IMPLEMENTATION OF BRITISH POLICY IN RAJPUTANA

ference from the British side.

The British involvement in the questions of the public appearance of the Raja and the assembly of the *thakurs*, as Metcalfe confessed, were due to ignorance of the local customs and traditions on the part of the British officials who were perhaps influenced by the European notions of feudal rights and obligations. But after investigation when Metcalfe became convinced about the mistake, he refrained from any further entanglements. For instance, he refused to distribute *khilats* to the *thakurs* in the assembly convened for the public appearance of the Raja and withdrew "entirely from all interposition between the Rani and the discontented chiefs," leaving them to settle their differences for themselves.[162] Thus the British interference in Jaipur, partial in principle but complete in practice, initiated by Ochterlony was at the end reversed by Metcalfe.

Metcalfe, however, realized that during his stewardship, the British Government interfered to a great extent both in Bharatpur and Jaipur. Particularly in such purely internal affairs as the constitution of the ministry, the removal of the Rani, the appointment of the regency in Bharatpur, and the convention of the assembly in Jaipur, the British Government had clearly crossed the limits prescribed by the treaties and had deviated from the policy of non-interference. But Metcalfe viewed non-interference as an instrument of political expediency, subject to modification and even abandonment, if circumstances warranted. It was not therefore thought of as a rigid dogma. In fact, he always advocated the right of the paramount power to interfere in extreme cases of anarchy and civil war. In such cases, he was of the opinion that "inferior considerations must yield to those of greater importance and the evils of direct interference must be endured to prevent greater evils of discord and disturbance".[163] But the exercise of this right was not to be allowed to degenerate itself into "obnoxious interference" in anything and everything concerning the dependent states. It was to be applied as judiciously and as sparingly as possible. Unless it became evident that evil was certain and was likely to be perpetuated, the

---

[162] Metcalfe to Stirling, January 17, 1827: *pol. cons.*, February 23, 1827, No. 10.

[163] Metcalfe to Low, April 10, 1826: *pol. cons.*, May 19, 1826, No. 12.

indulgence in interference, Metcalfe contended, would be impolitic. When once the first step in interference was taken, it would become difficult, if not impossible, to prevent further entanglements. The cases of Bharatpur, Jaipur, and all other states of Rajputana in which the British Government interfered prove this fact. Moreover, the result of interference in almost all these states was most disappointing, primarily due to the inevitable difficulties created by the existence of an external agency more powerful and authoritative than the ruler himself. "All our present embarassments., wrote Metcalfe, "it seems to me to proceed from our past interference. And what, it may be asked, have been its fruits to recommend its continuance. Whether the state of affairs in Jaipur would have been better or worse without it, no one can tell, but certainly the state in which they are after so many years of our endeavours to improve them affords little encouragement" to the prosecution of our labours."[164] This depressing spectacle further helped to strengthen his conviction in favour of the policy of non-interference.

In the execution of this policy in Rajputana Metcalfe had to content with certain inherent contradictions in the treaties of 1817-18. These treaties implied the Company's assumption of the *de facto* paramount authority with its wide range of interests and obligations on the one hand, and non-interference on the other. These two were mutually incompatible because the exertions of the British Government to preserve its interests and discharge its obligations would necessarily involve interference to a certain extent. Moreover, what came within the purview of internal affairs was always a point of dispute. This dilemma, in fact, accounts for the deviations and adjustments in the general policy towards the states of Rajputana.

---

[164] Metcalfe to Stirling, January 17, 1827: *pol. cons.*, 1827, No. 10.

6
The Cis-Sutlej States

THE CIS-SUTLEJ region to the north-west of Delhi was occupied by petty independent Sikh principalities. The most important of them were Patiala, Jind, Nabha, Kaithal, Ladwa, Khulsia, and Thanesar. Throughout the eighteenth century, incessant foreign invasions as well as the machinations of the unscrupulous military adventurers and freebooters had made the existence of these states precarious and miserable. During Sindhia's overlordship of Delhi, Perron had extended his influence to this area and controlled many of these chiefs, exacting considerable amount of money from them. But the treaty of Surji Arjangao, concluded in 1803, by which Sindhia conceded his rights and interests in this region to the British Government was a welcome relief, at least temporarily, to these states. The management of the British relations with them primarily due to their geographical proximity, was then entrusted to the Delhi Residency.

In the beginning the British Government was not interested either in extending its influence to this region or in realizing any tribute as Sindhia had done, even though the Governor-General was conscious of its strategic importance. In 1803, he had toyed with the idea of establishing close relations with these states in order "to frustrate any attempt of an invading army from the western side of the Indus."[1] The intention was not the extension of the territory, but the creation of a buffer zone. A closer study of their political set-up and mutual relationship convinced the Government that they could not by any arrangement be rendered efficient allies and auxiliaries against external enemies. The British Government, however, could not remain altogether indifferent to their turbulent nature and activities as the attitude of some of them threatened the security

---
[1] Montgomery Martin, *op. cit.*, iii, p. 211.

of the adjoining British territories. During the Anglo-Maratha war a few of them had fought against the British on the side of the Marathas and even after their defeat continued to entertain feelings of hostility, frequently plundering and pillaging the British domains. For the maintenance of peace and tranquillity in the British territories, it became an urgent necessity to curb their predatory incursions. According to David Ochterlony, this could be achieved by two ways: first, the assignment of the whole territory to the four important chiefs possessing paramount influence in this quarter (the terms the partition to be decided by the British Government);[2] and secondly, the complete establishment of British control over these states, exacting the tribute which was formerly collected by Perron.[3] The adoption of either of these measures was sure to entangle the Government in the internal affairs of these states and this was considered neither desirable nor profitable at that stage. The realization of the tribute, if imposed, would in all probability necessitate the presence of a military force which was not financially advantageous to the British Government in view of the meagre resources of these states. It was, therefore, decided to take only military precautions for the defence of the British territories without establishing any direct control over them.[4]

The political developments in the Cis-Sutlej states during this period were characterized by mutual aggrandizements, rivalries, internal dissensions and discord. "The internal dissensions among the chiefs," as Bhailal Singh, the Raja of Kaithal put it, "are perpetual. At times discord and contention prevail among them, and at times, they live together in accord and harmony."[5] In the absence of a restraining power, marked by the withdrawal of the Marathas and the reluctance of the British to fill the breach, avaricious tendencies soon gained ascendancy, creat-

---

[2] Sahib Singh of Patiala, Bhag Singh of Jind, Jaswant Singh of Nabha, and Bhailal Singh of Kaithal.
[3] Ochterlony to Edmonstone, November 7, 1804: *sec. cons.*, November 29, 1804, No. 306.
[4] Edmonstone to Ochterlony, January 13, 1805: *sec. cons.*, January 31, 1805, No. 243.
[5] Bhailal Singh to Seton, received on April 27, 1807: *pol. cons.*, August 4, 1807, No. 83.

ing anarchy and disorder in the whole region. The rulers were weak and financially bankrupt and their administration was inefficient and oppressive. Maharaja Ranjit Singh who had entertained hopes of creating a united Punjab discerned in this situation an opportunity to extend his power and authority. He had subjugated almost all the Trans-Sutlej states and was marking time to extend his domain to the Cis-Sutlej area.

In 1806 a boundary dispute between Rani Sudha Kaur of Patiala and Jaswant Singh of Nabha, which precipitated an armed conflict, gave Ranjit Singh the much desired opportunity to enter the arena. Bhailal Singh of Kaithal and Bunga Singh of Thanesar joined the Rani and Bhag Singh of Jind, uncle of Ranjit Singh, supported the Nabha ruler. Bhag Singh appealed to Ranjit Singh for help and the latter immediately agreed and crossed the Sutlej with an army of thirty thousand men.[6] Ranjit Singh gained quick military successes, occupied a portion of the Patiala territory, and invested the fort of Mansurpur in which Rani Sudha Kaur and Bhailal Singh had taken shelter. Ultimately peace was concluded and Ranjit Singh received Ludhiana in this deal. He repeated his onslaught in 1807 and acquired considerable power and prestige among the Cis-Sutlej chiefs.

The aggressive intentions of Ranjit Singh posed serious threat to the very existence of these weak and small states. The rulers of Patiala and Kaithal, who had refused to submit to his authority and had tried to resist his military might, were badly worsted. In fact, every one of them was appprehensive about the Maharaja's future moves and was frantically searching for assistance to ward off any possible attack. But even in the face of this common danger they could not sink their mutual jealousies and petty differences so as to offer a combined resistance. The only alternative was to appeal to the British Government for military assistance which was refused on the plea of non-intervention.[7] The adherence of the British Government to this policy deprived these states of the only source of assistance and helped Ranjit Singh to extend his influence in this quarter.

---

[6] Seton to Edmonstone, October 30, 1806: *sec. cons.*, November 20, 1806, No. 1.

[7] Monckton to Seton, August 4, 1807: *pol. cons.*, August 4, 1807, No. 84.

The political developments in Europe in the early nineteenth century, however, compelled the British administrators in India to revise this policy. The treaty of Tilsit concluded in 1807 raised the phantoms of Franco-Russian collaboration against England and the dangers of a possible invasion of India from the north. Napoleon had already gained considerable influence in the Persian court which, it was feared, was pregnant with dangerous possibilities to the British imperial interests in India. The Asiatic conquest was a dominant part of the Napoleonic grand design and the French diplomats were exploring the possibilities of a triple alliance between France, Turkey, and Persia for the purpose of opening out a road to India. After Tilsit, Napoleon incessantly pressed the Czar for a joint expedition against the English in India with the object of subverting their dominion and destroying the sources of their commercial prosperity. Lord Minto, the Governor-General, was alarmed by this prospect, especially because the north-western region was highly vulnerable to any such move. In order to foil this attempt he conceived the plan of establishing friendly and barrier treaties with the rulers of Persia, Afghanistan, and the Punjab. In pursuance of this policy John Malcolm, Mounstuart Elphinstone, and Charles Metcalfe were deputed to Persia, Afghanistan, and the Punjab respectively to conclude treaties with the rulers of these countries.

The negotiations with Ranjit Singh, whose diplomatic abilities elicited the admiration of the French traveller, Jacquement, dragged along a very tortuous path. The Maharaja was not inclined to accept the British proposals in the beginning and was prepared to conclude a treaty only on his own terms and conditions, the most important of them being an explicit sanction of the British Government to the extension of his territory across the Sutlej. This indeed was not acceptable to the British Government because, if conceded, it would make its territory coterminous with that of Ranjit Singh and would thereby subject its northern frontiers to a "chronic state of invasion and disturbance."[8] During these negotiations the Cis-Sutlej chiefs continued to repeat their earlier appeals for protection which now drew favour-

---

[8] Lepel H. Griffin: *The Rajas of the Punjab*, pp. 118-20.

able response from the British in view of Ranjit Singh's vacillation and clearly aggressive designs. The Maharaja had once again crossed the Sutlej and had captured the fort of Faridkote in Patiala. He then advanced towards Ambala. The British Government thereupon decided to afford open and immediate protection to the Cis-Sutlej states and employ a military force for that purpose.[9] In lieu of the protection against Ranjit Singh, it claimed from them the reciprocal benefit of introducing British troops freely into their territory.[10] The connexion with these states was also intended to secure to it "the advantages, facilities and resources of the country in the prosecution of any military arrangement and operation which might become necessary in the future."[11] The final settlement defining the exact nature of relationship with these states was, however, to be decided later on. Ochterlony was authorized to assure the chiefs about British protection and the decision of the Government to divest Ranjit Singh of his recent acquisitions on the right side of the Sutlej. He was instructed to obtain accurate information regarding "the disposition, character, condition and military strength of the several chiefs and the modes in which their power might be advantageously combined in any system of defensive arrangement against an invading enemy."[12]

Ranjit Singh quickly reacted to these moves as he realized that the extension of British authority to the Cis-Sutlej states would spell the doom of his cherished ambitions. He immediately tried to wean round the chiefs to his side and baulk the British intention of establishing a protectorate in this region.[13] Ochterlony, therefore, urged the Government to finalize the arrangements with these states and clarify "the exact nature of the relations of protection and dependence which shall permanently exist" with them.[14] He proposed that the arrangement

---

[9] Memorandum of Lord Minto: Kaye, *op. cit.*, i, p. 194.
[10] Edmonstone to Seton, December 26, 1808: *P. G. R.* ii, p. 4.
[11] Edmonstone to Ochterlony, December 29, 1808, *Ibid*, p. 13.
[12] *Ibid.*
[13] Seton to Edmonstone, January 18, 1809., *Ibid.*, p. 31.
[14] Ochterlony to Edmonstone, March 17, 1809, *Ibid.*, p. 82.

should provide for the exemption to these states from the payment of pecuniary tribute, non-interference in their internal arrangements, right of the British Government to requisition some military force for three months in every year without payment and their co-operation with the British troops at the event of an invasion of their country, and exemption from duties on European articles and horses purchased by the Company on the production of a passport from the Resident at Delhi.[15] In view of Ranjit Singh's procrastinations in concluding the treaty, Ochterlony's proposal was readily accepted by the Government and he was instructed to issue a proclamation to the Cis-Sutlej chiefs defining their future relations with the British power. The articles of this proclamation were to be as follows:

1. An assurance of permanent protection against the authority and control of Raja Ranjit Singh.
2. Exemption from all pecuniary tribute.
3. The exercise of the same rights and authority that the rulers had hitherto enjoyed within the limits of their respective possessions.
4. Facility and accommodation to the British troops whenever the Government shall judge necessary, for purposes connected with the general interests of the state, to march into their country.
5. Zealous co-operation with British power on any invasion of their territory.*

Ochterlony was also authorized to include an article regarding the exemption from duties on British goods, if he so desired.[16] These instructions of the Government differed from the proposals of Ochterlony only in one respect. Ochterlony wanted to reserve the right of the British Government to demand the services of a portion of their army for three months in a year without payment. This was not accepted by the Governor-General.

On the receipt of these instructions Ochterlony issued a proclamation to all the Cis-Sutlej states on May 2, 1809, on the

[15] Ibid.
[16] Edmonstone to Oehterlony, April 10, 1809: *P. G. R.* ii, p. 92.
* For the text of the proclamation see Appendix ii.

lines suggested by the Government. Meanwhile, on April 25, 1809, Ranjit Singh concluded the Treaty of Amritsar, according to which he undertook to abstain from committing any encroachments on the possessions or rights of the Cis-Sutlej states.[17] Thus the Cis-Sutlej states came under the protection of the British Government.

The relations of the British Government with these states stood on a peculiar footing. There was neither any treaty nor any written engagement between the two parties. The protective proclamation was a unilateral action on the part of the British Government and not an outcome of mutual negotiation and settlement. In fact, the Government did not want to establish a very intimate relationship with these states.[18] Its intention was to establish an autonomous and loyal confederacy of the chiefs who would be helpful to the protecting power in difficult times. It did not want to enmesh itself in their internal affairs as it was bound to be embarrassing and vexatious. Interference was neither a part of the policy nor was it necessarily connected with the obligations of general protection assured to them.[19] Rather, it was to be avoided as far as possible. But the British Government could not remain aloof from the developments in these states without abjuring the obligations of a protector. There were two types of problems that called for the attention of the British: first, extreme misgovernment; and secondly, mutual aggrandizement and usurpation. Patiala provides an example which clearly reflects the attitude of the British Government towards the first problem; the developments in Chichlondi and Tira illustrate their attitude towards the second.

Patiala

Raja Sahib Singh, the ruler of Patiala, was inefficient, weak, and an imbecile. His advisers and confidants were intriguers of low birth and vulgar character. He distributed favours to all

---

[17] Kaye, *op. cit.*, i, p, 221.
[18] Edmonstone to Ochterlony, April 10, 1809, *op. cit.*
[19] *Ibid.*

and sundry without any propriety or proportion.[20] The resources of the state were squandered away on silly and childish amusements.[21] He distrusted and disliked his wife, Rani Aus Kaur, a lady of considerable administrative efficiency.[22] Under him the administration of the state had degenerated into an instrument of oppression and misrule. He could not maintain his authority on the dependent *sardars* and law and order were hardly respected by the people. The attention of the British Government was drawn to this situation by an attack on Lieutenant White and his party in December 1809[23] by a body of horse and foot led by a person named Phula Singh.[24] The Government asked Sahib Singh to furnish a party of two hundred and fifty horsemen for punishing the offenders. The Raja ordered his *sardars* to provide it, but they treated his orders with contempt. At long last a force was provided which being inefficient was incapable of any effective action.[25]

This incident convinced Ochterlony that the conditions of Patiala needed immediate improvement. He urged Bhailal Singh and Jaswant Singh to use their influence with Raja Sahib Singh "to introduce a degree of order and regularity in his government". These chiefs, however, were not very optimistic about the outcome of their intervention and believed that the Raja would be amenable only to British influence. On their request, therefore, Ochterlony visited Patiala in January 1811, on the occasion of the wedding of Sahib Singh's son, to discuss the possibilities of introducing reforms in the admini-

[20] For instance he gave eight villages to Najabat Ali Khan in exchange for one elephant.
[21] One of his many amusements was to enact a fight between the British Government and Ranjit Singh. Two corps of boys clothed in broad cloth and provided with guns loaded with pieces of iron and lead represented the army of the British and Ranjit Singh. They were ordered to fire on each other as if a fight was going on between these two parties. The boys were paid for this and compensation was given for the killed and wounded.
[22] Seton to Edmonstone, August 11, 1807: *pol. cons.*, September 1, 1807, No. 9.
[23] White to Seton, December 24, 1809: *P. G. R.*, ii, p. 148.
[24] Seton to Lushington, December 28, 1809, *Ibid.*, p. 157. Lieutenant White was a surveyor in Patiala.
[25] Ochterlony to Edmonstone, March 9, 1811, *Ibid.*, pp- 246-47.

stration of the state.[26] Ochterlony made various suggestions to the Raja for improving the administration which the latter was prepared to implement with certain reservations. He agreed to withdraw the extravagant revenue-free grants, which had been previously made to the *zamindars*, to make new grants only to deserving parties, and to compel the *jagirdars* to keep their contingents ready for service. But he disagreed with Ochterlony on the selection of the person to whom the general control of the administration was to be given. He wanted Rani Khaim Kaur, his step-mother, to take charge of the administration. She was a profligate and rapacious woman whose pernicious influence on the Raja was believed to be a major reason for the malaise of the state. Ochterlony was, therefore, eager to exclude her from authority. He preferred Rani Aus Kaur who had administrative skill and capacity. As the Raja was adamant on his choice, he decided not to precipitate matters at that stage and sought the permission of the Government to invest the general control of the administration in the hands of Rani Aus Kaur.[26]

The Governor-General was not inclined to accept the suggestion of Ochterlony as it would involve the British Government in the internal administration of the state. The active British participation in administrative reforms which might save the state from possible ruin could indeed be a laudable task to undertake. But if the British Government were to act on considerations of justice and philanthropy, the Governor-General contended that its exertions would be needed in almost all these states, because all of them were labouring under conditions similar to those of Patiala. That would evidently enmesh the Government in the internal administration of these states which the Governor-General was eager to avoid. The British Government wanted to restrict its responsibility as a protector to the occasional exercise of its influence for securing to the protected states the enjoyment of their prescriptive rights.[28] Ochterlony was, therefore, instructed to refrain from participating in the measures of reform and limit the interference to mere advice and recommendation

---

[26] Ochterlony to Edmonstone, March 9, 1811, *op. cit.*
[27] *Ibid.*
[28] Edmonstone to Ochterlony, April 5, 1811: *P. G. R.*, ii, p. 256.

on points that might be submitted to his judgment.

Meanwhile Sahib Singh accepted the advice of Ochterlony and placed Rani Aus Kaur at the head of the administration. The Rani had insight into administrative matters and within a short period she effected vast improvements in the various departments, especially in the revenue. But the adherents of Sahib Singh, who had greatly benefited during the earlier period of his unrestrained autocracy, now started plotting against her. They succeeded in convincing the Raja that the Rani was planning to kill him by some foul means. They could easily prevail upon his weak mind and consequently on December 27, 1811, the Rani, her son, and Miser Nowdha, her Diwan, were arrested. She was, however, soon set free and asked to resume the administration. But the Rani wanted to obtain a guarantee against similar disgrace before accepting the office.

The removal of the Rani once again brought indolence, inefficiency and corruption into the high realms of the administration. The Raja was incapable of taking any active and useful interest in the affairs of the state as he had become almost deranged. He was naturally under the complete influence of his advisers, mostly selfish and contemptible, who squandered the resources of the state. This sorrowful state of affairs convinced the British Government that without its authoritative interference it would be impossible to improve the existing situation.[29] In case "the British Government remained an inactive spectator of the progress of the existing evils," it was feared that "the intermediate outrage, anarchy and confusion" would invite the interference of other powers "actuated by principles very different from those of British administration."[30] Sahib Singh was, therefore, divested of all power and authority and the administration was vested in the hands of the Rani.[31] She was exempted from paying tributes and *nazarana*. The civil and military officers of the state were informed that the Rani would protect, support, and continue them in their respective *jagirs* and offices, so long as they did not forfeit them by disobe-

---

[29] Ochterlony to Edmonstone, May 8, 1812, *op. cit.*
[30] Edmonstone to Ochterlony, July 4, 1812: *P. G. R.*, ii, p. 305.
[31] Ochterlony to Edmonstone, June 19 1812, *Ibid.*, p. 301.

dience or misbehaviour.[32]

However, the Government, wanted to limit the interference to a minimum. The Rani was to be supported by the British Government only if the external support really became indispensable. Once the administration was established on a sound footing, all control of the British Government should cease.[33] The Rani was not to appear before the public as a stooge of the Government, but as an independent ruler. This amply clarified the attitude of the Government towards misrule in the protected states.

Mutual Encroachments of the Chiefs

The invasion of Ranjit Singh from which protection was afforded by the proclamation of 1809 was only one of the many problems that the Cis-Sutlej states had to face. More serious threat than this to the peace and security of this region was the mutual usurpations and aggrandizements among the chieftains themselves. Rivalries resulting in violence were frequent among them before 1809, but then they had to contend with an external force like the Marathas or Ranjit Singh who used these occasions for their own advantage. The elimination of these forces by the intervention of the British left a clear field for the more powerful chiefs to try to increase their possessions. Though the British Government had not specified in the proclamation its obligations in the event of such incidents, it could not remain indifferent to them. In cases of Chichlondi and Tira, the British Government was confronted with such situations which compelled it to clarify its attitude and lay down a specific policy in this respect.

Chichlondi

Bungail Singh, the chief of Chichlondi, died in 1809 without leaving any direct heir. The principality according to custom belonged to Rani Ram Kaur, widow of Bungail Singh. But Jodh

---

[32] *Ibid.*

[33] Edmonstone to Ochterlony, July 4, 1812: *P. G. R.* ii, p. 309.

Singh, the ruler of Khulsia, took advantage of the situation and annexed this territory to his possessions. The Rani immediately solicited British interposition for restoring it to her.

Jodh Singh's relations with the British Government had not been very cordial. He was a close adherent of Ranjit Singh and during the British negotiations with the Maharaja he had openly expressed where his sympathies lay. He was the only important chief who had not met Ochterlony during his march to Ludhiana. It was certain that in the event of hostilities he would support Ranjit Singh against the British Government. The attitude of the Government towards him had, therefore, become very stern. Ochterlony had not even included him in the list of the chiefs to whom the proclamation of protection was initially addressed.[34]

Jodh Singh's past alignment with Ranjit Singh and his unfriendly demeanour to the British Government ruled out any possibility of a lenient treatment to him in this issue.[35] Without any hesitation the Resident named him the usurper and demanded the restitution of the principality to Rani Ram Kaur to whom it belonged by right. On Jodh Singh's non-compliance the Resident served an ultimatum demanding the restitution within five days or otherwise threatening the use of force to effect the same.[36] The preparations for military action against him were started with the approval of the Governor-General.

Jodh Singh was undoubtedly conscious of his limitations and the hazards involved in resisting the wishes of the British Government. He, therefore, tried to associate Ranjit Singh with this deal and take advantage of latter's influence and prestige for his selfish aggrandizement. He informed the Resident that he had already handed over Chichlondi to Ranjit Singh and had no longer any concern in that principality. In case the British Government wanted it to be restored to Rani Ram Kaur he advised the Resident to negotiate with Ranjit Singh as the territory was under his control.[37] This was viewed by the

---

[34] Ochterlony to Edmonstone, July 30, 1811, *Ibid.*, p. 265.
[35] Seton to Ochterlony, September 24, 1809: *sec. cons.*, October 17, 1809, No. 2.
[36] Seton to Jodh Singh, June 24, 1810: *pol. cons.*, July 14, 1810, No. 18.
[37] Seton to Edmonstone, July 6, 1810: *pol. cons.*, July 21, 1810, No. 48.

Government as a stratagem to avoid compliance with the British demand. It was doubtful whether any such transfer had taken place and even if it had, Ranjit Singh could not acquire it as the principality belonged by right to the Rani. The preparations for the contemplated military action were, therefore, continued without any detraction. The refusal of the British Government to accept these lame excuses and its determination to expel the usurper, preferably by peaceful methods and, if necessary, by force, convinced Jodh Singh that further evasion might prove harmful to his interests. He, therefore, agreed to hand over the territory to a confidential servant of the British Government.[38] But he was not sincere in his promise and tried to protract the proceedings as much as possible. He informed the Resident that the restitution could not be effected without a written order from Ranjit Singh. This attempt at prevarication contrary to his earlier professions, was viewed seriously by the Government and it was decided to take immediate compulsive measures for obtaining the submission of Jodh Singh. The troops were mobilized from Karnal and Meerut. On the appearance of the British army, Jodh Singh was alarmed and readily surrendered Chichlondi to British Government, which was eventually handed over to Rani Ram Kaur.[39]

Tira

On the death of Sangit Singh, the chief of Tira, in 1790 Durmo, his widow, took charge of the principality. She appointed her brother, Gujar Singh, as the manager. Gujar Singh being an ambitious man tried to usurp the authority, and his relations with his sister soon became strained, whereupon Durmo sought the help of Jodh Singh Khulsia to expel Gujar Singh from Tira. Jodh Singh assisted her to re-establish her authority for a monetary consideration. She then employed Fateh Singh and Jeet Singh, nephews of her husband, as managers and entrusted them the task of raising money for ful-

---

[38] Seton to Edmonstone, August 21, 1810: *pol, cons.*, September 6, 1810, No. 31.
[39] Seton to Edmonstone, November 6, 1810: *pol. cons.*, November 23, 1810, No. 42.

filling the financial commitment to Jodh Singh. Fateh Singh and Jeet Singh managed the affairs efficiently, collected money and soon discharged the obligation to Jodh Singh. They also protected Tira from external dangers, especially the exactions of Ranjit Singh. Their close association with the administration and efforts to protect the villages from enemies gave them considerable power and prestige which they utilized for their selfish ends. They took complete possession of the property, posed as the owners of Tira, and kept Durmo under restraint. Durmo then solicited the intervention of the British Government in her favour.[40]

The Resident at Delhi had no doubts about the legality of the Rani's claims and held that she was unjustly deprived of her property. She was kept under duress and in all probability even her life was in danger. The considerations of humanity and the obligations of the protector called for the interposition of the British Government. But the Resident was hesitant to intervene in this case as it was primarily a dispute between the two branches of the same family. In case the British took cognizance of family feuds, too trivial and too many among the Sikhs, it might involve them in petty quarrels, unworthy of their exertions. The Resident preferred these disputes to be settled by the parties themselves without the countenance of the British Government. But in the case of Tira he was not inclined to be altogether indifferent as the Rani was deprived of her personal liberty and was ejected from the principality which she had held for a period of twenty years. Fateh Singh and Jeet Singh were informed about the complaints preferred against them and were asked to explain their conduct.[41] They pleaded innocence of all the charges. They maintained that they had always been loyal to Durmo and had acted according to her wishes and promised to do so in future as well.[42]

An impartial investigation conducted by Ochterlony proved beyond doubt that the innocence of Fateh Singh and Jeet Singh was feigned and not real. They had actually seized the villages and were keeping Durmo under restraint. Further the Rani

[40] Statement by Durmo: *pol. cons.*, June 5, 1810, No. 36.
[41] Ochterlony to Fateh Singh and Jeet Singh, dated nil, *Ibid.*
[42] Fateh Singh and Jeet Singh to Ochterlony, dated nil, *Ibid.*

THE CIS-SUTLEJ STATES

disclaimed any kinship with them which, according to the Resident, altogether changed the complexion of the problem. It now became a case of the servants usurping the authority of the master.[43] The British Government, therefore, decided to interfere in favour of Durmo for a cause which, in the words of the Governor-General, was "just, creditable, and positively beneficial."[44] Fateh Singh and Jeet Singh were removed and the property was restored to Durmo.

Proclamation of Protection Against Mutual Usurpations

The cases of Chichlondi and Tira convinced the British Government that mere protection against external enemies would not help the peaceful existence of the states in this region. If the benefits of British protection were to be real and convincing, internal security and cordial mutual relations also had to be established. "If policy suggests the protection of the Sikhs south of Sutlej from external violence," wrote Ochterlony, "humanity and the honour of British name no less imperiously call upon us to shield them from the more disastrous consequences of their own base passions, their universal rapacity and their internal discord."[45] The Sikh chieftains, according to him, were eager to prey upon their neighbours for increasing their power.[46] This opinion carried conviction with the Government in the light of the developments in Chichlondi and Tira. It was, therefore, decided to restrain the chiefs from mutual aggressions. A proclamation was issued on August 22, 1811, clarifying the British attitude and policy in this respect.[47]

---

[43] Seton to Lushington, May 14, 1810: *pol. cons.*, June 5, 1810, No. 37.
[44] Edmonstone to Ochterlony, June 5, 1810: *pol. cons.*, June 5, 1810, No. 40.
[45] Ochterlony to Lushington, May 5, 1810: *pol. cons.*, June 5, 1810, No. 32.
[46] Ochterlony's estimate of Sikh character is as follows: " ... In my long acquaintance with mankind, I have never seen a race so strongly characterized by an almost brutal ignorance, selfish depravity, shameless falsehood, unprincipled cunning and a suspicion so excessive that even benefits must be felt before they are received as unconnected with some sinister design." Ochterlony to Edmonstone, March 28, 1809: *sec. cons.*, April 29, 1809, No. 33.
[47] Ochterlony to Edmonstone, September 2, 1811: *P G. R.* ii, p. 259.

According to this, the chiefs were prevented from forcibly taking possession of the estates of others. In case they did, the British Government claimed the right to interfere and effect restoration to the lawful owner. The offending party was to hand over to the lawful proprietor the revenues of the estate from the day of his ejection along with the compensation for losses which the inhabitants might sustain by the march of troops. Moreover, the British Government could also impose penalty on the offender.[48] Thus the Cis-Sutlej chiefs were assured protection both against external aggressions and their mutual encroachments.

This policy was successfully implemented by the Delhi Residency till 1834 with the active assistance of the Agencies at Ludhiana and Ambala. Afterwards the Cis-Sutlej states were separated from its political control and were placed under the Governor of the Agra Presidency.[49]

[48] Proclamation to the Cis-Sutlej States, *Ibid.*, pp. 269-71.
[49] Macnaughten to Scott, November 2, 1835: *pol. cons.*, November 2, 1835, No. 21.

7
The Question of the Royal Stipend

THE RAPID political changes in the first decade of the century relegated the Mughal Emperor to the position of a stipendiary of the Company. The Emperor had no other source of income for the maintenance of the royal family, except the stipend paid by the British Government and the revenue from a few personal *jagirs*. Shah Alam was unhappy about the financial provisions of the settlement of 1805, which he considered inadequate for upholding his status and those of his dependants. His feelings drew sympathetic response from the British officers, especially from the Governor-General who assured him without hesitation that the allowance would be enhanced when the depleted financial position of the Government due to the exigencies of war marked an improvement.[1] The Emperor harboured hopes on this promise, reminded the Governor-General at every possible opportunity, and waited with patience, of course, in vain, till his death.

During Akbar Shah's period this question became a live issue, considerably straining his relations with the British Government. On his accession the expenses of the royal household naturally increased due to his enlarged establishments and those of his wife and children. He found the allowance miserably insufficient for defraying his expenses and therefore immediately after his accession requested the Government for its augmentation.[2] The reaction of the Government was not the least favourable to him. Instead of increasing the stipend, as promised earlier, the Government decided to reduce it by cancelling the allowances formerly paid to the heir-apparent and Shah Nawaz Khan. It was held that these allowances were paid as a

---

[1] G.G. to H.M., July 29, 1805: *sec. cons.*, July 29, 1805, No. 7.
[2] H.M. to G.G received on February 6, 1807: *pol. cons.*, February 12, 1807, No. 98.

mark of personal attention and respect to the individuals and not to the offices they held. In protest Akbar Shah decided to decline the entire stipend, but was tactfully persuaded by the Resident to accept it as otherwise it might adversely affect his own interests.³

An augmentation of the stipend and the restoration of the allowances formerly paid to the heir-apparent and Shah Nawaz Khan now became the prepossessions of the Emperor. He wanted the stipend to be enhanced to Rs. 1,30,000 monthly which the royal family received during the time of Madhava Rao Sindhia. Apart from sending intermittent appeals to the Government to this effect, he tried to influence the Resident through the ladies of the palace and deputed Shah Haji to Calcutta to plead with the Governor-General directly.⁴ But all his attempts proved unsuccessful.

The attitude of the British Government to the question of the royal stipend had considerably changed since the departure of Wellesley from India and the death of Shah Alam. The Emperor's plea about the paucity of the allowance did no more elicit sympathetic response from the British officials because during the last two years of his life, Shah Alam had saved about five lakhs of rupees from his stipend. Moreover, six lakhs of rupees promised by Wellesley in 1803 was also paid to him, which was considered sufficient for all immediate needs of the Emperor. If in spite of this, he had any pecuniary problem, it was attributed by the Resident more to the mismanagement, than to the inadequacy of the royal funds; and the appointment of a person competent to regulate the expenditure of the royal family on principles of regularity, prudence and economy was urged to improve the situation.⁵ It was feared that to allow the Emperor to accumulate in his hands "resources exceeding the exigencies of the real comfort and convenience of the royal household," was pregnant with dangerous possibilities to the British interests as his allegiance and fidelity to the Government were of doubtful nature.⁶

---

³ Seton to Edmonstone, January 9, 1807: *sec. cons.*, January 22, 1807, No. 1.
⁴ Monckton to Seton, March 8, 1809: *pol. cons.*, March 13, 1809, No. 103.
⁵ Edmonstone to Seton, April 30, 1807: *sec. cons.*, April 30, 1807, No 15.
⁶ Edmonstone to Seton, April 9, 1807: *sec. cons.*, April 9, 1807, No. 8-D.

Decision of Minto

Lord Minto, who assumed the Governor-Generalship in 1807, viewed this problem from an entirely different perspective. The basic question, according to him, was whether the stipend was not enough to meet the reasonable requirements of the Emperor and his household. The British Government had, in fact, conceded its inadequacy in 1805 by agreeing to enhance the amount whenever the financial condition became favourable. Considered without reference to any unforeseen and contingent expenditure the total amount of Rs. 79,800 granted to the Emperor appeared quite substantial. But the Emperor had hundreds of dependents, the *salateens* or royal collaterals, who lived within the palace in a very miserable condition. Some of them received Rs. 2 or 3 as their personal allowances. The maximum amount received by any individual was Rs. 55.[7] In the absence of any external assistance, the only source to which they could look for help was the Emperor and whatever little he could give the Emperor did spare at least at the time of emergencies. Moreover, he had to defray the expenses on repairs of the palace and its gardens expend on account of birth, marriage, and on such other items. In view of these considerations Lord Minto came to the conclusion that the stipend granted by the Government was meagre for the comfort, convenience, and dignity of the Emperor.[8] The fact that Shah Alam could save five lakhs of rupees during his time was considered by Minto more as a proof of the wretched condition of the subordinate members of the royal family than of the adequacy of the stipend.

The various political and financial objections preferred by his predecessor were not regarded strong enough by Minto to decline an increase of the stipend. The Government had in 1805

---

[7] Edward Thompson describes their condition as follows: "If the gates opened to admit the Resident, these starving creatures would rush madly at him and mob him for the gift of a rupee or two. Government efforts to help them were useless. The only allevation of penury was a few blankets distributed in the cold weather nominally from the King, but in fact a private charity of Setons." Edward Thompson: *Life of Charles Metcalfe*, p. 141.

[8] G.G.'s minute, June 6, 1809: *pol. cons.*, June 17, 1809, No. 7.

conditionally promised to enhance the stipend and certainly going back on it without valid reasons was neither honourable nor decorous. It was urged, as we have already observed, that the stipend would be raised when the exegencies of the war would end and the revenue from the assigned territories would register an increase. The war with the Marathas was over, but the British officials argued that the revenue from the assigned territory fell far short even of the existing royal stipend,[9] though, while initially sanctioning the allowance had dismissed any correlation between the two, Wellesley had promised to enhance the stipend to one lakh of rupees whenever the assigned territory yielded an equivalent amount. Apart from the fact that the two conditions were not interdependent, the extent of the assigned territory itself was a point of dispute between the British Government and the Emperor. If it were to comprehend the territory on the right bank of the Jamna granted by Mahadaji Sindhia, as the Emperor believed it to be, the revenue realized from it considerably exceeded the amount of the royal stipend. In fact, even in 1805 the revenue of this area including the *jagirs* and *jaidads* alienated by the British Government exceeded one lakh of rupees.[10] That being the case, the only objection that remained for denying an augmentation could only be due to political expediency. Minto believed that it was as much fallacious as it was superfluous to apprehend that the Emperor could use his stipend for purposes injurious to the interests of the British Government. He, therefore, decided to fulfil the promise of Wellesley and enhanced the stipend to one lakh of rupees.[11] Out of this, the allowance of Rs. 7,000 assigned to the heir-apparent was suspended till the appointment was made to that office. The actual amount of augmentation was, therefore, only Rs. 13,200 which raised the Emperor's personal allowance to Rs. 82,200 inclusive of Rs. 3,000 commuted against his lands in the Doab.[12]

Though Minto believed that the augmented stipend would be sufficient to meet all reasonable needs of the royal family, the fact was that it neither satisfied the expectations of the Emperor,

[9] Seton to Edmonstone, April 13, 1809: *pol. cons.*, June 17, 1809, No. 1.
[10] G.G.'s minute, June 6, 1809, *op. cit.*
[11] Edmonstone to Seton, June 17, 1809: *pol. cons.*, June 17, 1809, No. 11.
[12] G.G.'s minute, June 6, 1809, *op. cit.*, para 72.

nor made any substantial improvement of his financial position. A comparative analysis of the augmented amount and the increase in royal expenditure would help to substantiate this point. On the demise of Shah Nawaz Khan, the post held by him was split into three separate offices—the *killedar*, the commander of the troops, and the steward of the household. Formerly, the salary of Shah Nawaz Khan was paid by the British Government, which was eventually discontinued. The Emperor had to provide for these three offices from his personal allowances. The Governor-General himself had conceded that the appointment of new personnel to these offices considerably increased the expenditure of the Emperor.[13] Secondly, during the time of Shah Alam the allowance of the heir-apparent used to be received by the Emperor himself and he distributed allowances among his sons and female members of the palace. On the reduction of this allowance the Emperor had to spare an equivalent amount from his stipend to meet their needs. After allocating the expenditure to these heads, amounting to Rs. 9,500, the augmentation, in effect, came to Rs. 3,700 only.

Apart from the increase in the personal establishment of the Emperor, his wife, Mumtaz Mahal, and the children were also to be maintained with dignity and comfort for they had attained a new status with the elevation of their father to the throne. To meet these expenses a paltry sum of Rs. 3,700 was all that was available. Lord Minto, who had admitted the inadequacy of the stipend as the main reason for its augmentation, unfortunately lost sight of the indirect drain on the resources of the Emperor by the reduction of the allowances of the heir-apparent and Shah Nawaz Khan. In the ultimate analysis, therefore, what Lord Minto could offer to the Emperor was not substantial. The sympathetic manner in which Minto set himself to the task had held out greater promises for the amelioration of the miserable condition of the Emperor and his relatives.

Pran Krishna's Mission

Though Akbar Shah greeted this decision of the Govern-

[13] *Ibid.*

ment with expressions of gratitude and goodwill, he was evidently disappointed. He was expecting a better deal. His demands were not entirely met and even the promise of Wellesley was not fulfilled in terms of actual augmentation. Without delay, therefore, he started making further endeavours to press his claims on the British Government. The first step in this direction was the employment of Babu Pran Krishna, a Bengali adventurer, to plead the case with the British authorities. Pran Krishna, who was then in Delhi in search of fortune, managed to convince the Emperor that he could obtain a favourable decision from the British Government through representations at Calcutta and, if necessary, at London. Akbar Shah appointed him as his accredited agent. He bestowed on him the title of "Raja",[14] and provided him with ample money to prosecute the mission. Pran Krishna immediately left for Calcutta, carrying letters of the Emperor, addressed to the Chief Justice, the Governor-General, and the King of England. The Emperor in these letters demanded the augmentation of his stipend and the restoration of certain privileges enjoyed by his ancestors.[15] He also denounced the conduct of Seton towards his family as more atrocious and derogatory than those of Gulam Qadir and Nadir Shah and desired him to be severely reprimanded.[16]

Pran Krishna was an impostor and he had neither any influence at Calcutta nor the capacity to undertake such an important task. His only interest was to squeeze as much money as possible from the Emperor who had no doubts about his *bona fide*. From Calcutta he sent to the Emperor very encouraging reports regarding his endeavours, concocting stories about the sympathetic attitude of the British officials. He wrote to the Emperor that the Chief Justice "wrung his hands with grief" on reading his letter, and promised to see justice done to him. Lord Minto and Seton were at that time embarking for the Eastern Archipelago. Pran Krishna availed of this opportunity

[14] Monckton to Metcalfe, July 22, 1811: *pol. cons.*, July 26, 1811, No. 105, para 8.
[15] H.M. to Lord Russel, August 22, 1810: *pol. cons.*, July 26, 1811, No. 106; and H.M. to G.G., August 22, 1810: *pol. cons.*, July 26, 1811, No. 107.
[16] H.M. to the King of England, dated nil: *pol. cons.*, July 26, 1811, No. 108.

THE QUESTION OF THE ROYAL STIPEND

and informed the Emperor that he was accompanying them to London. He requested him to give money to one of his friends at Delhi to defray the expenses on his trip to London.

The Emperor had arranged the mission with extreme secrecy and the Resident at Delhi had no knowledge about it. He was neither consulted about its propriety nor was his consent sought for its prosecution. The British Government took strong exception to this "disingenuous character of the Emperor's conduct" and refused to recognize the mission.[17] Pran Krishna was deprived of his title and his seal was confiscated in the presence of the *vakils* assembled from the various parts of the country.[18] Maulvi Gulam Mufstafa, Gulam Jalani, and Babu Goverdhan who were implicated in the prosecution of the mission were also dismissed from the service of the Emperor. The British Government was of the view that the Emperor had no just cause for complaint or discontent, and that he was to be grateful for the liberal provision which had been made for him.[19] The Governor-General, therefore, entirely disapproved his conduct and advised him to "relinquish that torment of his life, the worrying desire to effect impractical changes."[20] He was told that he was not empowered to confer titles on the Company's subjects without the knowledge and concurrence of the British Government, and that clandestine missions could "lead to no other result than certain disappointment, degredation and expense to His Majesty."[21] The Emperor immediately apologized, begging to be excused, as he was misled by his advisers. He solemnly promised to refrain from any such indulgence of ignoring the authority of the Resident in future.[22]

This promise of the Emperor was observed more in its breach than in its fulfilment. Immediately after the dismal failure of Pran Krishna's mission the Emperor endeavoured to solicit

[17] Monckton to Metcalfe, July 22, 1811, *op. cit.*
[18] *Ibid.*
[19] Metcalfe to Monckton, August 28, 1811: *pol. cons.*, September 20, 1811 No. 44.
[20] Kaye, *op. cit.*, i, p. 254.
[21] Monckton to Metcalfe, July 22, 1811, *op. cit.*
[22] H.M. to G.G., August 31, 1811, *pol. cons.*, September 20, 1811, No. 45.

the help of the Nawab of Awadh for the enhancement of his stipend and improvement of his status and dignity. Mirza Jahangir was sent to Lucknow apparently to attend a marriage but really to persuade the Vazir to use his influence with the British Government.[23] The proposed visit of Qudsia Begam, the Emperor's mother, to Lucknow to meet her son, Prince Sulaiman Shikoh,[24] was also believed to have been undertaken for the same purpose. The letters of the Emperor addressed to Mirza Jahangir fell into the hands of Colonel Bailey, the Resident at Lucknow, who brought the matter to the notice of the Government.

The reaction of the Government to this breach of faith was stern and severe. The augmentation of the stipend sanctioned in 1809 was immediately cancelled.[25] This decision of the Government completely outwitted the Emperor. He expressed his sincere regret and was prepared "to take solemn oath on the Quran or on the heads of his children that he would never again make any attempt to negotiate, except through the Resident stationed with him on the part of the British Government."[26] He earnestly implored the Resident to use his good offices with the Governor-General and, as Metcalfe reports, he "called himself a fool, he called himself a wretch, he pulled his own ears in token of deserving punishment and humbled himself in a manner it was painful to see."[27] He offered to apologize to the Resident in public "with his hands together in a posture of supplication."[28] In short, there was no course which he was not prepared to adopt for securing the goodwill of the British Government.

The whole episode is a sad commentary on the feeble character of the Emperor. It is surprising that he should chose to use "strange, unwarrantable, unjust and absurd"[29] language about Seton who always held him in high veneration and was too cautious and respectful in his dealings. He had made no

[23] Metcalfe to Adam, April 9, 1813: *pol cons.*, April 30, 1813, No. 4, para 7.
[24] Sulaiman Shikoh, the second brother of the Emperor, was then staying at Lucknow as a guest of the Nawab.
[25] Metcalfe to Adam, May 20, 1813: *pol. cons.*, June 4, 1813, No. 20.
[26] Metcalfe to Adam, April 9, 1813, *op. cit.*, para 9.
[27] *Ibid.*, para 17.
[28] *Ibid., op, cit.,* para 19.
[29] Metcalfe to Monckton, August 20, 1811, *op. cit.*

complaint against Seton while he was in office. The real motive perhaps was to gain the sympathy of the higher authorities by harping on the ungenerous conduct of the erstwhile Resident. Moreover, he did not possess any strength of conviction or consistency of opinion. His mean demeanour after the failure of Pran Krishna's mission and the reduction of his stipend, and his desperate anxiety to absolve himself of any duplicity of conduct make a very pathetic and miserable reading.

The remonstrance of the Resident and the reduction of the stipend had a singular effect on the Emperor. The most important point that the Resident impressed on his mind was that the increase or decrease of the royal stipend depended entirely on the pleasure of the British Government.[30] It seemed that the Emperor was convinced of this and, according to Metcalfe, this was the object which induced the Government to reduce the stipend. He, therefore, recommended the immediate restoration of the full allowance, as otherwise the advantages gained by the reduction were liable to be weakened. A permanent reduction of the allowances would naturally occasion despair and perpetual discontent and keep the Emperor in a state of constant irritation. This, it was feared, might drive him into further intrigues. Hitherto his intrigues had been directed towards negotiation with the British Government. In case of permanent reduction of the stipend he might plot against the British Government, if men succeeded in influencing his weak mind which was undoubtedly bordering over desperation. To forgive and to restore the allowance were, to Metcalfe the best guarantee of the Emperor's good behaviour in future.[31]

Though sensible of the force of Metcalfe's arguments, the Governor-General nevertheless thought it advisable to delay the restoration of the full stipend in order to confirm the impression produced by its suspension.[32] However, the reduced amount was restored after three months.[33] The restoration was sanctioned with retrospective effect i.e., from May 1, 1813, thereby causing

---

[30] Metcalfe to Adam, April 9, 1813, *op. cit.*
[31] *Ibid.*, para 31.
[32] Adam to Metcalfe, April 30, 1813; *pol. cons.*, April 30, 1813, No. 5.
[33] Adam to Metcalfe, July 16, 1813: *pol. cons.*, July 15, 1813, No. 46.

no pecuniary loss to the Emperor.³⁴

But the Emperor did not entirely give up hopes. He continued to press the Government through oral and written representations to sanction an augmentation which was at least proportionate to the increase in the revenue of the assigned territory. He supposed that the settlement of 1805 held out an assurance that the whole of the revenue of the assigned territory would be used exclusively for the maintenance of the royal household. In 1827 when Lord Amherst met him at Delhi, he reiterated his demands. In a memorandum which he transmitted to the Governor-General³⁵ through the Secretary, he demanded the augmentation of his stipend on the lines agreed to in 1805, the in addition to restoration of the salary of Shah Nawaz Khan, complete liberty in domestic affairs, benefit of receiving *nazar* from the rajas and nobles through the Resident on the occasion of *Id* and other festivals, discretion to entertain as many horse and foot as may be thought necessary for the purposes of state, right to strike coins in the royal name and put in currency in Delhi and *khalsa mahals*, the prerogative of conferring titles and *khilats* on the chiefs and nobles and to receive *peshkush* from them. The Emperor also wanted the Resident and all the Englishmen in general to receive titles according to custom.³⁶ The Governor-General immediately referred these demands to Metcalfe, for his views and observations.³⁷ He was instructed to ascertain three points, namely the extent of the territory originally assigned to the Emperor, the actual revenue of this area after deducting the expenses of administration, including the salary of European officers and police establishments, and the availability of any private fund of the Emperor for repairing the palace.³⁸

Metcalfe made a detailed analysis of the various demands of the Emperor. The enhancement of the royal stipend, according to him, was "the chief or almost the chief object of His

---

³⁴ *Letters to the Court of Directors (pol.)*, October 1, 1813, para 203.
³⁵ The heir-apparent and *the salateens* also presented papers of requests, *pol. cons.*, June 15, 1827, No. 7 and No. 10
³⁶ The paper of requests presented by H.M.: *pol. cons.*, June 15, 1827, No. 6.
³⁷ Stirling to Metcalfe, May 12, 1827, *op. cit.*
³⁸ *Ibid.*

THE QUESTION OF THE ROYAL STIPEND

Majesty's desires to which all the other wishes expressed were merely auxiliary and subordinate."[39] He examined this question from two angles, first, as an obligation of the British Government arising out of the promise made in 1805; and secondly, as a right of the Emperor in relation to the increase in the revenue of the assigned territories.

The obligation of the British Government to the Emperor, in Metcalfe's view, was very limited in scope. It involved, in the first place, an adequate provision for the support of the Emperor and the royal household as embodied in the resolution of 1805; and secondly, the fulfilment of the promise made by Wellesley to Shah Alam. The resolution of the Government, however, was not an engagement binding its future conduct since it "never did intend to enter into any compact with His Majesty."[40] The provisions then held out to the Emperor, who had nothing to offer in return for the benefits conferred on him except his ailing, decrepit self, were more gratuitous in nature than claims arising out of a mutual engagement. This being the spirit of the settlement, the obligation of the British Government became restricted to the grant of a "liberal stipend, but fixed, and limited according to the exigencies of the royal family and the available resources of the Government."[41] While effecting the augmentation in 1809, Lord Minto had taken into consideration the adequacy of the stipend and had also fulfilled the promise of Wellesley. Metcalfe, therefore, thought that this question had been finally disposed of.

The second point to be considered was the claim of the Emperor to the whole revenue of the assigned territory. The assigned territory comprised the territory on the right bank of the Jamna to the north-west of Kabulpur, ceded to the British Government by the treaty of Surji Arjangao. In course of time this territory underwent some mutilations and additions without any reference to the Emperor. According to Metcalfe, this modification could not have been made, if this territory had belonged to the Emperor in consequence of an engagement

---

[39] Metcalfe to Stirling, June 26, 1827: *pol. cons.*, July 27, 1827, No. 7.
[40] *Ibid.*, paras 6 and 19.
[41] *Ibid.*, para 23.

on the part of the British Government.[42] These changes effected in the extent and composition of the assigned territory were unilateral measures taken by the Government in spite of the Emperor's protests.

The resolution of 1805 put a maximum ceiling of one lakh of rupees on the personal allowances which the Emperor could receive.[43] Metcalfe contended that such a restriction could not have been prescribed, had it been settled that the whole of the net revenue should belong to the Emperor. This particular paragraph (para 12) of the Government's resolution,[44] if taken separately, does not warrant any other interpretation. But it has to be read in the context of the entire resolution. Colonel Ochterlony, the then Resident at Delhi, proposed the payment of a personal allowance of one lakh of rupees to the Emperor. But the Government sanctioned an allowance of sixty thousand rupees. This reduction was made on two considerations. First, the revenue of the assigned territory was not adequate enough even for the payment of sixty thousand rupees. Secondly, the resources of the Government were impoverished by the exigencies of war. The Government, however, made a promise to enhance it to the level suggested by the Resident, if the revenues of the assigned territory registered an increase.

The notes of instructions to the Resident at Delhi issued on November 10, 1804, leave no one in doubt that the revenue of the assigned territory was to be treated as a part of the Emperor's fixed stipend. In 1804 the British Government definitely intended to appropriate the whole revenue of the territory to the Emperor.[45] There is nothing in the resolution of 1805 in refutation of it in plain terms, rather it stands confirmed. According to this resolution, "the revenue shall be collected and justice be administered in the name of His Majesty."[46] Further,

---

[42] *Ibid*, para 14.
[43] Lumsden to Ochterlony, May 23, 1805, *op. cit.*, para 12.
[44] It reads: "If the produce of revenue of the assigned territory should hereafter admit of it, the monthly sum to be advanced to His Majesty for his private expenses may be increased to the extent of one lakh of rupees." See Appendix I
[45] Notes of Instructions to the Resident, November 17, 1804: *sec. cons.*, November 29, 1804, No. 302.
[46] Lumsden to Ochterlony, May 23, 1805, *op. cit.*, para 2.

THE QUESTION OF THE ROYAL STIPEND

the Emperor was given the right "to appoint a *dewan* and other inferior officers to attend at the office of collection for the purpose of ascertaining and reporting to His Majesty the amount of the revenues which may be received and the charges of the collection, and of satisfying His Majesty's mind that no part of the produce of the assigned territory shall be misappropriated."[47] This by implication meant that the Emperor possessed certain interest in the territory. In the light of this, even Metcalfe had to concede that it was not clear as to whether the Emperor was to enjoy the revenue accruing from the assigned territory, or that his stipend was to be limited to the maximum mentioned.[48] It is, therefore, clear that the Emperor was entitled to his due share in the increase of the revenue from the assigned territory. Among British officers, it was only Ross who saw the point clearly that the Government, by the arrangement which it adopted in 1805, intended to appropriate to the Emperor and his household the entire produce of the assigned territory.[49]

A close scrutiny of Metcalfe's letter gives the impression that he treated the subject with callous indifference. His arguments in refutation of the Emperor's claims, were mainly based on memory as he was not in possession of precise and detailed information.[50] It lacked both cogency and consistency. He was never sympathetic towards the claims of the Emperor and always objected to the veneration and consideration shown towards him by the British Government. The fate of the representation, in fact, became a foregone conclusion when it was referred to Metcalfe, because his views were seldom overruled by the authorities at Calcutta. The Governor-General agreed with him[51] and turned down the requests of the Emperor.[52] The practice of presenting *nazars* to the Emperor on the part of

---

[47] *Ibid.*, para 5.
[48] Metcalfe to Stirling, June 26, 1827, *op. cit.*
[49] Ross to Swinton, February 25, 1823: *pol. cons.*, June 13, 1823, No. 45.
[50] Metcalfe to Stirling, June 26. 1827, *op. cit.*
[51] Stirling to Swinton, October 5, 1827: *pol. cons.*, February 1, 1828, No. 1.
[52] G.G. to H.M. dated nil: *pol. cons.*, February 1, 1828, No. 2.

the Governor-General was also discontinued.[53] The Mughal Emperor had not quietly resigned himself to his lot and it was not found desirable to encourage his false pretensions.

Mission of Raja Ram Mohun Roy

The failure to achieve his aims, through direct representations to the Governor-General, prompted the Emperor to seek redress from the King of England. Ram Mohun Roy, well-known for his intellectual attainments, scholarship, and zest for the cause of social reforms, was preparing at this time to leave for England to be present there at the time of the renewal of the Charter Act by Parliament and its discussion regarding the practice of *sati*. He was approached by a *vakil* of the Emperor to act as his envoy and present his case to the King of England. Ram Mohun agreed. The Emperor consequently appointed him as his agent to the court of England and instructed him to prepare a letter to be presented to the King of England.[54] The title of "Raja" was bestowed upon him which Ram Mohun Roy was reluctant to accept as he was not anxious for such distinctions.[55] But the Emperor, out of consideration for the dignity of the royal house and the importance of the mission, insisted that Ram Mohun should accept the title. The Governor-General, however, did not recognize the title.[56]

Ram Mohun Roy, according to the wishes of the Emperor, drew out an *arzee* to the King of England in which the demands and grievances of the Emperor were very ably presented.[57] The Emperor claimed the entire revenues of the *"mahals* originally assigned for the support of the royal family, but unjustly alienated from the rightful owner and appropriated for themselves by the Honourable Company" and the restitution of the allowances which the royal family were deprived of in past

[53] Swinton to Colebrook, Resident, February 1, 1828: *pol. cons.*, February 1, 1828, No. 3.
[54] H.M. to Ram Mohun Roy, dated nil: *pol. cons.*: March 26, 1830, No. 97
[55] Ram Mohun Roy to G.G. dated nil: *pol. cons.*, January 22, 1830, No. 51.
[56] Stirling to Ram Mohun Roy, dated January 15, 1830: *pol. cons.*, January 22, 1830, No. 52.
[57] H.M. to the King of England, dated nil: *pol. cons.*, March 13, 1829, No. 20.

years.[58] He urged upon the King to assign him the gross revenues of the assigned territories or alternatively, grant him a fixed annual stipend of thirty lakhs of rupees. He claimed it as a matter of right and not as a favour to be conferred by the magnanimity of the King.

The attitude of the Government to the mission of Ram Mohun was least helpful. It refused to provide him the copies of the official correspondence regarding the royal affairs and also to recognize him as the accredited agent of the Emperor.[59] The Governor-General, in fact, was annoyed by "the unmeasured and unfounded accusations" levelled against the Government in the petition to the King of England. He was eager to obstruct the mission and even to defeat it, if possible. Ram Mohun, therefore, disowned his official status and declared that he was going to England in the capacity of a private individual.[60] He sailed from Calcutta on November 15, 1830, by the *Albion* bound for Liverpool and reached there on April 8, 1831. In England he was received courteously and both his mission and title were recognized by the Home Government. He was introduced to the King by Charles Grant, the President of the Board of Control, and at the coronation of William IV he was assigned a seat among the ambassadors of the crowned heads of Europe.

Ram Mohun Roy did not leave a "single stone unturned" to seek redress of the grievances of the Mughal Emperor. He presented a printed statement regarding the claims of the Emperor to the Court of Directors and circulated it among the influential persons in England. He undoubtedly succeeded in creating a public sentiment in favour of the Emperor. His endeavours, however, did not bear fruit immediately as the members of the Court of Directors and the Board of Control were engaged in more important political matters, namely the Reform Bill and the renewal of the Company's Charter.[61] But soon after, the Court

---

[58] *Ibid.*, para 12.
[59] *Letters to the Court of Directors* (*pol.*), October 14, 1830.
[60] Brajendra Nath Banerjee: *Raja Ram Mohun Roy's Mission to England*, p. 20.
[61] Hamilton, Officiating Secretary, North-Western Provinces, to Macnaughten, Secretary to Government, April 18, 1837: *pol. cons.*, May 8, 1837, No. 25, Encl. 5.

of Directors sanctioned an increase of three lakhs of rupees annually to the stipend of the Emperor. It was stipulated that the pecuniary grant was to be received by the Emperor in full satisfaction of all claims that the royal family might be supposed to possess.[62] The Emperor, on the advice of Ram Mohun Roy, declined the grant as his claims deserved better consideration.[63] Ram Mohun, who had great faith in the liberality of the British Parliament, was preparing an appeal to it for more favourable terms, but unfortunately he died on September 27, 1833, without accomplishing his mission.

The death of Ram Mohun Roy and the pecuniary difficulties to which the Emperor was subjected by the expenses incurred on the mission to England compelled him to reconsider his decision. He now decided to accept the grant, not as a final settlement of all his claims but only as a partial relief. He also wanted complete liberty in the allocation of the grant among the various members of the royal family.[64] The Government, however, insisted on "unqualified acceptance without conditions and equivocations" which was eventually submitted by him.[65]

A large number of British officers in India were opposed to any further increase in the stipend of the Emperor. Charles Metcalfe, who, on the formation of the Agra Presidency in 1834, had taken over as the Governor was the most vehement of them. He was of the opinion "that a further annual stipend of three lakhs of rupees in addition to the twelve and more which the King now enjoys is an unwarrantable permanent waste of large sum of public money, which would be much better applied to the reduction of debt or the relief of revenue payers or the education of the people or any other public purpose."[66] Though the Governor-General agreed with these sentiments, he decided to implement the orders of the Court of Directors without any further delay, especially as the Emperor had accepted all the

[62] Macnaughten to Fraser, Agent, June 21, 1833: *pol. cons.*, June 21, 1833, No. 1.
[63] H.M. to Fraser, dated nil: *pol. cons.*, August 2, 1833, No. 13, Encl. 2.
[64] H.M. to Fraser, October 14, 1834: *pol. cons.*, December 31, 1834, No. 15.
[65] H.M. to Fraser dated nil: *pol. cons.*, October 16, 1834, No. 22.
[66] Macsween to Macnaughten, January 14, 1835: *pol. cons.*, December 31, 1834, No. 13.

THE QUESTION OF THE ROYAL STIPEND

conditions prescribed by the British Government.[67]

The Political Agent at Delhi immediately started discussions with the Emperor regarding a satisfactory mode of allocation of the grant among the members of the royal family. This, however, proved to be a very difficult matter due to the conflicting views held by the Emperor and the British Government. In the distribution proposed by Akbar Shah, he apportioned a major part of the grant for his personal expenses and to his favourites, including the sons of Ram Mohun Roy.[68] The British Government did not agree to this suggestion as a portion of the grant was assigned to the individuals who were not members of the royal family, and who had, therefore, no claim on the bounty of the British Government. The Agent made an alternative proposal which was indeed not acceptable to the Emperor.[69] In this proposal there was no provision for the Emperor, his sons, and his devoted servants. The Emperor, therefore, declined the grant. He insisted on having complete liberty in this matter if he were to accept it.[70] The Governor-General thereupon decided to abstain from any further negotiation till the Emperor renewed his application for payment.[71]

The decision of the Government on this issue, it has to be admitted, was not very fair. The proposed increase was of no practical advantage to the Emperor personally and to his favourite

---

[67] Macnaughten to Macsween, January 28, 1835: *pol. cons.*, January 28, 1835, No. 14.

[68] The amount was to be distributed as follows: Roy Radha Prasad and Roy Rama Prasad, sons of Ram Mohun Roy: Rs. 1,875; Prince Mirza Salim and Sohanlal: Rs. 1,875; Helpless and poor people: Rs. 250; Repairing of Delhi Palace: Rs. 800; Prince Abu Zafar: Rs. 1,104-2-2; Brothers of the King: Rs. 2,955; Sisters of the King and *salateen* at an average rate of 20 per cent added to their former allowances: Rs. 8,166; for His Majesty: Rs. 8,000; Total: Rs. 25,000. (Rs. 25,025—2—2) *pol. cons.*, May 8, 1,837, No. 25.

[69] The distribution recommended by the Agent was: Anour Mahal Rs. 320; Mirza Abu Zafar: Rs. 6816-14-0; King's sons and grand sons Rs. 3944; Sons of the King's brothers: Rs. 3615-05-3; Sons of the King's sisters: Rs. 1317-11-9; Sons of the *salateen*: Rs. 3430-06,9; Repairs of Palace: Rs. 5000; Expenses of College: Rs. 555-10-3; Total: Rs. 25,000

[70] H.M. to G G., dated nil: *pol. cons.*, May 8, 1837, No. 26.

[71] Bushby to Thomas Metcalfe, February 18, 1837: *pol. cons.*, May 8, 1837, No. 25, Encl. 3.

son Mirza Salim, whereas an undue proportion of the grant was reserved for the repair of the palace. There was a time when the British Government had even harboured the designs of removing the Empreror from his royal residence at Delhi, thereby depriving his claims to it. It was therefore paradoxical that the British Government should now reserve a considerable portion of the increased allowances for the care and maintenance of that very edifice. It was too much to expect the Emperor to accept an arrangement which completely overlooked his claims. It was true that the condition of the *salateens* and other royal collaterals called for immediate amelioration. That, however, could not justify a total disregard of the Emperor who, in reality, was the pivotal figure. At the discussions in the Executive Council, A. Ross, one of the Councillors, maintained that the Emperor had been rather harshly dealt with.

Bahadur Shah II

Akbar Shah died on September 28, 1837 at the old age of 82 years. Upon his death Mirza Abu Zafar ascended the throne under the name Abdul Muzaffar Sirajuddin Muhammed Bahadur Shah Badshah Gazi. Immediately after his accession the new Emperor reopened negotiations regarding the royal stipend. The Governor-General was prepared to grant him the increase provided he agreed to the terms offered to his late father. They were of course not acceptable to Bahadur Shah and he declined to accept the augmentation on those conditions. The Governor-General, who was eager to end these protracted negotiations, referred it to the Court of Directors for a final decision.[72]

The Court of Directors took a sympathetic view of the case and decided to renew the offer to the Emperor. They instructed the Governor-General to propose an arrangement under which some portion of the amount could be assigned to the Emperor for his own use. The Emperor, however, was required to assign to the junior branches of the family reasonable allowances that could not be altered without the previous consent of the British

---

[72] *Letters to the Court of Directors (Pol.),* February 8, 1839.

Government and to remove his distant relatives from the palace.[73] He was also required to execute an *Ibranama* to the effect that the augmentation was in satisfaction of all his claims on the British Government. The Emperor, however, stuck to his earlier decision and agreed to accept the augmentation only if no condition was attached to it.[74] He also wanted the palace to be completely repaired and his debts paid by the British Government. The Governor-General suggested the transfer of his *tyool* lands to the Government, the revenue of which could be used to pay off the debts. This was not acceptable to the Emperor as the transfer of his private lands would deprive him of an important source of personal income.[75] He was, however, prepared to accept the additonal allowance if the arrears of the augmented amount from the date of the sanction by the Court of Directors could be made use of for clearing a part of the debt. The rest he urged could be paid to him as a loan recoverable from his *tyool* lands at the rate of fifty thousand rupees per annum. This was accepted by the Government and it did not insist on the execution of an *Ibranama* either.

The distribution of the increased amount now became a stumbling block in the way of a satisfactory settlement. With the assistance of his ministers the Emperor prepared a schedule of distribution, which proposed a capricious allotment to his favourites.[76] A sum of Rs. 6,000 was reserved for his privy purse. Mirza Fakhr-ud-Din and Mirza Jawan Bakht, his two favourite sons, were to receive Rs. 400 each, whereas his other sons were granted only Rs. 217 each. His favourite wife, Zinat Mahal, was also to receive Rs. 400 apart from Rs. 4,000 per per month she was already receiving. The Agent objected to this mode of distribution as "the intention of the augmentation was to provide for such members of the royal family who had no assigned allowance or were insufficiently provided for." It was not meant for the benefit of those who already enjoyed

---

[73] *Letters from the Court of Directors (Pol.)* December 4, 1844.
[74] *Pol. cons.,* November 15, 1845, No. 16-A.
[75] *Ibid.*
[76] Thomas Metcalfe to Allen, Officiating Secretary, North-Western Provinces, December 6, 1848: *pol. cons.,* October 11, 1850, No. 200.

a reasonable amount.[77]

In the allocation suggested by Akbar Shah, he had excluded all the concubines, his own and those of his sons. But Bahadur Shah made provision for them also. He classified the concubines under two heads—those who had children and those who had not. A provision of Rs. 46 for the former and Rs. 18 for the latter of his own concubines and Rs. 18 and Rs. 10 for those of his sons was provided.[78] The concubines of his nephews and other *salateens*, however, were disregarded. The Agent was in favour of excluding all concubines who had no children and to treat the money thus saved as a fund for the help of the *salateens* having family. The Emperor had allowed the *salateens* merely an allowance of Rs. 14 which was considered very inadequate by the Agent.

The allocation of the grant suggested by the Agent[79] considerably differed from the Emperor's proposal. Apart from effecting a reduction in the amount set aside for his personal expenses, the Agent treated all royal children on a parity. No preferential treatment to the favourites of the Emperor was accorded. The instructions of the Court of Directors to effect the distribution with the concurrence of the Emperor prevented him from suggesting further changes like the exclusion of all the concubines, whether with or without children from the schedule and adding the amount thus saved for the *salatens*.[80] The Emperor, however, was not inclined to make any changes in the schedule of distribution prepared by him.

Matters stood thus when Lord Dalhousie became the Governor-General. He viewed the matter from an entirely

[77] Thomas Metcalfe to Allen, December 6, 1848, *op. cit.*
[78] *Ibid.*
[79] Allocation of the grant suggested by the Agent was: Heir-apparent: Rs. 2,000; His Majesty's sons (10): Rs. 1195; Daughters (20): Rs. 1271-04; Grandsons (22): Rs. 774; Sons and grandsons' wives: Rs. 147-13-6; Grand-daughters (9,): Rs. 407-08-9; Wives (2): Rs. 10; Concubines who have children (8): Rs. 78; Sons' concubines who have children (16): Rs. 145; Daughters' sons (32): Rs. 575; Grand children (45): Rs. 978-14; Children of the above including all the *salateens* (669): Rs. 10,097-11-7; Nickah wives and concubines (196); Rs. 997-06-9; Wife of the late King Akbar Shah: Rs. 250; For His Majesty's privy purse: Rs. 5,000; Surplus to be appropriated for the repairs of the palace: Rs. 1,090,05-4: Total: Rs. 25,000.
[80] Thomas Metcalfe to Allen, December 6, 1848, *op. cit.*

different perspective and finally settled it in a rather summary manner which did no justice to the claims of the Emperor. According to him, the Emperor had not accepted the conditions proposed by the Government and was, therefore, not entitled to further consideration. He held that "the King having rejected each and all of the conditions on which the munificent offer of an increased stipend was made by the Court, that offer so rejected is at an end and ought not to be resumed." He considered it an act of favour, an offer made to the King for his personal benefit. In his opinion there was no question of any obligation of the British Government to increase the stipend of the Emperor. The position and circumstances of the Emperor and the royal family did not demand any augmentation, as the liberal allowance of twelve lakhs of rupees per annum was ample for all their needs. He was convinced that it was neither good policy nor justice towards the people to renew the offer. He, therefore, recommended to the Court of Directors to consider the refusal of the Emperor to accede to the conditions to be final and not to renew the offer. The Court did not give any definite reply and contented themselves by asserting that the details of the conditions had not been satisfactorily worked out between the Emperor and the Government.[81] This was sufficient for Lord Dalhousie to keep quiet about the entire matter and the Emperor's allowances remained fixed at twelve lakhs of rupees per annum.[82]

The question of the royal stipend clearly brings out the attitude of the British Government towards the Mughal House. Lord Minto was the last Governor-General who evinced a sympathetic attitude to the Emperor. After him the Government was unduly influenced by Metcalfe who considered the stipend to be adequate for the maintenance of the royal family. Ellenborough and Dalhousie had no veneration for the past glory of the Mughals. Whether the Emperor lived in penury or in splendour was no concern for them till he did not interfere with the affairs of the British Government. This indifference was the result of the power and prestige that the Government had acquired in India. The times had changed and it was no longer necessary to take note of the Emperor as it did in 1803.

[81] *Letters from the Court of Directors* (*Pol.*), June 18, 1851.
[82] Minute by G.G. August 26, 1852: *pol. cons.*, September 24, 1852, No. 257.

8
The Status of the Mughal Emperor

THE SETTLEMENT of 1805 as discussed earlier, created an *imperium in imperio*. The Mughal Emperor was recognized as a titular sovereign with regal prerogatives within certain prescribed limits. He had a territory of his own and enjoyed immunity from law. He was also given the authority to sanction or deny capital punishments in the assigned territory. He could hold durbar, receive *nazars*, and bestow *khilats* and titles. The coins struck in his name were in Currency. Thus he was "more than a pensioner, a pageant and a puppet. He was to be a king and yet no king—a something and yet nothing—a reality and a sham at the same time."[1] The position of the Emperor was a political paradox.

Lord Wellesley had undoubtedly cherished the ambition of placing the Company on the throne of Delhi which was then the symbol of the sovereignty of India. But he refrained from executing this imperialist move and allowed the Emperor to maintain the sovereign status inside the palace mainly because he apprehended opposition from the Home authorities to his plans.[2] His immediate successors adopted conciliatory attitude and allowed the Emperor to enjoy the privileges and prerogatives sanctioned in 1805. The first two Residents, Ochterlony and Seton, too, did not suggest any drastic deviation from this policy because during that period it was in the interest of the British to venerate the Emperor. Their success in the second Anglo-Maratha war had not made them the unchallenged masters of the country. Their might and superiority could still be contested by Indian powers. A summary dismissal of the Emperor or cold indifference to his welfare and authority were sure to arouse great indignation among the Indians against them.

[1] Kaye and Malleson: *History of the Indian Mutiny*, ii, p. 4.
[2] *Ibid.*, p. 3.

THE STATUS OF THE MUGHAL EMPEROR

But the paradoxical position of the Mughal Emperor was embarrassing and inconvenient for both parties. The Emperor could not easily reconcile himself to his changed position and strove to extend his power and authority beyond the prescribed limits. The mission of Shah Haji and the Emperor's desire to bestow *khilats* on the Governor-General and the important princes of the country were some of his attempts in this direction. The British Government naturally could not encourage his pretensions to sovereignty. It was, therefore, considered necessary to adopt sterner attitude towards him without injuring his sentiments and resist his endeavours to resuscitate the regal authority of the imperial Mughals.

Views of Charles Metcalfe and Lord Moira

The views of Charles Metcalfe and Lord Moira clearly reflected this attitude of the British Government. Metcalfe had thoroughly disapproved of the obsequious manner of Seton and was in favour of obliterating the "shadow" of the Mughal Emperor in case the interests of the Government so warranted. He believed that the lenient attitude and submissive conduct observed by his predecessors, beyond the respect and attention warranted by a "humane consideration for the fallen fortunes of a once illustrious family" would only help to create complications and embarrassments. According to him, the privileges granted to the Emperor were purely out of sympathy for his feelings. He could have no claim on the British Government as a matter of right.[3]

Lord Moira shared Metcalfe's opinion. Moira came to India

---

[3] Metcalfe wrote as early as 1807: "... As it is evident that we do not mean to restore imperial power to the King, we ought not to pursue a conduct calculated to make him aspire to it. Let us treat him with the respect due to his rank and situation, let us make him confortable in respect to circumstances and give him all the means, as far as possible, of being happy; but unless we mean to establish his power, let us not encourage him to dream of it. Let us meet his first attemps to display imperial authority with immediate check and let him see the mark beyond which our respect and obedience to the shadow of a King will not proceed." Metcalfe to Sherar, June 16, 1807: Kaye, *op. cit.*, i, p. 155.

as the Governor-General when the Charter Act of 1813 was passed by Parliament, which bestowed the sovereignty of the Company's possessions in India on the British Crown. Hence he was eager to end the "pretensions for preeminence in the Court of Delhi" and "the fiction of the Mughal Government."[4] He naturally considered it impolitic to concede the prerogatives of paramountcy to the Emperor.

In the light of this Moira found it necessary to resist the attempts of the Emperor to assume imperial authority and also to discourage the Indian princes from observing the "empty, unbecoming form of acknowledging fealty to the pageant throne of Delhi."[5] It was a political necessity since Lord Moira had decided to make the British Government paramount in name as in authority, a position which the Mughals enjoyed for about two centuries. It was possible neither to appear paramount nor to conduct British relations with Indian states on a sound foooting until the influence exercised by the Mughals on the mind of the Indian princes withered away. If the British Government were to acquire the position of the paramount power, it should be imperative to renounce all traces of its vassalage to the Mughal Emperor. Lord Moira, therefore, initiated a policy of denying the Emperor the royal prerogatives enjoyed by him, which conceded him a status superior to that of the British Government. Of course this was not to be effected by a blatant use of force. The policy adopted by the Government was to discourage the prerogatives of the Emperor step by step, and to usurp his authority gradually, thereby making him absolutely innocuous and insignificant in the political life of the country. This became clearly evident from the attitude of the Government towards the intercourse of the Governor-General with the Emperor, regarding the presentation of *nazars* and the conferring of *khilats* and titles.

Lord Moira's Steps

In 1814 Lord Moira got an opportunity to implement his policy. When the Governor-General was on a tour of the Upper Provinces, the Emperor expressed his desire to meet the head of

[4] *Hastings' Private Journal.*, i, pp. 55 & 79.
[5] Prinsep's note, March 6, 1830: *pol. cons.*, April 2, 1831, No. 35.

the British Government. Moira also was desirous of paying his "personal attention to His Majesty". But the footing on which the interview was to be arranged turned out to be a matter of great disagreement. The Emperor regarded the Governor-General to be his subject and, hence, insisted that he should appear before him as his subject during the meeting and present the usual *nazars*.[6] He expected the compliance of the Governor-General with a "ceremonial which was to imply His Majesty being the leige-lord of the British possessions."[7] Moira refused to meet him except on a footing of equality. A long and tedious negotiation followed in which Charles Metcalfe, who held similar views as the Governor-General, discarded the ceremonial suggested by the Emperor, which implied his suzerainty over the Company's territories. The meeting was, therefore, dropped and a deputation was sent to offer the compliments of the Governor-General to the Emperor.[8]

Moira followed this with more vigorous measures. Faiz Muhammad Khan, the chief of Kanond, applied to the British Government for *khilats* and titles formerly held by his father. Because the bestowal of *khilats* and titles was a prerogative of the sovereign power, Moira thought that if he complied with Faiz Muhammad Khan's request, it would be a serious step towards curbing the pretensions of the Emperor and asserting the sovereign rights of the British Government.[9] The Vice-President-in-Council agreed with the Governor-General that the step could be adopted as a measure for the gradual exclusion of the nominal supremacy of the Emperor.[10] It was, therefore, decided to confer *khilats* and titles on Faiz Muhammad Khan on behalf of the British Government.[11] Though a

[6] Percival Spear, *op. cit.*, p. 45.
[7] *Hastings' Private Journal.*, i, p. 318.
[8] The deputation consisted of Mr. Ricketts, Mr. Adam and Mr. Swinton, Secretaries to the Government; Mr. Thomson, private secretary, Major Doyle, military secretary, Hon. Major Stanhope, first aide-de-camp and Hon. Williams Moore, the nephew of the Governor-General. *Hastings' Private Journal.*, i, p. 323.
[9] Swinton to Monckton, September 23, 1814: *sec. cons.*, November 18, 1814, No. 14.
[10] Monckton to Swinton, November 18, 1814: *sec. cons.*, November 18, 1814, No. 20.
[11] Swinton to Charles Metcalfe, January 4, 1815: *sec. cons.*, January 24, 1815, No. 33.

public proclamation was not made to this effect, the assumption of this prerogative was undoubtedly meant to put the British Government in the position of the paramount power.

Another attempt in this direction was the attitude adopted by the Governor-General towards the relationship between the Emperor and the Nawab of Awadh. The Nawab was tradionally the *Vazir* of the Mughal Emperor and was considered one of his dependants. In spite of the fallen fortunes of the Mughal House he continued to pay respects due to its members.[12] The Governor-General discouraged him from observing any marks of inferiority and induced him to end his dependence on the Mughal House.[13] The Nawab then assumed the kingly title and became an independent ruler.[14] The Emperor received this news with "undisguised indignation."[15]

Another expression of Lord Moira's policy was the abolition of Delhi Mint in 1818 on the recommendation of Charles Metcalfe. The practice of striking coins in the name of the Emperor, an important royal prerogative, was stopped along with it.[16] But a limited number of some coins was issued in his name as a compliment on the anniversaries of his acces-

[12] Two brothers of the Emperor were staying in Lucknow on the bounty of the Nawab. When he met these Mughal princes in the streets he paid them homage by making the elephant on which he rode kneel before them. Marquess of Hastings: *Summary of the Administration of the Indian Government.*, p. 116.

[13] ". . . I caught at the opportunity of saying to the Nawab Vizier, that to continue such demonstration of inferiority must rest with him alone, for the British Government did not require the manifestation of such submission to the Delhi family and had itself dropped those servile forms with which it had heretofore unbecomingly complied. Having reason to think that this instigation would work upon the Nawab Vizier's reflection, I directed the Resident to watch and encourage any apparent disposition in that prince to emancipate himself." Marquess of Hastings, *op. cit.*, p. 117.

[14] Report prepared by J. Paton, First Assistant to the Resident of Awadh, about the relation between the British Government and the Kingdom of Awadh (1764-1835). *For. Misc.*, i, pp. 153-58. This document is also available in print—Bisheshwar Prasad (ed.): *British Government and the Kingdom of Awadh*, (1764-1835).

[15] Marquess of Hastings, *op. cit.*, p. 118.

[16] Charles Metcalfe to Stirling, June 26, 1827, *op. cit.*, p. 55.

THE STATUS OF THE MUGHAL EMPEROR 141

sion. During his second term as the Resident, Ochterlony suggested the re-establishment of the mint.[17] But the Governor-General did not accept it as it would have meant a reversal of the Government's policy.[18] The Emperor's request to revive this practice[19] was also treated similarly.[20] However, the coins of the Company, continued to bear the name of the Emperor till 1835.[21]

The policy of Lord Moira was also intended to discourage any communication between the Emperor and the rulers of Indian states which could "tend to keep alive or resuscitate the expiring notions of his supremacy and their dependence."[22] The confirmation of their succession to the throne by the Emperor was anomalous in the existing political situation in India, according to Moira. The requests from Indian princes to this effect was, hence, discouraged. In fact, the British Government was assuming this right of the paramount power. The application of Jaipur for a *tika* from the Emperor on the occasion of the succession of Sawai Jai Singh in 1819 is an instance in point. The Jaipur court solicited the permission of the British Government to perform the ceremony of *tika* on the part of the Mughal Emperor.[23] The Resident recommended a compliance with this request as its refusal could be "most humiliating to His Majesty, and to Jaipur, a dimunition of that independence

---

[17] Ochterlony to Adam, February 7, 1819: *pol. cons.*, March 13, 1819, No. 36.

[18] Adam to Ochterlony, March 13, 1819: *pol. cons.*, March 13, 1819, No. 38.

[19] Emperor's paper of requests, *op. cit.*

[20] Swinton to Colebrooke, February 1, 1828, *op. cit.*

[21] In 1835 the name of the Emperor was removed from the coins and the following pattern was introduced: "on the obverse, the head and the name of the reigning sovereign of the United Kingdom of Great Britain and Ireland and on the reverse the designation of the coin in English and Persian and the words East India Company in English with such embellishments as shall from time to time be ordered by the Governor-General-in-Council." *Bengal Regulations*, iii, 1834-35, pp. 8-10.

[22] Charles Metcalfe to Ochterlony, May 6, 1820: *pol. cons.*, May 6, 1820, No. 21.

[23] Bhairisal to Ochterlony, Received on April 9, 1820: *pol. cons.*, May 6, 1820, No. 20, Encl.

which they hoped to retain, even in a protective alliance."[24] But the Governor-General did not share the feelings of the Resident. The Emperor could confirm the Raja's succession by performing such a ceremony only if he held the paramount authority. The British Government had already exercised that power by formally recognizing the succession. It naturally could not sanction the same indulgence on the part of the Emperor. It was, therefore, decided to refuse permission to the ceremony.[25] By adopting these steps Lord Moira uneqivocally proclaimed the British Government's intention to strip off the regal prerogatives of the Mughal Emperor in order to assume them to itself.

Emperor's Interview with Lord Amherst

The policy of Lord Moira was successfully carried forward by Lord Amherst. In 1827 the Emperor desired to meet the Governor-General while he was on his tour of the Upper Provinces. Charles Metcalfe, who had in 1814 stubbornly resisted the pretensions of the Emperor for a status superior to that of the Governor-General, was still the Resident at Delhi, serving his second term. During the negotiations he insisted that the interview should be conducted only on a footing of equality. The Emperor now reluctantly agreed to this condition. He believed that a personal meeting with the Governor-General would help to ameliorate his situation. Moreover, the measures taken by Moira were still fresh in his memory. He considered them vindictive, arising from his refusal to meet him on terms suggested by the British Government. He was apprehensive of similar consequences in case he persisted in his course.[26] Consequently, a meeting was arranged which ruled out all expressions of inferiority on the part of the Governor-General.

The Emperor sent Mirza Salim, his son, to Mathura to convey a complimentary message to the Governor-General and

[24] Ochterlony to Charles Metcalfe, April 13, 1820, *pol. cons.*, May 6, 1820, No. 20.
[25] Metcalfe to Ochterlony, May 6, 1820, *op. cit.*
[26] Martin to Prinep, December 7, 1831: *pol. cons.*, January 13, 1832, No. 9

express his desire for an interview with him.[27] Lord Amherst accepted the Emperor's invitation and visited Delhi on February 15, 1827. Mirza Abu Zafar and Mirza Salim met him at the Lahore Gate and the latter conducted him to the Residency. On the 17th morning the Governor-General proceeded to the palace accompanied by Mirza Salim and all the important British officers. At the *tusbeeh khana* the Emperor met and embraced the Governor-General, bidding him to be seated on a state chair in front of the throne, a privilege which none but the heir-apparent had enjoyed so far. No *nazars* were presented to the Emperor, but the Emperor took a handsome string of pearls and emeralds from his neck and placed it around that of Lord Amherst. The members of the Governor-General's staff and suite, however, presented *nazars* and received *khilats*. At the time of departure the Emperor took the Governor-General by the arm and led him to the door of the *tusbeeh khana*. A salute of 19 guns was fired from His Majesty's artillery park, both upon the entry and departure of the Governor-General.[28]

On the 24th the Emperor returned the visit at the Residency where "he was received with every demonstration of respect and honour". The Governor-General presented to the Emperor 101 trays of jewels, shawls, and garments of various kinds, two elephants richly caparisoned and six horses with costly trappings valued at a total amount of Rs. 82,690.[29] This was followed by a visit of the heir-apparent and other sons of the Emperor who were also given appropriate presents amounting to Rs. 41,963.[30] The Governor-General in return visited the heir-apparent. Lady Amherst visited Mumtaz Mahal Begam and the wife of Mirza Salim and presented them a precious necklace and a pair of ear-rings[31] respectively.

This was to be the first and the last meeting of the the Emperor and the Governor-General. In 1831 when Lord Bentinck was on his usual state tour of the Upper Provinces the

[27] *P.G.R.*, i, p. 337.
[28] *Ibid.*, p. 338.
[29] *Ibid.*, p. 340.
[30] *Ibid.*, p. 341.
[31] *Ibid.*, p. 339.

Emperor expressed his desire to meet the Governor-General.³² Bentinck was as vehemently opposed as his predecessors to the imperial pretensions of the Emperor.³³ He was neither prepared to make any concessions nor concede anything that could imply a superior status to the Emperor over the Governor-General. He also did not contemplate any innovations in the existing practice and expressed his readiness to meet him on the precedence established by Lord Amherst.³⁴ But the Emperor had by then complained through the mission of Raja Ram Mohun Roy against the arrangements adopted by Lord Amherst. Bentinck, therefore, decided to suspend all intercourse and communication with the Emperor till a decision was taken by the Home authorities on his petition.³⁵ The proposed interview was abandoned.³⁶

This question was again discussed in 1838. Lord Auckland was desirous of visiting the Emperor if an interview could be arranged on terms of "perfect equality" and without the presentation of *nazars* and other marks of inferiority.³⁷ No presents were to be offered as at the time of Lord Amherst's visit and the Emperor was required to pay a return visit to the Governor-General.³⁸ But Bahadur Shah was not prepared to concede anything more than what was observed by his father during his interview with Lord Amherst.³⁹ Consequently, Lord Auckland decided to "forgo the pleasure he had promised himself of

[32] H.M. to G.G., received on October 28., 1831: *pol. cons.*, March 11, 1832, No. 7.

[33] He wrote: " . . . to continue to acknowledge in this pageant any of the attributes of sovereignty or to do more than kindness and generosity may claim for an ancient and fallen dynasty is not only a questionable but a very objectionable policy".

[34] Prinsep to Martin, November 20, 1831: *pol. cons.*, January 13, 1832, No. 4.

[35] Martin to H.M., November 23, 1831: *pol. cons.*, December 30, 1831, No. 15.

[36] Prinsep to Martin, December 2, 1831: *pol. cons.*, January 13, 1832, No. 6.

[37] Macnaughten to Thomas Metcalfe, January 26, 1838: *pol. cons.*, May 2, 1838, No. 22.

[38] Thomas Metcalfe to Macnaughten, February 6, 1838: *pol. cons.*, May 9, 1838, No. 22.

[39] H.M. to Thomas Metcalfe, received on February 5, 1838: *pol. cons.*, May 9, 1838, No. 22, Encl.

becoming personally acquainted with His Majesty.⁴⁰"

In 1942 when the details of the visit of Lord Ellenborough were being discussed, the British Government pressed for a new convention. The Emperor was now expected to pay the first visit to the Governor-General and the latter would in turn return the visit.⁴¹ These changes in the forms of ceremony are instructive of the Government's attempt to diminish gradually the status of the Emperor. At the time of Hastings the interview was demanded on a "footing of equality." But Lord Auckland wanted "perfect equality" without offering any presents and Ellenborough demanded "most perfect equality", with the Emperor paying the first visit.⁴² Ellenborough's stipulation was undoubtedly meant to relegate the Emperor to a position of inferiority *vis-a-vis* the Governor-General.

Forms of Address

According to the forms of correspondence observed by the Governor-General in the beginning of the nineteenth century, the Indian princes could be classified into three categories: superior, equal, and inferior. The Mughal Emperor and the members of the royal family were accorded the status of superiors in this respect and the Governor-General's letters addressed to them were called *arzee*.⁴³ The Governor-General designated himself as *fiducee* of the Mughal Emperor both in his letter and on his seal. His letter to the Emperor began as follows: "It is humbly represented to those who make obeisance at the auspicious and sublime threshold of the Lord of the earth and the age, the Kibbeh⁴⁴ of the world and its in habitants, the Kabbah⁴⁵

---

⁴⁰ Macnaughten to Thomas Metcalfe, February 12, 1838: *pol. cons.*, May 9, 1838, No. 123.

⁴¹ Thomas Metcalfe to Hamilton, December 2, 1842; *pol. cons.*, March 22, 1843, No. 81.

⁴² Thomas Metcalfe to Hamilton, December 15, 1842: *pol. cons.*, March 22, No. 93.

⁴³ Note by Swinton, dated nil, August, 1820: *For. Misc.*, vol. 139.

⁴⁴ Kibbeh signifies the quarter to which the Mohammedans turn their face in prayer.

⁴⁵ The temple at Mecca. The use of these terms implies the utmost possible veneration for the party to whom they are applied.

of the universe, His Majesty, the shadow of the Almighty, etc. etc". The letters of the Emperor, on the other hand, were styled "gracious mandates" and he addressed the Governor-General as "the chosen and faithful servant".

This style of correspondence was considered by Lord Moira as inconsistent with the comparative status of the royal family and the Governor-General. Even the most insignificant member of the family was to be addressed by him in the humble form of an *arzee*.[46] It was a strange contradiction in terms that the letters of the royal princes soliciting a pension from the bounty of the British Government should be called mandates while the letters from the Governor-General denying or conferring the boon should be termed petitions. Lord Moira considered this form of vassalage highly derogatory to the status of the head of the British Government. He decided to remove the term *fiducee* from his seal. The epistolary correspondence between the Governor-General and the Emperor was also suspended along with it.[47] The Emperor was greatly disappointed at this decision and strongly resented it. He tried several times to revive the friendly intercourse, but in vain.[48]

This deadlock was resolved by Lord Amherst. His interview with the Emperor had established equality of status on formal occasions. In conformity with this change, Amherst considered it necessary to change the existing style of correspondence with the Emperor in a manner which would not include any expression of vassalage on the part of the Governor-General, and persuaded the Emperor to agree to a form of address, which was not derogatory to him.

[46] An example quoted in this respect is that of Muzaffar Bakht, the elder brother of Akbar Shah. He was believed to be a person of ignoble birth and was living on a subsistence allowance of Rs. 750 per month from the British Government. He visited Lord Moira at Fatehgarh, but the Governor-General did not even repay the visit. Letters of the Governor-General to him, however, were superscribed as *arzee*. His sons also were expected to receive the same treatment.

[47] This happened in 1820. No formal resolution seems to have been recorded on the subject. Note by Persian Secretary to Government, September 6, 1827: *pol. cons.*, September 21, 1827, No. 68.

[48] Prinsep to Ochterlony, March 10, 1821: *pol. cons.*, March 17, 1821, No. 74.

The new style of address adopted by Lord Amherst was strikingly different from the former. According to the mode now suggested, the letters of the Governor-General commenced with a prayer or invocation of prosperity: "May the Almighty perpetuate the reign of the pearl of the Crown of Royalty, the ornament of the throne of the Empire, the sovereign of the realm of justice and compassion. Be it known to your enlightened mind resplendent as the Sun etc."[49] He designated himself the "suppliant of the throne of Almighty" and his letters were qualified as *wasikah*.[50] The Emperor now addressed the Governor-General as "the chief of high and exalted dignity" and began his letters as follows: "May the chief of the high dignity and titles, the most excellent and distinguished of the support of the throne, the pillar of the state, he who is appointed to rule over and administer the affairs of Empire, be the object of God's grace and the Royal favour." His letters were termed as "illustrious epistles".[51]

The changed style of address was similar to that prevailed between the Governor-General and the ruler of Persia. It acknowledged the superior rank of the Emperor as possessing kingly dignity, but did not contain any term indicating vassalage or subordination on the part of the Governor-General. This, of course, was not considered by the Government entirely unobjectionable as it conceded a superior status to the Emperor. But it was not possible to achieve complete equality in the style of correspondence since the British Government unequivocally recognized the Emperor as a titular sovereign.[52]

The new form of correspondence came into force when the Governor-General addressed a letter to the Emperor announcing the appointment of Edward Colebrooke to succeed Charles Metcalfe as the Resident and the Civil Commissioner in 1827.[53] The Emperor did not immediately object to this change, but acknowledged the receipt of this letter without any remonstrance.[54]

[49] This is a form common between equals.
[50] *Wasikah* merely means a letter or writing generally used for a treaty
[51] Note by Persian Secretary to Government, September 6, 1827, *op. cit.*
[52] *Ibid.*
[53] G.G. to H.M., July 28, 1827: *pol. cons.*, July 28, 1827, No. 64.
[54] H.M. to G.G., Received on September 1, 1827 : *pol. cons.*, September 21, 1827, No. 67.

But later on he expressed his resentment against it through the mission of Raja Ram Mohun Roy.[55]

It would, however, be wrong to think that these measures were intended to injure the feelings of the Emperor as is evident from the attitude of the Government towards the handling of the royal affairs by Francis Hawkins.[56]

Hawkins came to Delhi with exaggerated notions of the importance of the Resident and misconceived ideas about his relative position *vis-a-vis* the royal family. He failed to comprehend the Government's policy of honour for the Emperor, "within and disregard without the Mughal palace". Moreover, he was overwhelmed by a consciousness of the superiority of the British and hence could not reconcile to the age-old customs and ceremonies observed in the Mughal palace.

During his first visit to the palace Hawkins took umbrage at the treatment meted out to him by the Emperor and the members of the royal family. The Emperor, he observed, neither expressed satisfaction at his arrival nor asked him any question. The heir-apparent did not offer him a seat when he called on him.[57] He considered these as personal insult and slight to his authority. He therefore adopted an indifferent and hostile attitude towards the Emperor and the members of his household.

Immediately after assuming office, Hawkins recommended to the Government to abolish the practice of presenting *nazars* to the Emperor. He also sought the permission of the Government to stop the customary practice of firing salute by the British artillery every time the Emperor went out and returned to the palace. He wanted to limit it to four occasions in a year. They were the two *Ids* and the anniversaries of the Emperor's birthday and accession to the throne.[58] Another suggestion of his was to discontinue the petty presents given by the Resident to the menial servants of the royal household on the occasion

[55] H.M., to the king of Britain dated nil: *pol. cons.*, March 13, 1829, No. 20.
[56] Hawkins was the Resident at Delhi after Colebrooke. His appointment, etc., is discussed in Chapter IX.
[57] Hawkins to Swinton, February 1, 1830: *pol. cons.*, March 19, 1830, No. 6.
[58] Hawkins to Swinton, October 23, 1829: *pol. cons.*, November 13, 1829, No. 13.

THE STATUS OF THE MUGHAL EMPEROR 149

of the *Dashehra* festival.[59]

These suggestions would have considerably lowered the status of the Emperor had they been implemented. But William Bentinck did no wish to make any sweeping innovations that would injure the feelings of the Emperor and yield no political advantage.[60] The Resident was, therefore, instructed to observe the usual ceremonies and manners so far maintained towards the Emperor and the members of the royal family.

This, however, did not induce the injured Resident to observe propriety in his conduct. On more than one occasion Hawkins was guilty of injuring the feelings of the Emperor and violating the customs and etiquette observed in the palace. He presented *nazars* to the heir-apparent by one hand, insisted on sitting in the presence of Mumtaz Mahal, refused the dishes sent by the heir-apparent and the nosegayes by the Emperor, and returned a *shukka* sent by Banu Begam, the Emperor's niece.[61] Accompanied by a friend, he even entered the gateway of *Diwan-i-Khas*, commonly called the gate of red curtain (*Lal Purdah*), on horseback in spite of the remonstrance of the sentry stationed there.[62] This was a breach of etiquette that had never before occurred in the Mughal palace. When informed about this, the Emperor's "unaccountable grief and remorse" knew no bounds and he complained to the Governor-General about the insolent conduct of Hawkins.[63] The Governor-General immediately

[59] Swinton to Hawkins, November 13, 1829: *pol. cons.*, November 13, 1829, No. 14.

[60] Swinton to Hawkins, October 30, 1829: *pol. cons.*, October 30, 1829, No. 3; and Swinton to Hawkins, December 26, 1829: *pol. cons.*, December 26, 1829, No. 11.

[61] H.M. to G.G., received on January 1, 1830: *pol. cons.*, January 8, 1830, No. 42.

[62] H.M. to G.G., received on January 1, 1830, *op. cit.*

[63] He wrote: "On receiving this intelligence we were smitten to the soul with grief and shame and cannot describe to your lordship the affliction of spirit under which we have since laboured. All the world know that up to this time no Resident, nor other British officers of rank, ever committed a grave offence and studied insult of this nature towards our Royal Self. Alas! alas! woe is me! that Hawkins should have knowingly, wilfully and deliberately been guilty of such a dereliction of duty and outrage. We entreat your lordship to reflect what a situation we are reduced to, if the Resident who is the channel of conducting all affairs and by whose advice and counsel we are bound to act and always have acted, insults and degrades the royal dignity and authority."

relieved Hawkins of the charge of the palace affairs[64] and called for his explanation about the complaints preferred against him.[65] He submitted his explanation in a lengthy despatch which remains a monument of unpardonable arrogance and utter ignorance of Indian sentiments, etiquette, and customs.[66]

The explanation of Hawkins failed to remove from the mind of the Governor-General the impression that from the very beginning he had been wanting in the proper observance of the etiquette expected of the British representative towards the royal family.[67] Even if disrespect were shown towards him, the Governor-General pointed out that he should have shown proper restraint and attributed that to error. In any case, the wiser policy should have been to ignore it rather than make it the subject of an undignified controversy. The Governor-General disapproved of the Resident's conduct and consequently removed him from office.

Hawkins' conduct was not merely a crude expression of the ignorance and arrogance of a misguided and capricious individual. It had a deeper significance. It actually represented the changing British attitude not only towards the Mughal Emperor but also towards things Indian.[68] Hawkins felt the pulse

[64] Thomas Metcalfe was ordered to take over the charge of the palace affairs and the Emperor was requested to conduct matters with him till final arrangements were made. Swinton to Thomas Metcalfe, January 5, 1830: *pol. cons.*, January 8, 1830, No. 46, and G.G. to H.M. January 5, 1830: *pol. cons.*, January 8, 1830, No. 47.

[65] Swinton to Hawkins, January 5, 1830: *pol. cons.*, January 8, 1830, No. 45.

[66] An example may be quoted in this respect. The Emperor complained that the Resident did not send a *choubdar* to enquire about his health. In his explanation Hawkins stated that he did not find any necessity of sending a *choubdar* to enquire about the health of the Emperor as he did not hear of his being indisposed. Hawkins to Swinton, February 1, 1830, *op. cit.*

[67] Swinton to Hawkins, March 19, 1830: *pol. cons.*, March 19, 1830, No. 7.

[68] A masterly analysis of this change by Percival Spear is worth quoting: "The utilitarian spirit was silently creeping into the British ranks even in India, and romance paled in the dawn of common sense. The possession of the Mughal name, which to Wellesley had seemed worth so much, came to be regarded more and more as an encumbrance. What before was a prize was becoming a nuisance. The officials who

of this change at Delhi. Naturally he considered the manners and etiquette observed by his predecessors as obnoxious and unbecoming of the representative of the British Government. "What was almost a pleasure for Seton and a matter of courtesy and policy to Metcalfe was for Hawkins an occasion for shame." Though the Emperor conceded equlity of status to the Governor-General, his assumption of royal authority in his relations with the Resident was considered by Hawkins humiliating and degrading. He found to his dismay that the Resident was still to appear before the Emperor as his subject and subordinate. He was to stand in front of the members of the royal family and was expected to enquire about the health of the Emperor everyday. He was to offer *nazars* in obeisance and was not even at liberty to refuse petty presents from the members of the royal family. Hawkins was violently opposed to these servile forms of inferiority and he had, in fact, sought the permission of the Government to end them immediately.

But the Government did not encourage the Resident to treat the Emperor and his family lightly in matters of etiquette and intercourse. It was not its intention to violate the usual customs and manners that would injure the feelings of the Emperor or introduce changes that would yield no political harvest. The Emperor was to be left to himself and allowed "to live as a king" at least within the palace. The removal of Hawkins from Delhi made the position quite clear that the King was entitled to due recognition and dignity within the four walls of his residence.

> had before debated on means of improving the king's condition were now coming to say, "to what purpose is this waste?" What was to be preserved as an interesting survival was now to be abolished as a fantastic imposition ... All over India the British attitude to things Indian was changing. The old interest in and respect for Indian civilization was changing to criticism and detest. New intellectual and moral gods had arisen in Europe who frowned upon the gorgeous East. Once men had looked to India as the home of the natural man, of a culture closer to nature than that of Europe and had idealized the simple and pious Hindu. Now through the twin eyes of utilitarian reason and Evangelical religion the scene was changed. To the glance of the one, all was superstition and denial of natural morality, in the view of the other, all was idolatry and darkness." Percival Spear; *op. cit.*, p. 50-51.

This, however, was only the "pensionary courtesy" which Lord Minto had conceived as obligatory on the part of the British Government to the Emperor. It did not in any way retard the policy of gradual reduction of his authority and privileges. The steps taken by Bentinck himself in respect of *khilats* and titles and the attitude of his successors to the presentation of *nazars* amply illustrate this.

Khilats and Titles

The bestowal of *khilats* and titles was an important royal prerogative widely in vogue in India. The princes and chiefs applied to the Emperor for the grant of these honours which were generally complied with in return for *nazars* and presents. The grant of *khilats* to a prince on his accession to the throne was considered a sanction of the paramount power to his succession.

The settlement of 1805 did not make any stipulation about this prerogative. The Emperor continued to enjoy his regal authority and freely distributed *khilats* and bestowed titles on British officers, the subjects of the Company, and the Indian princes and chiefs. Lord Lake had received a *khilat* and a title from Shah Alam. The Residents invariably received titles when they were inroduced to the Emperor.[69] It was necessary to discourage this practice in the interest of the British Government as it implied a paramount status to the Emperor. The attempt of Akbar Shah to bestow *khilat* on the Governor-General and important princes of India in 1807 was, therefore, thwarted by the Government. The investiture of *khilats* on the occasion of succession of the princes and nobles was also disallowed. On the accession of Malhar Rao Holkar the Goverment decided not to allow the investiture of *khilat* on the part of the Emperor should the Prince apply to that effect.[70] In case of titles the Government did not assert itself so vigorously

---

[69] Ochterlony and Seton were given the titles of "Nazim-ud-Daula" and Charles Metcalfe "Mumtuzum-ud-Daula, Mukhtiar-ul-Mulk Ikhtias Yar Khan Bahadur Soulat Jung."

[70] Edmonstone to Metcalfe, November 27, 1811: *pol. cons.*, November 29, 1811, No. 15.

THE STATUS OF THE MUGHAL EMPEROR 153

in the early period. Malhar Rao Holkar and Sahib Singh, the Raja of Patiala, were allowed to receive titles from the Emperor.[71] But the subjects of the British Government were not permitted to receive similar honours,[72] as it would imply the acceptance of the Emperor's suzerainty over its possessions. The British Government, in fact, was assuming these prerogatives for itself. In 1813 titles were granted to Faiz Mohammad Khan[73] and *khilats* were bestowed on Nawab Sams-ud-din Khan[74] and the Raja of Bikaner in 1828.[75]

The Emperor was naturally unhappy about these restrictions imposed on him. In the letter of requests presented to Lord Amherst he raised these issues and demanded once again the restoration of these privileges to him.[76] The Government then decided that he could enjoy these prerogatives only in the case of royal servants.[77] His desire to bestow *khilats* and titles on the chiefs and nobles of Delhi on their succession was also disallowed by the Government.[78] He was, however, allowed to grant titles to the Residents and the members of the royal family.[79]

This decision of the Government was put to test in 1832. Rao Lachman Singh of Patan, a feudatory of Jaipur state, was long endeavouring to obtain titles and *khilats* from the Emperor. The Residents continuously discouraged him from this indulgence. In 1832 he approached the Emperor again for obtaining

---

[71] Metcalfe to Edmonstone, April 28, 1813: *pol. cons.*, May 21, 1813, No. 6.
[72] The case of Aadit Narain, the Raja of Benares, may be quoted as an example. He was a dependant of the British Government. In 1828 he applied to the Emperor for a title. The British Government disallowed it. Stirling to Colebrooke, February 22, 1828: *pol. cons.*, February 29, 1828, No. 40.
[73] Swinton to Charles Metcalfe, January 4, 1815, *op. cit.*
[74] Colebrooke to Swinton, August 21, 1828: *pol. cons.*, September 13, 1828, No. 11.
[75] Swinton to Colebrooke, September 13, 1828: *pol. cons.*, September 13, 1828, No. 13.
[76] The paper of requests presented by the Emperor, *op. cit.*
[77] Swinton to Colebrooke, February 1, 1828: *pol. cons.*, February 1, 1828, No. 3.
[78] *Letters to the Court of Directors* (*Pol.*), July 3, 1828.
[79] Metcalf to Stirling, June 26, 1827: *pol. cons.*, July 27, 1827, No. 7.

these honours. In spite of the Resident's remonstrance the Emperor now decided to comply with this request,[80] and conferred *khilats* and titles on the Rao.[81] The exercise of this prerogative by the Emperor, much against the declared decision of the Government, was viewed by the Governor-General very seriously.[82] It was decided to maintain the Government's earlier decision to confine this privilege to the members of the royal household.[83] The Emperor was advised to recall these honours as the British Government considered their conferment "improper and impolitic."[84] The Emperor promised to abstain from similar indulgence in future, but wanted to be excused this time as the resumption of royal favours was "contrary to the usage of the house of Timur."[85] But Bentinck was not prepared to make any adjustment in this case and asked the Patan chief to return the *khilat* through the Rajputana Agency.[86]

The adamant attitude of the Government notwithstanding, the Emperor continued to press this prerogative. In 1835 Simon Fraser was entrusted with the investigation of William Fraser's murder. On the conclusion of the investigation the Emperor conferred a title on him in appreciation of his efficient discharge of duties.[87] This was in violation of the Government's decision of 1828, which did not recognize the right of the Emperor to confer titles on British subjects. Since Fraser was a public functionary of the Government, it was entirely within its purview to appreciate and acknowledge his services.[88] The Agent was, therefore, instructed to forbid the receipt of titles from the Emperor by the officers of the British Government in future.[89]

The Emperor exercised this prerogative again in 1837 on

[80] H.M. to Blake, Assistant to the Resident: *P.G.R.*, i, p. 360
[81] Fraser to H.M., April 3, 1833: *pol. cons.*, May 16, 1833, No. 29, Encl.
[82] Swinton to Macnaughten, July 30, 1832: *pol. cons.*, July 30, 1832, No. 17
[83] Macnaughten to Swinton, July 5, 1832: *pol. cons.*, July 30, 1832, No. 15.
[84] Fraser to H.M., April 10, 1833: *pol. cons.*, May 16, 1833, No. 29, Encl.
[85] H.M. to Fraser, April 10, 1833: *pol. cons.*, May 16, 1833, No. 29, Encl.
[86] Fraser to Macnaughten, April 17, 1833: *pol. cons.*, May 16, 1833, No. 29.
[87] Scott to Macnaughten, September 5, 1835: *pol. cons.*, September 28, 1835, No. 18.
[88] *Ibid.*
[89] Macnaughten to Scott, September 28, 1835: *pol. cons.*, September 28, 1835, No. 19.

THE STATUS OF THE MUGHAL EMPEROR

the occasion of the visit of the Commander-in-Chief to Delhi.[90] The Government took very serious note of it and called for the explanation of the Agent for not acquainting the Commander-in-Chief about the instructions of the Government in this respect.[91] During the visit of the Commander-in-Chief the Agent was out of Delhi and his assistants overlooked the orders of the Government. In order to prevent any further departure from the Government's instructions the Emperor was informed that he could no more bestow titles on any one except his immediate servants.[92] Thus the Emperor was ultimately deprived of one of the most important royal prerogatives.

Presentation of Nazars

Shah Alam and his successors tenaciously adhered to their right to accept *nazars*, which was another important imperial prerogative. The settlement of 1805 did not make any stipulation in this respect also. But the British officials and the Indian princes and chiefs presented *nazars* and received *khilats* in return. *Nazars* were presented on behalf of the Governor-General, the Commander-in-Chief, and the Resident on all important festivals. Apart from this, whenever British officers visited Delhi and met the Emperor, they invariably presented *nazars* to him.

The practice continued without any change till 1813. Lord Moira, who had insisted on equality of status in all intercourse with the Emperor, considered this custom of observing "public testimony of dependence and subservience as irreconcilable to any rational policy."[93] He could not reconcile himself to this abject form of presenting *nazars* as "a homage to his liege-lord,"[94] which implied a superior status to the Emperor. He instructed his staff to refrain from presenting *nazars* on his

---

[90] Lumley, Adjutant General to Casement, Military Secretary, December 9, 1837: *pol. cons.*, January 31, 1838, No. 77.

[91] Maenaughten to Hamilton, December 21, 1837: *pol. cons.*, February 21, 1838, No. 67.

[92] Thomas Metcalfe to Hamilton, January 10, 1838: *pol. cons.*, July 4, 1838, No. 66.

[93] *Hastings' Private Journal*, i, p. 323.

[94] *Ibid.*

behalf when they went to meet the Emperor. The *nazars* presented by the Resident four times in a year on the part of the Governor-General were, however, allowed to be continued. But he completely stopped this practice on behalf of the Commander-in-Chief.[95]

The Emperor was unhappy about these decisions. In 1823 when Edward Paget arrived in India as the Commander-in-Chief, the Emperor demanded an explanation from the Resident for the omission of the customary *nazars* on the part of the Commander-in-Chief.[96] The Resident enquired of the Government if this practice, observed till 1813, was to be revived. The Government thought it impolitic to retrace the steps already taken[97] and the Court of Directors gave the sanction for the abolition of this practice.[98]

The presentation of *nazars* to the Emperor by Indian princes and chiefs considerably diminished during this period. It was quite natural as the Emperor no more wielded any practical authority. Such prerogatives as the grant of *khilats* and titles formerly exercised by him were gradually assumed by the British Government. The Emperor raised this question in 1827 in the letter of requests presented to Lord Amherst. He requested the Governor-General to induce the princes with whom the British Government had treaty relations to offer him the usual *nazars*.[99] The Government took the attitude that it had not prohibited this practice by the princes and nobles. It was left to them to observe it or not. However, the policy of the Government was to discourage any notion of allegiance or inferiority to the Emperor on the part of the Indian princes. Naturally therefore the Government could not comply with

[95] Elliot, Agent at Delhi to Swinton, August 27, 1823: *pol. cons.*, November 7, 1823, No. 21. *Nazars* were presented four times in a year on behalf of the Commander-in-Chief, two *Ids* and the anniversary of the Emperor's accession and birth. Fifty-one gold mohars were presented each time.

[96] Elliot to Swinton, August 27, 1823: *pol, cons.*, November 7, 1823, No. 21.

[97] Swinton to Elliot, November 7, 1823: *pol. cons.*, November 7, 1823, No. 22.

[98] *Letters from the Court of Directors (Pol.)*, December 12, 1827.

[99] The paper of requests presented by the Emperor, *op. cit.*

his wishes.[100]

Lord Amherst also introduced innovations in this respect. During his interview with the Emperor he had avoided the presentation of *nazars*.[101] After that he decided to stop this practice altogether on the part of the Governor-General,[102] and substituted an annual *nazar* of equal amount to be presented by the Resident.[103] This was intended to avoid any pecuniary loss to the Emperor.

Further changes were effected in 1836. It was then decided to discontinue *nazars* at the expense of the Government except those presented by the Resident to the Emperor, the Queen and the heir-apparent on customary occasions.[104] The assistants at the Agency and other British officers at Delhi could present *nazars*, if they so desired, at their own expense.[105] The Emperor was highly mortified to learn about this decision of the Government and sought the help of the Agent to reverse it.[106] The Agent, of course, could not offer him any help. In compliance with this order when Captain Graham joined the Agency as an assistant he was neither presented to the Emperor nor any *nazar* was offered. He was expected to conduct the royal affairs while the Agent was away on tour. The Emperor considered it highly derogatory to his dignity to transact business with a person who had not paid him the wanted honours.[107] When Graham was taken to the Court the Emperor refused to acknowledge him unless he presented a *nazar* and received a *khilat* in return. He was so insistent that Graham had to pay the *nazar* from his private funds.[108] The Government then ordered that an assistant, if required to look after the palace affairs, could present a *nazar* at the public expense.[109]

[100] Metcalfe to Stirling, June 26, 1827: *pol. cons.*, July 27, 1827, No. 7.
[101] Stirling to Swinton, March 3, 1827: *P.G.R.*, i, p. 338.
[102] Note by Seton Carr, September 8, 1852: *pol. cons.*, October 29, 1852, Nos. 195-96.
[103] *Letters to the Court of Directors (Pol.)*, July 3, 1828, para 65.
[104] Bushby to Thomas Metcalfe, February 17, 1836: *P.G.R.*, i, p. 388.
[105] Bushby to Thomas Metcalfe, May 14, 1836: *P.G.R.*, i, pp. 391-92.
[106] H.M., to Thomas Metcalfe, March 21, 1835: *P.G.R.*, i, p. 389.
[107] H.M., to Charles Metcalfe, October 27, 1835: *P.G.R.*, i, pp. 393-94.
[108] Thomas Metcalfe to Hamilton, November 23, 1837: *P.G.R.*, i, p. 395.
[109] Hamilton to Thomas Metcalfe, November 15, 1837: *P.G.R.*, i, pp. 394-95.

It was Lord Ellenborough who dealt the final blow. He disliked half measures and was highly indignant to learn that the Resident still continued to offer *nazars* to the Emperor. He considered this token of feudal submission inconsistent with the relative position of the Emperor and the British Government. He had neither sympathy for the Emperor nor any regard for his feelings of. He knew that in 1829 the Resident had suggested the total abolition of *nazars*, motivated mainly by two considerations.[110] First, it was degrading and humiliating to the status and authority of the British representative; and secondly, it involved considerable expenditure to the British exchequer.[111] William Bentinck had then decided to maintain the *status quo*.[112] But these recommandations suited Ellenborough's purpose. He decided to implement the Resident's proposals and immediately ordered the disconstinuance of presentation of the *nazars*.[113] The Emperor was very much perturbed at this decision and in his appeal to the Governor-General to repeal this measure he laid much stress on the drain it would cause to his already strained financial resourses.[114] The Governor-General thereupon sanctioned an addition of Rs. 10,000 annually to the royal stipend,[115] which, however, was never paid as the Emperor declined to receive anything in place of *nazars*.[116]

When referred to them for approval, the Court of Directors took a humane view of the situation. They were not inclined to introduce any change during the life-time of Bahadur Shah and, therefore, ordered to continue the practice.[117] Lord

[110] Hawkins to Swinton, October 8, 1829: *P.G.R.*, i. p. 378.
[111] From August 1828 to July 1829 the British Government spent about Rs. 11,350 on this account (*P.G.R.*, i, p. 381). This cannot be said as a huge amount.
[112] Swinton to Hawkins, October 30, 1829: *pol. cons.*, October 30, 1829, No. 3.
[113] *Letters to the Court of Directors (Pol.)*, July 26, 1843.
[114] H.M. to the G.G., March 26, 1843: *pol. cons.*, October 29, 1852, No. 183.
[115] Thomas, Secretary to Government to Thomas Metcalfe, April 17, 1843: *pol. cons.*, October 29, 1852; No. 185.
[116] Bahadur Shah to Ellenborough, May 5, 1843: *pol. cons.*, October 29, 1852, No. 188.
[117] *Letters from the Court of Directors (Pol.)* May 1, 1844, para 26.

THE STATUS OF THE MUGHAL EMPEROR

Hardinge, who succeeded Ellenborough, did not implement the orders of the Home authorities.[118] He addressed them a careful and strong protest against the revival of the practice and vehemently pleaded against the repeal of the decision of his predecessor. He suggested that this decision would be made applicable only to persons in the service of the Government. All others visiting the Emperor were at liberty to present *nazars*. But the Agent or any other British official was not to be present on such occasions.[119] The Court of Directors agreed to this change.[120]

The Emperor strenuously endeavoured to revive this prerogative. He sent representations to the Governor-General[121] and to the Court of Directors for reversing this decision.[122] But by then Lord Dalhousie had assumed charge as the Governor-General. He was more vehemently opposed to the Emperor's regal prerogatives than his predecessors and was, in fact, waiting for Bahadur Shah's death to effect some sweeping innovations. He followed the steps taken by Lord Ellenborough and even turned down the request of the Emperor for the arrears of the commutation earlier promised against the *nazars*.[123] This step of Lord Dalhousie closed the question for ever.

With the discontinuance of *nazars* the policy initiated by Lord Moira was almost complete. By slow degrees the Government succeeded in depriving the Emperor of all royal prerogatives and in making him a cypher in the political life of the country. What was left to him were only the kingly title and the royal palace at Delhi.

---

[118] *Press List of Punjab Government Records*, p. 106.
[119] *Letters to the Court of Directors (Pol.)* November 5, 1847.
[120] *Letters from the Court of Directors (Pol.)* November 18, 1848.
[121] H.M. to G.G., September 18, 1849: *pol. cons.*, December 15, 1849, No. 19.
[122] H.M. to the Court of Directors, September 18, 1849: *pol. cons.*, December 15, 1849, No. 20.
[123] G.G.'s minute, October 19, 1852: *pol. cons.*, October 29, 1852, No. 195.

9
The Final Phase

THE TWENTIES and early thirties of the century saw quick changes in the personnel, status, and jurisdiction of the Residency. Charles Metcalfe who was summoned from Hyderabad in 1825 to clean the Augean stables, remained in Delhi only for a period of two years. The "golden age" of the Residency came to an end with his departure. His successors were unfortunately of much less calibre and efficiency. The unflinching integrity of Ochterlony, the devotion to duty of Seton, and the adroit statesmanship of Metcalfe were never again to be seen at the Delhi Residency. Metcalfe's successor, Edward Colebrooke[1] considerably lowered its prestige by indulging in corruption and nepotism, for which he was suspended[2] and later on dismissed[3] on a complaint from Charles Trevelyan, an assistant in the Residency.[4] Francis Hawkins succeeded him.[5] He also proved to be a wrong choice as he could neither carry on well with the Emperor nor manage the relations efficiently with the Rajput and Sikh states.

[1] Colebrooke took charge of the Residency on July 31, 1827, Colebrooke to Swinton, July 31, 1827: *pol. cons.*, August 17, No. 65.
[2] Swinton to Colebrooke, July 17, 1829: *pol. cons.*, July 17, 1829, No. 22.
[3] This case has been dealt with in detail by Percival Spear in *Twilight of the Mughals*, pp. 167-81.
[4] Trevelyan to Swinton, June 30, 1829: *pol. cons.*, July 17, 1829, No. 20.
[5] Hawkins took charge of the Residency on September 18, 1829. Hawkins to Swinton, September 18, 1829: *pol. cons.*, October 14, 1829, No. 22.
After the suspension of Colebrooke, William Fraser was appointed to officiate as the Resident. But after six weeks of his assumption of the office he was also removed on a complaint from Trevelyan about his partiality and consideration towards Colebrooke which made the enquiry against the latter ineffective. Trevelyan to Swinton, August 3, 1829: *pol. cons.*, August 21, 1829, No. 32; and Swinton to Fraser, August 21, 1829, *pol. cons.*, August 21, 1829 No. 34.

THE FINAL PHASE

He was consequently removed and W.B. Martin was appointed in his place.[6]

In 1832 William Bentinck considered it necessary to separate the Rajput states from the control of the Delhi Residency. The border disputes and certain internal difficulties which called for immediate action could not be effectively handled from Delhi due to its distance from these states.[7] A separate Agency was established for Rajputana and the Delhi Residency was now left with the management of the relations with the Sikh chiefs and the Mughal Emperor.[8] As a result the duties and responsibilities of the Residency considerably diminished and it was no longer necessary to continue it on its former status. It was, therefore, relegated to the position of an Agency and the Civil Commissioner of Delhi was entrusted with the political duties. He was designated "the Civil Commissioner and Agent to the Governor-General at Delhi". He was given an additional allowance of Rs. 500 and two assistants.[9] Martin was relieved of his post and William Fraser, then the Civil Commissioner, assumed the charge of the Agency.[10] Fraser, however, was not destined to remain in office for long. He was murdered on March 22, 1835, on the instigation of Nawab Sams-ud-Din of Firozpur.[11] Thomas Theophilus Metcalfe, the younger brother of Charles Metcalfe, then took over the charge and held this office till his death in 1853.

Meanwhile, vital changes had taken place in the Company's Indian administration. The Charter Act of 1833 divided the Presidency of Bengal into the Presidency of Fort William in Bengal and the Presidency of Agra.[12] The immediate effect

---

[6] Swinton to Hawkins, June 18, 1830: *pol: cons.*, July 18, 1830, No. 7. Martin joined the Residency on November 25, 1830. Martin to Swinton, November 25, 1830: *pol. cons.*, December 10, 1830, No. 7.

[7] G.G.'s minute, March 30, 1832: *pol. cons.*, April 16, 1832, No. 22.

[8] *Ibid.*

[9] G.G.'s minute, March 30, 1832, *op. cit.* The assistants could be employed either as assistants to the Commissioner or the Agent as required by circumstances.

[10] Martin to Swinton, March 10, 1832: *pol. cons.*, March 26, 1832, No. 9.

[11] Thomas Metcalfe to Macnaughten, March 24, 1835: *pol. cons.*, April 13, 1835, No. 9. Murder of Fraser has been examined in detail by Percival Spear in *Twilight of the Mughals*, pp. 128-90.

[12] *Letters from the Court of Directors (Pol.)*, December 17, 1833.

of this change on the Delhi Agency was that the Agent was subordinated to the Governor of Agra and designated the "Agent to the Governor of Agra."[13] In 1836 the Presidency of Agra was converted into the North-Western Provinces under a Lieutenant-Governor with all the political duties formerly attached to the Governor of Agra.[14] The Agent at Delhi naturally came under him. He was designated the "Agent to the Lieutenant-Governor of the North-Western Provinces."[15] Till now the Delhi Residency was the very centre of political activities in this part of the country. But from 1834 onwards the Agent at Delhi was relegated to a comparatively insignificant position. The Cis-Sutlej states were also placed under the Agra Government[16] and the Resident was required to manage only the relations with the Mughal Emperor.

Ellenborough's Proposals

Bahadur Shah II, who ascended the throne in 1837, was allowed by the British Government all privileges enjoyed by his predecessor. But by then the consensus among the British officers in India had increasingly turned against the lenient and considerate treatment accorded to the Mughal Emperor. They were sceptical about his loyalty to the British Government and were apprehensive about the wisdom behind the policy of perpetuating a political nonentity at a considerable cost to the exchequer. But Lord Auckland was then so much engrossed in Afghan affairs that he had hardly any time to devote to the affairs of the Mughal Emperor. On the conclusion of the Afghan War in 1843, his successor, Lord Ellenborough, decided to make sweeping changes in the privileges enjoyed by the Mughals.

On account of the heavy expenditure incurred on the Afghan War Lord Ellenborough was compelled to devise some

[13] Macnaughten to Scott, May 25, 1835: *pol. cons.*, May 25, 1835, No. 23
[14] Macnaughten to Charles Metcalfe, Lieutenant Governor, N.W.P., March 28, 1836: *pol. cons.*, March 28, 1836, No. 5.
[15] *Ibid.*
[16] Macnaughten to Scott, November 2, 1835: *pol. cons.*, November 2, 1835, No. 27.

economy measures. He turned his attention first to the charges connected with the Political Agencies with native chiefs, especially with the Mughal Emperor. He considered such formalities as the presentation of *nazars* and grant of titles unnecessary and altogether inconsistent with the new position of the Emperor under the British Government.[17] The exercise of these sovereign prerogatives by the Emperor, Ellenborough thought, was nothing but an "attempt to preserve the unreal image of the past."[18] In order to put an end to this image he thought that the Emperor should be denied all these privilages as well as his title. He, therefore, ordered the discontinuation of the presentation of *nazars*[19] and instructed the Agent to refrain from undertaking any step on the demise of Bahadur Shah, which might imply the recognition of the title of Emperor to his successor, without specific authority from the Governor-General.[20] It was feared that "the King being a Mohammedan, he may one day place himself at the head of a factious party and cause much annoyance to the British Government." To forestall such a possibility the Governor-General suggested the reduction of the royal stipend to Rs. 50,000 per month. Further, on the demise of Bahadur Shah Ellenborough proposed to fix a total sum of two lakhs of rupees annually for the maintenance of the royal family.[21] He also wanted to abolish the Agency at Delhi and stop the attendance of a British officer at the Emperor's durbar.[22]

The Emperor, who came to know about these proposals through a subordinate official of the Agency and later confirmed by the Agent himself, was greatly agitated about the future of his family. He knew that an appeal to the Governor-General would be of no avail and he immediately decided to seek redress from the Queen of England by sending a trust-

[17] Report of Lord Ellenborough to the Council, February 22, 1843: *pol. cons.*, May 24, 1843, No. 10-B.
[18] *Letters to the Court of Directors (Pol.)*, July 26, 1843.
[19] Thomson, Lt. Governor, to Thomas Metcalfe, February 26, 1843: *pol. cons.*, March 22, 1843, No. 117.
[20] Thomson to Thomas Metcalfe, February 26, 1843: *pol. cons.*, March 22, 1843, No. 118.
[21] Report of Lord Ellenborough, February 22, 1843, *op. cit.*
[22] Thomson to Thomas Metcalfe, May 2, 1843: *pol. cons.*, May 24, 1843, No. 10.

worthy agent to London. About this time George Thompson, an Englishman of repute and philanthropic inclination, had come to India on the invitation of Dwaraka Nath Tagore. His services were solicited to present the claims and grievances of the Emperor to the various tribunals in England.[23] Thompson agreed to accept the assignment.[24] The Emperor then deputed Hakim Asanullah Khan Bahadur, one of his confidential servants, to Calcutta with an imperial *sanad*, appointing George Thompson his envoy.

Thompson reached Delhi on July 9, 1843 and was formally presented to the Emperor on August 12. On that occasion a *khilat* and a title were conferred on him.[25] The Emperor had plans to send his son, Mirza Fateh-ul-Mulk, also to England with Thompson in order to give the mission more weight and make it more representative in character.[26] But he was not given permission as the Governor-General considered it an impolitic measure, involving huge expenditure and indeed without any real benefit. The Emperor also had, by then, abandoned the idea of sending his son.[27]

The Government's reaction to the employment of Thompson as the royal envoy, however, was slightly different. The Governor-General refused him an interview at Allahabad[29] and insisted on receiving all communications from the Emperor through the prescribed official channel.[29] But the Government agreed to the appointment of Thompson as the agent and conceded the honorary distinctions conferred on him by the Emperor.[30] Thompson left for England in November

[23] George Thompson to the Earl of Ripon, the President of India Board, March 1844: *Letters from the Court of Directors (Pol.)*, May 1, 1844, Encl. 1.

[24] Thomas Metcalfe to Thomson, April 18, 1843: *pol. cons.*, May 10, 1843, No. 13.

[25] H.M. to the Queen of England: *Letters from the Court of Directors (Pol.)*, May 1, 1844, Encl.

[26] H.M. to Thomas Metcalfe, received on August 25, 1843: *pol. cons.*, September 23, 1843, No. 21.

[27] Hamilton to Thomson, October 11, 1843: *pol. cons.*, November 25, 1843, No. 24.

[28] George Thompson to the Earl of Ripon, March 19, 1844, *op. cit.*

[29] Thomson to Hamilton, September 23, 1843, *op. cit.*

[30] George Thompson to the Earl of Ripon, March 19, 1844, *op. cit.*

THE FINAL PHASE

1843 carrying with him a personal letter from the Emperor to the Queen of England. In that letter the Emperor contrasted, almost pathetically, his miserable condition to the past glory and grandeur of his illustrious ancestors, and expressed his anxiety for the future of his successors. "I am now old", he wrote, "and have no ambition left for grandeur. I would devote my days entirely to religion, but I feel anxious that the name and dignity of my predecessors should be maintained, and that they may descend to my children unimpaired, according to the original engagements made by the British Government."[31]

After his arrival in England, Thompson addressed a letter to the Earl of Ripon, the President of the Board of Commissioners for the affairs of India, and another to the Court of Directors. In the first letter he solicited an interview with the Earl of Ripon and sought his advice about the method by which he could submit the letter of the Emperor to the Queen of England.[32] The interview was refused and he was informed that all representations to the Board should proceed through the Court of Directors.[33] The Court of Directors held a similar view and refused to recognize Thompson as the agent of the Emperor and to "hold communications through any other channel than that of the Indian Government."[34]

At the same time the proposals of Ellenborough were not favourably received by the Court of Directors. They were not inclined to make any change till the demise of Bahadur Shah and the Governor-General was instructed to refrain from implementing his proposals till the Court of Directors discussed and took a final decision about the matter.[35]

In refusing permission to the proposals of Lord Ellenborough, the Court of Directors were actually trying to avoid any possible injury to the feelings of the Emperor. Bahadur Shah was fairly advanced in years—he was seventy-five—devoid of energy, perhaps even of any ambition and was mainly given

[31] H.M. to the Queen of England: *Letters from the Court of Directors (Pol.)*, May 1, 1844, Encl.
[32] George Thompson to the Earl of Ripon, March 19, 1844, *op. cit.*
[33] *Letters from the Court of Directors (Pol.)*, May 1, 1844, Encl.
[34] *Ibid.*
[35] *Ibid.*

to literary pursuits. He was weak in health and was likely to die very soon. If it were so, considerations of humanity called for the continuation of the privileges and prerogatives so far enjoyed by him. But the Government was not prepared to extend the same consideration to his successor. It was, therefore, almost certain that Bahadur Shah's death would be the occasion for drastic changes in the affairs of the Mughals.

The British Government had not so far taken a decision on the nature and extent of these changes. The Agent was eager to finalize them, so that in the event of the Emperor's death the succession could be smooth and without any complication. He suggested certain terms to be offered to the next incumbent, Prince Dara Bakht, which implied drastic changes in the existing privileges of the Mughal House. The most important of them related to the power and dignity of the successor-prince and the ownership of the palace at Delhi. He was in favour of allowing the Prince the income enjoyed by his father. The powers of the Emperor, limited though they might be, were to be discontinued. The continuation of the title of Emperor, the Agent suggested, should be made conditional to the transfer of the palace to the British Government.[36]

The palace, popularly known as the Red Fort, had both political and military importance to the British Government. Along with the large fortified town, sheltering within its walls a numerous population, turbulent and exposed to intrigues, it was always considered an inconvenience by the Government.[37] With the disappointed Emperor and the disgruntled members of the royal family occupying it, the Government was apprehensive that on the occasion of some disaffection this important fortress might easily fall into the hands of an enemy. Apart from this, the palace could be militarily useful. The powder magazine of the Government was then located in a very populous part of the city, most unsuitable for the purpose and full of dangers to the life and property of the people.[38] The Government was looking

---

[36] Minute by Thomas Metcalfe, February 17, 1848: *pol. cons.*, February 24, 1848, No. 21.

[37] Thornton, Secretary, North-Western Provinces, to Elliot, Secretary to Government, March 31, 1848: *pol. cons.*, February 24, 1848, No. 20.

[38] Kaye and Malleson, *op. cit.*, ii, p. 13.

for a suitable place for this. No better place, of course, was available in Delhi than the imperial palace of the Mughals.

The political considerations were much stronger. Right from the beginning, the British Government had been trying to reduce the importance of the city of Delhi and the prominence of the Mughal Emperor in its life. In 1803, while suggesting the transfer of the Emperor to Monghyr, Wellesley was animated by this feeling. In creating a separate Agency for Rajputana in 1821 the Government had the same end in view.[39] The Rajput rulers had been sending their vakils to Delhi to transact business with the Resident, thereby perpetuating the impression that that city continued to be the centre of political activities in India. And Delhi, needless to say, was synonymous with the Mughal Emperor, his power and his authority. The Governor-General was eager to end this practice and draw away the attention of the Indian feudatories from the imperial city. The British Government by 1848 had by slow degrees deprived the Emperor of the various prerogatives of sovereignty and assumed them largely to itself. Now, apart from the royal title, the palace was the only remnant of imperial dignity left to the Emperor. Its occupation by the British Government would then symbolize the final transfer of sovereignty from the Mughals to the British.

Metcalfe wanted to effect this change by persuasion. The Prince was to be requested to evacuate the palace and take up his residence at Qutab on his accession to the throne. If he agreed to this, the Agent suggested that "he be permitted to retain the title of *badshah* and that on his periodical visits to the great mosque of the city, to the *Idgah* in the environs and contiguous shrine of the Saint Nizam-ud-Din, he be at liberty to fire his own salute and that he be allowed to maintain a bodyguard of horse and infantry, the strength of each to be fixed by the British Government."[40] To ensure ready compliance with this arrangement, a portion of land in the vicinity of Qutab could be assigned to him as a personal *jagir*, of which the management would be entrusted to the Agent. If the Prince objected to these arrangements the title of Emperor and all other

---

[39] *Letters to the Court of Directors* (*Pol.*), June 13, 1833.
[40] Minute by Thomas Metcalf, February 17, 1848, *op cit.*

special considerations like salutes during his visit to *Idgah* and elsewhere were to be discontinued.⁴¹ The members of the royal family, however, were to be compelled to vacate the palace and reside wherever they liked within the jurisdiction and subject to the laws of the British Government.

Prince Dara Bakht, the heir-apparent, was fifty-seven years old and "in appearance and constitution scarcely less feeble than his father." The possibility of his outliving Bahadur Shah seemed to be very remote. If he were to die before the Emperor, the next claimant to the throne was Mirza Fakhr-ud-Din who was about thirty years old, in "good health, quick and intelligent, partial to European society and likely to be less manageable than his elder brother in the event of his becoming the head of the fallen dynasty."⁴² On such a contingency, the Agent was of the opinion that it would not be necessary to extend to Mirza Fakhr-ud-Din the same consideration, as it was necessary for Prince Dara Bakht, who as the acknowledged heir-apparent, cherished expectations of succeeding to the power, income, and dignity of his father.

Lord Dalhousie's Views

When the future of the Mughal House was thus being debated, Lord Dalhousie became the Governor-General of India. He embodied "the progressive go-ahead spirit of the Victorian age" and had no regard for Indian tradition because he considered Indian culture to be effete and hidebound. He had no doubts about the goal of the British in India. The overwhelming military and political superiority of the Government, highlighted by the subjugation of Sindh and the Punjab, convinced him of the necessity of a more forthright and dynamic policy towards all Indian problems. He was opposed to the policy or rather the impolicy of bolstering up "semblances of royalty without royal powers."⁴³ It was natural that he became sceptical about the propriety, even the wisdom, of the deference so far shown to the Mughal Emperor. The various privileges

---

⁴¹ *Ibid.*
⁴² *Ibid.*
⁴³ William Lee-Warner: *The Life of the Marquis of Dalhousie*, ii, p. 134.

THE FINAL PHASE

and considerations granted to him by the British helped to perpetuate the notions of the past grandeur and status of the Mughals in Indian polity. Though the paramountcy of the British Government was not in dispute, to allow even in name a rival in the person of a sovereign whose ancestors once held the paramount authority was inconsistent with the realities of the existing situation.[44] The Emperor by himself, according to Dalhousie, might not endanger the position of the British Government, but the intrigues of which "he might, and not infrequently, be the nucleus might vex" the latter. In view of these considerations he was of the opinion, that "it is fitting that we (the British) should appear before India to all futility as being paramount in name as also in authority and right."[45] For effecting this the abolition of the royal dynasty as well as the title of *badshah* was deemed inevitable.

Dalhousie would have taken immediate action on the receipt of Metcalfe's proposals. But before doing so he wanted to discuss the matter with the Agent and acquaint himself with all details of the royal affairs, which he did during his journey to the North-West Frontier region. Meanwhile, on January 11, 1849, Prince Dara Bakht died. This facilitated the introduction of the changes contemplated by the Agent and the Governor-General. Dalhousie now freely gave vent to his feelings in a minute which was to figure later on as a great controversial document.[46]

In agreement with Metcalfe's views, Dalhousie proposed to leave the old Emperor undisturbed with the possession of his nominal throne, income and all the honours of sovereignty which he had so far enjoyed. But the event of his demise was to be the time for the introduction of fundamental changes in the position of the head of the royal family. Had Dara Bakht been alive, the Governor-General believed, propriety and decorum would have required the British Government to show some consideration to the dynasty, since he was the last of the family whose memory went back to the time when the Emperor of Delhi still sat on the throne as the paramount potentate in India. His

[44] G.G.'s minute, February 10, 1849: *pol. cons.*, February 24, 1849, No. 25.
[45] *Ibid*.
[46] *Ibid*.

death ruled out any concessions. Consequently, the Governor-General proposed an end to the royal privileges of the House of Timur on the demise of Bahadur Shah.[47] Prince Fakhr-ud-din, the next incumbent, was not to be accorded recognition as the heir-apparent. With the death of Bahadur Shah the title of Emperor was to be put into abeyance and the head of the family to be styled simply as Prince. He was not to be allowed any royal privileges but was to be treated on the footing of other Indian princes, with a meagre grant and a salute. He was to be compelled to leave the palace at Delhi with the whole *salateen*, the head of the family residing in the royal palace at Qutab and the *salateen* in the city or elsewhere as they pleased. The Court of Directors was requested to sanction these changes.[48] Meanwhile, the Agent at Delhi was instructed not to take any steps which could be construed into a recognition of Prince Fakhr-ud-din as the heir-apparent.[49]

The plan of Dalhousie was, in fact, an enlargement of the proposals of the Agent. As far as the payment of the stipend was concerned, the Governor-General was in complete agreement with him. Both considered the transfer of the palace to the British Government an imperative necessity. The difference was only in its execution. Animated by a regard for the feelings of the Prince, Metcalfe was in favour of persuading him to comply with the wishes of the Government. But Dalhousie did not rule out compulsion. The title, according to Metcalfe, was to be abolished only if the Prince refused to move out of the palace on his accession. But Dalhousie suggested a preremptory end of the dynasty and the title.

These differences in the proposals of the Agent and the Governor-General could be explained by the change in the circumstances. When Metcalfe framed his proposals, Prince Dara Bakht, the recognized heir-apparent, was alive. While making his suggestions, he had taken into consideration the status, dignity, and sentiments of the Prince. But when Dalhousie took up the matter, Prince Dara Bakht was dead. There was no recognized

[47] *Ibid.*
[48] *Letters to the Court of Directors (Pol.)*, February 16, 1849.
[49] Elliot to Allen, February 15, 1849: *pol. cons.*, February 24, 1849, No. 26.

heir-apparent and therefore no commitment on the part of the British Government. Metcalfe himself had asserted that it was not necessary to give the same consideration to the next incumbent, in case Dara Bakht were to die before the Emperor.

These recommendations of the Governor-General were the subject of a major controversy between the Court of Directors and the Board of Control. Nineteen out of the twenty-three Directors opposed these proposals. They feared that they would foster discontent among the Muslim population and, above all, inflict a grievous injury to the feelings of the Emperor. It was, therefore, decided to turn down the proposals of the Governor-General.[50] Sir A. Gelloway, the Chairman of the Court, wrote to Dalhousie: "As to depriving the lawful heir of the title of Badshaw, the Court was most strongly opposed to it. They perceive no object that can be gained by it of any moment; while it is possible that much evil may arise out of it by the indignity it would offer to the Mohammedan nationality. I fear that if the title were abolished the evacuation would become hopeless. The Prince would of course be enraged by the indignity; and if he has one drop of the blood of Timur in his veins, he would rather sacrifice his life than quit the palace of his ancestors by compulsion."[51] The Board of Control, on the other hand, supported the views of Dalhousie and were in fovour of enforcing the proposed measures. Though the Directors made an appeal to the Board to reconsider this decision, Hobhouse, the Chairman of the Board, used his authority to compel them to sanction the proposals of the Governor-General.[52] He was surprised that the Court should attach so much importance to a question which appeared insignificant to him. He acquainted the Governor-General of the various objections raised by the Court and authorized him to implement the changes or modify them as he deemed fit.

The Executive Council of the Governor-General was also divided on this issue. The Council then consisted of Sir Fedrick Currie, Sir John Littler, and John Lewis. Sir Littler was apprehensive about the consequences of the proposals and pleaded

[50] Kaye & Malleson, *op. cit.*, i, p. 4.
[51] William Lee-Warner, *op. cit.*, ii, p. 136.
[52] *Letters from the Court of Directors (Pol.)*, January 16, 1850.

for caution and delay.⁵³ Currie considered the change to be necessary, but proposed it to be deferred till the demise of the Emperor.⁵⁴ Lewis, however, stood for the immediate abolition of the title and the evacuation of the palace.⁵⁵

In view of the objections of the Directors and the opinion of his colleagues in the Council, Dalhousie decided to modify the proposed changes. The opinion of some members of the Court, who had long experience and knowledge of Indian affairs, would indeed be impolitic to disregard. In deference to their views, the Governor-General agreed to recognize the Prince as the Emperor on the demise of Bahadur Shah.⁵⁶ He would also not be compelled to vacate the palace, but could be persuaded to quit it voluntarily and reside at Qutab, on the condition of an addition of Rs. 25,000 to his personal income. It was stipulated that the Prince, on succession, should meet the Governor-General on terms of perfect equality and entrust his *tyool* lands to the British Goverment, the proceeds of which, over and above the expenses of management, would be paid to him. Only his children and grandchildren would be allowed to reside within the palace and exempted from legal process. All others were to be removed from it and subjected to the rules and regulations of the British Government.⁵⁷ The Court of Directors accorded sanction to these modified proposals.⁵⁸

The Governor-General immediately started negotiations for a final settlement on these lines. According to the right of primogeniture which the British Government was eager to uphold, the successor of Bahadur Shah was his eldest surviving son, Mirza Fakhr-ud-Din. But the Emperor, due to the influence of his favourite wife, Zinat Mahal, recommended her son, Mirza Jawan Bakht. He objected to Fakhr-ud-Din on grounds of illegitimacy and mutilation. The first, on enquiry, was found

---

⁵³ Minute by Littler, April 4, 1850: *pol. cons.*, April 10, 1850, No. 2.
⁵⁴ Minute by Currie, April 4, 1850: *pol. cons.*, April 10, 1850, No. 3.
⁵⁵ Minute by Lewis, April 5, 1850: *pol. cons.*, April 10, 1850, No. 4.
⁵⁶ Minute by Dalhousie, September 10, 1850: *pol. cons.*, October 11, 1850, No. 199.
⁵⁷ Elliot to Thornton, November 30, 1851: *pol. cons.*, February 27, 1852 No. 54.
⁵⁸ *Letters from the Court of Directors (Pol.)*, June 18, 1851.

to be correct, but the Government held the opinion that in the Mughal House illegitimacy was no bar to succession. Even Bahadur Shah himself was reported to be illegitimate. The second reason was nothing but a flimsy excuse, if not a pretext. Since Humayun's time, according to Bahadur Shah, no Mughal Prince had been circumcised, except Mirza Fakhr-ud-Din. An exception was made in his case due to some physiological reasons. The Emperor asserted that, according to the custom followed by the Mughals, this debarred the Prince from succession. The Government overruled these objections, but decided to withhold his formal recognition as heir-apparent so that the feelings of the Emperor were not injured.[59] He was merely to be assured that he would be acknowledged as the successor to the throne on the death of his father.[60]

Mirza Fakhr-ud-Din agreed to these conditions including the evacuation of the palace, provided the British Government upheld for the House of Timur, the imperial title and the royal privileges so far enjoyed by his predecessors.[61] An agreement to this effect was executed by the Prince on January 23, 1852.[62] But immediately after this, on the same day, he urged a revision of the condition with respect to his rights and privileges as the heir-apparent. Though he did not specifically press for an open declaration of his appointment, the demands put forward by him, if complied, would have indirectly amounted to that. The demands were as follows:

1. The Prince should receive for the future the salary of the heir-apparent with the arrears now in deposit.
2. The guards at the palace gate be drawn out to salute him whenever passing to and from the palace.
3. The Agent be instructed to visit him.
4. The Prince be entrusted with the distribution of the stipend on his accession.[63]

---

[59] *Letters from the Court of Directors* (*Pol.*), June 18, 1851.
[60] Elliot to Thornton, November 30, 1851, *op. cit.*
[61] Thomas Metcalfe to Thornton, January 24, 1852: *pol. cons.*, February 27, 1852, No. 57.
[62] The Agreement executed by Fakhr-ud-Din, January 23, 1852: *pol. cons.*, February 27, 1852, No. 57, Encl.
[63] Thomas Metcalfe to Thornton, January 24, 1852, *op. cit.*

The British officials, including the Governor-General, were inclined to acknowledge the Prince as the heir-apparent because it would help to increase his respectability, confirm him in his gratitude to the British Government, and defeat the machinations of Zinat Mahal directed against him.[64] But the Governor-General could not take any positive step in this direction as the orders of the Court of Directors precluded him from taking such a step. However, the whole case was submitted to the Court for reconsideration. In view of the acceptance by Prince Fakhr-ud-din of all the conditions laid down by the British Government, the Court of Directors agreed to his recognition as the heir-apparent in a "manner least calculated to give umbrage to the Emperor."[66] Fakhr-ud-din was then recognized as the heir-apparent, granting him the stipend with the arrears and permitting him to receive the usual honours attached to that dignity.[67] He, however, was not to be entrusted with the distribution of the stipend among the members of the royal family when he succeeded to the throne.[68]

The terms of the agreement between Prince Fakhr-ud-din and the Government created great consternation in the palace circles.[69] By this settlement Fakhr-ud-din had not only resigned his rights and privileges but had also signed off those of the other members of the royal family, without caring for their future security and proper maintenance. The Government was, though not specifically, responsible for finding accommodation for the sons and grandsons of the Emperor only.[70] The other members of the family were to make their own arrangements for which they were absolutely ill-equipped. More-

[64] Thornton to Elliot, January 28, 1852: *pol. cons.*, February 27, 1852, No. 56.
[65] *Letters from the Court of Directors* (*Pol.*), June 18, 1851.
[66] *Letters from the Court of Directors* (*Pol.*), June 2, 1852.
[67] Allen to Muir, September 4, 1852: *pol. cons.*, September 24, 1852, No. 260.
[68] G. G.'s minute, February 24, 1852, *pol. cons.*, February 23, 1850, No. 58.
[69] Thomas Metcalfe to Muir, July 18, 1852: *pol. cons.*, December 23, 1853, No. 68.
[70] Elliot to Thornton, November 30, 1851: *pol. cons.*, February 27, 1852, No. 54.

THE FINAL PHASE

over, the agreement marked an end to the way of life and privileges enjoyed by them since their birth. By a single stroke they were being thrown out from the membership of a great and illustrious family to the position of commoners. Of course, they had been living in the palace under great financial difficulties. But they had comfortable shelter in the palace and privileges associated with the royal family. The person most vexed was Zinat Mahal. Even Fakhr-ud-din was not happy at the whole arrangement. The British Government had taken maximum advantage of the existence of a rival to his claims in Mirza Jawan Bakht.[71] Fear of losing his position, in case he resisted the demands of the British Government, induced him to agree to the proposals.

However, it appeared that the question of succession and the related problems were going to be settled once for all. But Fakhr-ud-din unexpectedly died on July 10,1856, so it was reported, striken by cholera.[72] To Zinat Mahal and her adherents, who were all the while endeavouring to obtain the appointment of Jawan Bakht as the heir-apparent, the death of Fakhr-ud-din afforded a golden opportunity. The very next day of the death of the Prince, the Emperor, induced by Zinat Mahal, expressed his desire to elevate Jawan Bakht to the office of the heir-apparent.[73] He produced a document signed by all his sons, except Mirza Koeash, the eldest surviving son, containing a request in favour of Jawan Bakht as the heir-apparent.[74] Mirza Koeash, however, presented a separate memorial in which he advocated his claims to be recognized as the heir-apparent.[75]

---

[71] Elliot to Thornton, November 30, 1851, *op. cit.*

[72] Simon Fraser, Agent, to Thornhill, Officiating Secretary, North-Western Provinces, July 11, 1856: *pol. cons.*, August 29, 1856, No. 181. It was suspected that Mirza Fakhr-ud-din was poisoned. He took some bread with cury gravy and was immediately seized with deadly sickness and vomiting. Extreme prostration and debility ensued and in spite of medical attention the Prince passed away. Kaye and Malleson; *op. cit.*, i, pp. 20-21.

[73] H.M. to Simon Fraser, July 12, 1856: *pol. cons.*, August 29, 1856, No. 184.

[74] *Pol. cons.*, August 29, 1856, No. 185.

[75] Mirza Koeash to Simon Fraser, July 18, 1856: *pol. cons*, August 29, 1856, No. 188.

Zinat Mahal tried to influence the Governor-General through a private agent. Thomas Cavendish Fenvick, an Englishman of considerable legal knowledge, was then seeking employment at Delhi. The Begam appointed him as her law attorney for advocating the claims of Mirza Jawan Bakht at Agra and Calcutta.[76] The Agent tried to dissuade her from this indulgence as the claims of Jawan Bakht had been earlier dismissed by the Government.[77] The Emperor, however, believed that the appointment of Fenvick would be highly beneficial to the cause of Jawan Bakht and did not anticipate any opposition from the British Government.[78] Fenvick was sent to Calcutta to obtain a decision in favour of the Prince. Zinat Mahal and Mirza Jawan Bakht entrusted him memorials addressed to the Governor-General in which the claims of the Prince to the office of the heir-apparent were strongly advocated.[79] They objected to Mirza Koeash on grounds of illegitimacy whereas Jawan Bakht had no such drawback.[80] Nevertheless, the Governor-General rejected their plea.[81]

Meanwhile, changes in personnel had occurred both at Delhi and Calcutta. Simon Fraser had taken over the charge of the Agency after the death of Thomas Metcalfe.[82] And at Calcutta Canning had replaced Dalhousie. These changes facilitated the adoption of a fresh approach without inhibitions imposed by

[76] Simon Fraser to Thornhill, October 29, 1856: *pol. cons.*, November 21, 1856, No. 69.
[77] Simon Fraser to H.M., October 13, 1856: *pol. cons.*, November 21, 1856, No. 70.
[78] H.M. to Simon Fraser, October 22, 1856: *pol. cons.*, November 21, 1856, 71.
[79] Memorial of Zinat Mahal and Mirza Jawan Bakht to the G.G., October 20, 1856: *pol. cons.*, November 21, 1856, No. 64.
[80] The Emperor signed and forwarded a document to this effect to the Agent. Fenvick to Edmonstone, Secretary to Government, October 31, 1856: *pol. cons.*, November 21, 1856, No. 65.
[81] Edmonstone to Thornhill, November 19, 1856: *pol. cons.*, November 21, 1856, No. 72.
[82] Thomas Metcalfe died on November 3, 1853. During his long association with Delhi he had earned the affection of a large group of people. A huge number, both Europeans and Indians, attended his funeral. Hakim Asanullah Khan was one of those who attended it. Palace intelligence, November 4, 5 and 24, 1853: *For Misc.* Vol. 361.

past experience. Fraser could view matters with considerable detachment and assess the situation as it stood, specially because he was not in possession of all the records connected with the royal affairs.[83] Lord Canning had been in India for just a few months and had no personal experience, worth the name, of Indian affairs and sentiments. His information was based purely on official documents. Moreover, the Governor-General's Council had also been recently reconstituted. These factors proved to be an advantage from the British point of view in effecting the final settlement with the Mughals.

The death of Mirza Fakhr-ud-Din also provided an opportunity to the British Government to reconsider the future of the Mughal dynasty. According to the arrangement finalized with Fakhr-ud-Din, almost all the privileges of the members of the royal family were to be withdrawn on Bahadur Shah's death. Yet the Prince was promised certain prerogatives, namely, the title, stipend and legal exemption. The Agent, now on a reappraisal of the problem, was not inclined to grant the same terms to the next incumbent. None of the Emperor's sons, according to him, possessed the influence, character, and qualifications necessary for recognition as the heir-apparent.[84] He was, therefore, in favour of leaving the question of succession in abeyance till the death of the Emperor. Mirza Koeash could then be informed that the British Government would be prepared to recognize him as the head of the family, provided he agreed to all the conditions laid down by the British Government. Apart from the terms concluded with the late heir-apparent, the Agent recommended the abolition of the title and changes in the style of address, salute, and such other formalities. The continuation of the title of Emperor to the Mughal representative who had "no retainers, power or influence was unnecessary for any object of justice or policy", especially in the existing political situation in India.[85] The Mughal Emperor had outlived his usefulness to the British. He asserted, though wrongly, that the people of India, including the Mohammedans, had no interest in the

---

[83] Simon Fraser to Thornhill, July 14, 1856: *pol. cons.*, August 29, 1856, No. 183.
[84] *Ibid.*
[85] *Ibid.*

fortunes of the royal family. He, therefore, suggested that Mirza Koeash on succession be designated "His Royal Highness the Prince, the exalted head of the family of Timur", and that the style of address adjusted accordingly. The salute was not to exceed nineteen guns. An allowance of Rs. 15,000 per month was considered adequate for his personal expenses. The other members of the royal family could draw their allowances direct from the treasury, subject to revision on the death of the incumbents.[86] He also suggested that the representative of the Government should be allowed a seat during his interviews with the head of the family.

Lord Canning held almost identical views. He did not entertain the considerations which had prompted Dalhousie to defer the implementation of his original plan, nor was he aware of them as they were not on records in India.[87] He was unable "to see any reason why the Government of India should not refuse to give a new and solemn sanction to a sham, which answers no good purpose and which will soon cease to be defensible upon the only ground on which such a fiction can be defended, consistently with his own dignity and truthfulness, a respect mainly for the personal feelings, recollections and associations of the members of a fallen house."[88]

The supremacy of the British in India had by now been established beyond doubt and, therefore, to the mind of Canning, the preservation of a titular King paramount of Hindustan, appeared a serious anomaly. He asserted that the Emperor had become insignificant, and even the Mohammedans were indifferent towards the royal house of Delhi. He completely accepted the proposals of the Agent and instructions were issued for the prosecution of the proposed measures without delay.[89] In this Canning had the unanimous support of his Council.[90] This decision of the Government, it was resolved, would be

[86] *Ibid.*
[87] G.G.'s minute, August 12, 1856: *pol. cons.*, August 29, 1856, No. 189.
[88] *Ibid.*
[89] Edmonstone to Thornhill, August 29, 1856: *pol. cons.*, August 29, 1856, No. 193.
[90] Minute by George Anson, Dorin, Grant and Peacock, Councillors, August 14, 1856: *pol. cons.*, August 29, 1856, No. 190, 191 and 192.

THE FINAL PHASE

communicated to the Prince, "not in the way of inviting negotiation or bargaining, but as the declaration of the mature and fixed determination of the Government of India."[91]

It was in this summary fashion that the future of the Mughal dynasty was ultimately decided. This was the culmination of the process that had started at the time of Wellesley. Canning merely tried to fix the last nail on the Mughal coffin. But fate willed otherwise. The tragic course of the revolt of 1857 and the part played by Bahadur Shah and the members of the royal family interrupted the proceedings of the British Government. When the revolt was at its height the Lieutenant-Governor of the North-Western Provinces was instructed "neither to make any promise to the King and the royal family nor to enter into any engagements regarding them."[92] The revolt provided a convenient opportunity to end the royal privileges of the Mughal dynasty without conditions and guarantees.

---

[91] G.G.'s minute, August 12, 1856, *op. cit.*
[92] Edmonstone to Thornhill, June 20, 1857: *sec. cons.*, June 26, 1857, No. 39.

10
Conclusion

IN THE early morning of May 11, 1857, when the imperial city was still in slumber about two thousand sepoys from Meerut, who had revolted on the previous day, crossed the Jamna. They killed the toll-keeper, set the toll-house on fire, and marched towards the Red Fort. They thronged the palace gates soliciting the help of the Emperor and trumpeting their deeds at Meerut. Followed by an excited crowd, they entered the palace through the Rajghat gate and were immediately joined by the palace guards. The revolt started in Delhi. Simon Fraser, the Agent, and captain Charles Douglas, the commandant of the palace guards, who were inside the palace on a summons from the Emperor, tried to control the sepoys both by advice and remonstrance. But the sepoys were in no mood to heed. They were defiant, violent, and thirsting for European blood. Moghal Beg, an orderly of the palace guards, mercilessly attacked Fraser and murdered him on the spot. The last British Agent at Delhi thus fell at his post.

The course of the revolt in Delhi and Bahadur Shah's participation in it need no recapitulation. About fifty-four years ago young Bahadur Shah had witnessed his grandfather welcoming Lord Lake to the imperial palace and conferring *khilats* and titles on him. Shah Alam was not then sure about the attitude of the new conquerors, but had no fears about his own future. But Bahadur Shah, who had taken refuge in Humayun's tomb after the fall of Delhi, had a different fate. He did not know what was in store for him and was apprehensive even about his life. In fact, Zinat Mahal had to bribe captain Hodson for a promise to spare their lives. They were conducted from their hidings and imprisoned in a most humiliating manner and later, tried and deported to Burma. To the relief of many British officials in India and to the sorrow of thousands in Delhi "the shadow, the sham" was ultimately obliterated. The Mughal

CONCLUSION

ruling dynasty came to an end and thus the policy initiated by Wellesley in 1803 reached its inevitable culmination.

With the Emperor removed from Delhi as a prisoner and the imperial city no more imperial, and thus deprived of its political importance, it was unnecessary to maintain a British representative at Delhi. The Agency was abolished. The revolt of 1857 thus marked the end of the Agency as well as of the Mughal ruling dynasty.

The Residency at Delhi fulfilled a major position in the British political set-up in North India for about fifty-four years. Coming into existence at a time when the British Government was struggling for superiority, it made significant contribution to the expansion and consolidation of British power in this region. Though the management of British relations with the Emperor formed the primary charge of the Resident, it was only a part of the multifarious duties entrusted to him. He was, at one time or other, the channel of British relations with the rulers of Kabul, Lahore, Indore, the states of Rajputana and the Cis-Sutlej, Multan, Bhawalpur, and Firozpur.[1] Till 1832, with the exception of period of a seven years from 1818, the administration of the assigned territory was also under his charge.

In discharging these duties the Residency was very ably served by officers like Charles Metcalfe, David Ochterlony, Archibold Seton, W.B. Martin, and Thomas Metcalfe. They had under them political agents and news-writers at the various courts, who assisted them by furnishing information and by implementing their decisions. Cobbe, Low, Coulfield, Murray, Ross, among others, admirably filled this role. At the headquarters the Resident had assistants to lessen his burden of onerous duties. A well organized intelligence department and a trained staff of *munshis* and other lower servants completed the establishment of the Agency. In fact, the Residency with its "espionage everywhere, agents and news-writers at other courts" was a state in itself.[2]

The importance which was formerly attached to the

---

[1] Metcalfe to Adam, May 6, 1816: *pol. cons.*, June 1, 1816, No. 12.

[2] Thompson, *op. cit.*, p. 142.

Mughal palace slowly shifted to the Residency. The vakils from the various states of Rajputana and the Punjab daily attended the Residency, imparting to it the appearance of a medieval Indian darbar. Residents like Ochterlony and Fraser, who were half-Asiatic in their habits, liked it and maintained the pomp and pageantry of these durbars. The Resident had come to be looked upon by the people of Delhi, and even by the members of the royal family, as the seat of power and authority. This was inevitable due to the restrictions imposed upon the Emperor and the control and power wielded by the Resident. The Emperor had to seek the permission of the Resident for the regulation of his domestic affairs. He could not go out for extensive excursions without his approval. The members of the royal family were forbidden from pilgrimage to Mecca and other holy places even when the Emperor had already granted them permission.[3] Their best efforts notwithstanding, Akbar Shah and Bahadur Shah could not have their final say in the appointments of the heirs-apparent. The personal servants of the Emperor were more than once removed by the interposition of the Resident and their maltreatment was resented by him.[4] The Resident enquired into various cases that occurred inside the palace. All these naturally were the gossip of the bazar which, as is true of all gossips, gave them different colour and exaggeration.

The Supreme Government at Calcutta greatly helped its representative in Delhi in maintaining his position and prestige. It refused to accept any memorial or representation from the Emperor or other chiefs without the knowledge of the Resident. All attempts of the Emperor to influence the Governor-General through the Nawab of Awadh and some private agents were systematically discouraged. The failure of Shah Haji's mission and the harsh treatment meted out to Pran Krishna showed the determination of the Government to uphold the Resident as the only acceptable channel of communication with the powers

[3] Charles Metcalfe to Adam, September 25, 1813: *pol. cons.*, October 15, 1813, No. 30; and Adam to Charles Metcalfe, October 15, 1813: *pol. cons.*, October 15, 1813, No. 31.

[4] Metcalfe to Adam, November 19, 1813: *pol. cons.*, December 10, 1813, No. 48; and Elliot to Prinsep, August 29, 1823: *pol. cons.*, October 3, 1823, No. 46.

CONCLUSION

under his charge. It created an impression that the authority of the Resident was indomitable.

In spite of all this, the position of the Resident in comparison with the royal family continued to be, in some respects, of a subordinate nature. In the royal durbar he was nothing more than an important noble. In the presence of the Emperor he stood in obeisance, bare-footed and bare-headed. Even during his interviews with the Queen, who always conversed with him from behind a screen, he kept on standing. Seton had to show considerable tolerance in the name of courtesy when he was once scolded and told by the Queen that "his kindness was simply the duty of a servant to his master."[5] Ochterlony and Seton admirably adjusted themselves to these circumstances. Charles Metcalfe suffered it out of sympathy for the Emperor. But the later Residents did not entertain the same consideration. Hawkins wanted to end these forms of inferiority once for all. He even insisted on sitting in front of the Queen during his interviews with her.

The Resident, working as a direct subordinate of the Governor-General, had considerable initiative and liberty of independent action. He could call for the services of the army if the circumstances so warranted.[6] On many occasions he took action in anticipation of the sanction of the Government and his suggestions were generally accepted by the Governor-General. The appointment of Major Lockett as the Political Agent at Bharatpur is a case in point. But there are numerous instances when his proposals were turned down and he was admonished for improper conduct. Ochterlony's suggestions for the enhancement of the royal stipend and for re-starting the Delhi Mint were not accepted by the Governor-General. Seton was reprimanded for his lenient attitude towards the Emperor. Colebrooke's initiative in the case of Jodhpur was disapproved.[7] Hawkins'

---

[5] Edward Thompson: *Life of Charles Metcalfe*, p. 139.
[6] Stirling to Colebrooke, June 13, 1828: *pol. cons.*, June 13, 1828, No. 5. Seton had done so on the death of Shah Alam II to avoid any possible breach of peace in the city.
[7] In 1828 a few *thakurs* of Jodhpur state revolted against the authority of Raja Man Singh. Colebrooke authorised Cavendish, the Superintendent of Ajmer, to use British troops, if necessary, for saving "the capital and

treatment of the Emperor was considered highly unbecoming and he was even removed from office. These, however, were only exceptions. Generally the Resident's proposals found favour with the Government.

The office of the Resident in relation to the subordinate Political Agents was of an appellate character.[8] He directed and supported the Agents in the administration of the interests committed to their charge. He did not deal directly with the chiefs, but through the channel of the Agent.[9] The Agent, in turn, communicated with the Government through the Resident. All his letters and reports were received by the Resident, scrutinized and then forwarded to the Government with his remarks.[10] He upheld the prestige and authority of the Agent as his own was upheld by the Governor-General.

The foregoing analysis attempts to highlight in the form of a case-study the influence of the British Politicals in the evolution and execution of the Company's policy towards Indian powers. The broad features of British policy in India were indeed determined by the Home authorities but in its execution, the general policy had to be adjusted according to the prevailing circumstances which in India differed from one quarter to the other. A uniform application of the policy was certainly impossible. In order to meet the political exigencies, often adjustments within the framework of the general policy and sometimes total deviation from it were called for. The decision-making in this respect was influenced by the subordinate officers who

the Maharaja's person from insult." The Governor-General reprimanded the Resident for delegating the discretionary powers to a subordinate officer to use the military force according to his notions of emergency Colebrooke to Cavendish, May 28, 1828: *pol. cons.*, June 13, 1828 No. 4; and Stirling to Colebrooke, June 13, 1828: *pol. cons.*, June 13, 1828, No. 5.

[8] Macnaughten to Fraser, August 22, 1833: *pol. cons.*, August 22, 1833, No. 27.

[9] William Fraser addressed a letter directly to Megh Singh of Boorea. The Governor-General called for his explanation for doing so. Macnaughten to Fraser, August 16, 1833: *pol. cons.*, August 16, 1833, No. 17.

[10] In spite of repeated instructions Ross, Deputy Superintendent for Hill and Sikh states, sent his letters directly to the Governor-General. He was severely reprimanded for this.

were responsible for apprising the Government of the local requirements. Their recommendations which were based on local knowledge and personal experience formed the basis of the governmental decisions. The Resident at Delhi performed this task in respect to the Mughal Emperor, the states of Rajputana, and the Cis-Sutlej States.

A few instances may be restated here to illustrate the point. In early nineteenth century the Company's official policy towards Indian states was the policy of non-intervention. Lord Hastings, who was himself a non-interventionist in the beginning, decided to depart from the prescribed policy and revise the existing political alliances. Though Hastings' wrangles with the Court of Directors and his ultimate decision in this respect are familiar themes in Indian historical writings, the influence of a large number of subordinate officers in this decision-making has not attracted proper attention. Charles Metcalfe, the Resident at Delhi, was an advocate of this change even before Hastings came to India. In the case of Rajputana, as discussed earlier, it was he who systematically opposed the policy and outlined a plan for the revision of the existing political alliances, which was later on accepted and implemented by Hastings.

The British relations with the Mughal Emperor further prove the point. Almost all important decisions of the Government, whether in respect to the royal stipend, the presentation of *nazars* or the future of the Mughal dynasty, had originated with the Resident. The settlement of 1805 was on the lines suggested by him. Lord Ellenborough's much criticized decision to stop the *nazars*, was earlier recommended by the Agent. The provisions of the final settlement of 1856 were entirely his suggestion. This is also true of the British policy towards the Cis-Sutlej states. The protection offered to them in 1809 was urged by the Resident as early as 1805.

In conclusion, it may be emphasized that within the given limitations, the policy of the British Government towards the Mughal Emperor, the states of Rajputana, and the Cis-Sutlej states had its origin at Delhi.

Appendix I

Letter from J. Lumsden, Chief Secretary to Government, to David Ochterlony, the Resident at Delhi regarding the arrangement with Shah Alam (2 June, 1805 : Sec. Cons., 20 June, 1805, No. 422.)

THE ESTABLISHMENT of a permanent arrangement for the support of His Majesty Shah Allum, and of the royal household at Delhi having been under the consideration of the Governor-General-in-Council, with reference to the Notes of Instructions transmitted to you on the 16th of November 1804 — and to the observations contained in your letters, dated the 30th of the same month, the 8th of December following, and the 9th of February 1805—I am directed to communicate for your information, and guidance, the final determination of His Excellency in Council on this important question.

2. The objections stated in your despatches of the 30th November and 8th December 1804, to the transfer of the Land to be assigned for the support of the royal household to the management of native officers to be appointed by His Majesty and subject to His Majesty's sole control, are extremely forcible—His Excellency in Council has accordingly been pleased to determine that territory to be assigned to the royal family shall remain under the charge of the Resident at Delhi, and that the revenue shall be collected, and justice be administered in the name of His Majesty and under regulation to be prescribed by authority of the British Government.

3. The territory to be assigned to His Majesty is to comprise all that portion of the territory on the right bank of the Jumna ceded to the Hon'ble Company under the Treaty of Surge Augengaum, which is situated to the north west of a town or village named Kaboolpore, in the map of the ceded and conquered provinces constructed by Lieut. Colonel Colebrooke. All the lands in the Dooab under your management are

to be transferred to the Collectors of Seharanpore or of Alighar, and the lands on the right bank of the Jumna, to the south east of Kaboolpore, which may have been committed to your charge, are to be made over to the Collectors of Alighur or Agra. The districts, to which these lands are to be respectively annexed, must be determined with reference to the local position of the several pergunnahs to be transferred.

4. The territory assigned for the support of His Majesty and the royal family, is to continue as at present under your management; and you are authorized to let the lands in farm for a period of three years on the best terms which can be obtained reporting your proceedings in the execution of this arrangement for the confirmation of the Governor-General-in-Council. The general arrangements to be required from the farmers will be stated to you in a separate despatch.

5. You will communicate this arrangement to His Majesty, Shah Alam, and you will at the same time signify to His Majesty, the request of the Governor-General-in-Council that His Majesty will be pleased to appoint a Dewan, and other inferior officers to attend at the office of collection for the purpose of ascertaining and reporting to His Majesty the amount of the revenues which may be received, and the charges of the collection, and of satisfying His Majesty's mind, that no part of the produce of the assigned territory shall be misappropriated.

6. Two courts of Justice will be required for the administration of civil and criminal justice, according to the Mahomedan law to the inhabitants of the city of Delhi and of the assigned territory lying without the precincts of the city. The Judges of each of these courts must be selected from amongst the most respectable and learned of the Mussulman inhabitants of Delhi, and no sentences of the criminal courts extending to death ought to be carried into execution without the express sanction of His Majesty to whom the proceedings in all trials of this description are to be reported, by the Judge of the court before whom the prisoner may be tried, through the channel of the British Resident.

7. No criminal must in future suffer the punishment of mutilation, under sentences of the courts to be established in the

assigned territory. When a prisoner shall be sentenced under the Mahomedan Law to lose two limbs the sentence must be commuted for imprisonment, and hard labour for the term of fourteen years, and when the sentence shall adjudge the prisoner to lose one limb, it is to be commuted for imprisenment and hard labour for seven years.

8. A civil servant of the Company will be appointed your assistant for the special purpose of aiding you in superintending the collection of the revenue, and the administration of justice.

9. You are desired to report for the consideration, and orders of the Governor-General-in-Council, your sentiments with respect to the subsidiary regulations which ought in your judgment to be adopted for the administration of justice in civil and criminal cases, and with respect to the establishments which may be required for each of the courts.

The system to be introduced will necessarily be defective and the utmost circumspection will therefore be required in the selection of the judges, on whose character, and integrity, the equity of their decisions must in a great measure depend.

10. You will signify to His Majesty that if the arrangements now to be introduced into the assigned territory, shall be found to be ill calculated to promote the improvement of the country, and to ensure realization of the public revenues, the Governor-General-in-Council will hereafter submit for His Majesty's approbation such modifications of the proposed system as shall in his judgment appear to be necessary, to ensure to His Majesty all the advantages which the country is capable of yielding, and at the same time to secure the happiness and prosperity of the people.

11. To provide for the immediate wants of His Majesty, and of his royal household, the Governor-General-in-Council has been pleased to determine that the following sums shall be paid monthly in money from the treasury of the Resident at Delhi:—To His Majesty for his private expenses Rs. 60,000; To the heir-apparent exclusive of the revenues of Cote Cossim his Jagheer Rs. 10,000; To Mirzalzzut Buksh, His Majesty's son by his favourite wife, Mobarreck Mahl Rs. 5,000; To Mirza Monym Bukht Rs. 1,000; To his brother Rs. 500; To His Majesty's fifty younger sons and daughters at Rs. 200 each, say

APPENDIX I   189

Rs. 10,000; To Shah Newaz Khan Rs. 2,500; To Syed Reza Khan Rs. 1,000; Total per mensem Rs. 90,000.

12. If the produce of the revenue of the assigned territory should hereafter admit of it, the monthly sum to be advanced to His Majesty for his private expenses may be increased to the extent of one lakh of rupees.

13. You are likewise authorized to pay to His Majesty at the great festivals of the *Jeshun*, the *Edes*, *Nouraze*, *Bussunt*, *Holy*, and at the *Ramzaaun* the sum of ten thousand rupees according to ancient established usage.

14. In the negotiation of this arrangement as it respects the heir-apparent and His Royal Highness Mirza Izzut Buksh, it must be stipulated that the jagheers now held by those princes in the Dooab shall be surrendered to the British Government.

15. The arrangements proposed in your letters to the Right Hon'ble the Commander-in-Chief, dated the 16th of March, and to His Excellency the Governor-General dated the 23rd of the same month for the establishment of a military force, for the protection of the assigned territory, and of the North West Frontier of our possessions in Hindostan is considered to be judicious. The Governor-General-in-Council is however of opinion, that it would be expedient to substitute for the three Nadjeeb battalions proposed to be stationed at Carnaul, or Panipat, and at Nurnole, three of the battalions heretofore in the service of Ambajee Inglia, and now employed in Bundelcund, and to attach to these corps, a sufficient proportion of European officers, from the officers heretofore in the service of Dowlut Row Scindiah, and now in the pay of the British Government.

16. The sentiments of the Governor-General-in-Council on the arrangement have been communicated to the Right Honourable the Commander-in-Chief, by whom you will be furnished with instructions for the regulation of your proceedings. The Commander-in-Chief will also determine whether in consequence of the vicinity of the assigned territory, to the possessions of the Sicks, it may be necessary to maintain any irregular cavalry on the frontier.

17. The pay of the troops of every description to be employed in the assigned territory is to be regularly issued to them from the treasury of the Resident at the Court of Delhi, under

proper regulations to be determined hereafter.

18. Your suggestion that the forts of Goenlghur, Madooghur, and Ranoor should immediately be dismantled appears to the Governor-General-in-Council to be judicious. You will not however demolish the fortifications until you shall have obtained the previous sanction of the Right Hon'ble the Commander-in-Chief to that measure.

19. When the arrangements prescribed in this dispatch shall have been carried into effect, you will submit for the consideration, and orders of the Governor-General-in-Council a detailed report of your proceedings in the introduction of the system proposed to be established in every branch of the administration of the territory assigned to His Majesty, and you will furnish regular monthly accounts of all your receipts, and disbursement according to forms, which will be transmitted to you from Fort William. You will likewise submit to the Governor-General-in-Council, frequent reports of all matters connected with the administration of the affairs of the Territory placed under your superintendence, and management, in every department of the public service.

20. The success of your administration will in a great measure depend on the prudence and circumspection which may regulate your choice of the native officers to be employed in the immediate charge of the revenues, and of the police of the assigned territory, and on your own vigilance in the detection of abuses. The reputation, and permanent interests of the British Government require that the administration of the affairs of the assigned territory should be established, and maintained, on a basis of justice and moderation, and the Governor-General-in-Council entertains a confident expectation that the important trust committed to your charge will be executed in such manner as shall impress on the minds of all descriptions of persons under your authority, a just sense of the inestimable advantages they will receive from their transfer from the lawless dominion of a marhatta despot, to the mild, and equitable authority of the British Government.

Appendix II

Proclamation to the Cis-Sutlej Chiefs

IT IS clearer than the sun and better proved than the existence of yesterday that the marching of a detachment of British troops to this side of the river Sutledge was entirely at the application and earnest entreaty of the several Chiefs, and originated solely from friendly considerations in the British Government to preserve them in their possessions and independence. A treaty having been concluded on the 25th of April, 1809, between Mr. Metcalfe on the part of the British Government and Maharaja Runjeet Sing, agreeably to the orders of the Right Hon'ble the Governor-General-in-Council, I have the pleasure of publishing for the satisfaction of the Chiefs of the country of Malwah and Sirhind, the pleasure and resolutions of the British Government as contained in the seven following articles :—

1. The country of the Chiefs of Malwah and Sirhind having entered under the British protection, they shall in future be secured from the authority and influence of Maharaja Runjeet Sing conformably to the terms of the treaty.

2. All the country of the Chiefs thus taken under protection shall be exempted from all pecuniary tribute to the British Government,

3. The Chiefs shall remain in the full exercise of the same rights and authority in their own possessions which they enjoyed before they were received under the British protection.

4. Should a British force on purposes of general welfare be required to march through the country of the said Chiefs, it is necessary and incumbent that every Chief shall within his own possessions assist and furnish to the full of his power such force with supplies of grain and other necessaries, which may be demanded.

5. Should an enemy approach from any quarter for the purpose of conquering this country, friendship and mutual

interest require that the Chiefs join the British army with all their forces, and exerting themselves in expelling the enemy act under discipline and proper obedience.

6. All European articles brought by merchants from the eastern districts for the use of the army shall be allowed to pass by the *thannadars* and *saverdars* of the several Chiefs without molestation and the demand of duty.

7. All horses purchased for the use of the Cavalry regiments, whether in the district of Sirhind or elsewhere, the bringers of which being provided with sealed *rahdaries* from the Resident at Dehlie or Officer Commanding at Sirhind, shall be allowed to pass through the country of the said Chiefs without molestation or the demand of duty.

Glossary

Arzee	Petition.
Choubdar	An attendant carrying a short staff or mace.
Diwan-i-Khas	Private audience chamber.
Durbar	Royal Court.
Gaddi	Throne.
Ibra-nama	A written acquittance or relinquishment of claim.
Ikranama	A deed of assent.
Jaidad	Assets.
Khalsa lands	Crown lands.
Kharita	Special letter.
Khilat	Dress of honour presented by the superior authority to an inferior.
Khilledar	Governor of a fort.
Mahal	Palace; District.
Malik	Master.
Mirza	Prince.
Mukhtiar	Chief Minister.
Munshi	Writer.
Mumtazim-ud-Dowla	Administrator.
Musnud	Throne.
Najib	A body of irregular infantry.
Nazar	A present, especially from an inferior to a superior.
Nazim	Administrator.
Nazir	Supervisor.
Pargana	District.
Peshkush	Tribute.
Poojari	Priest.
Rabia-ul-Awal	The first of the two months termed Rabia, the third of the Mohammedan year.
Razinama	A deed of assent.
Salatin (Salateen)	Designation of the younger members of a royal family.
Sanad	A grant or charter.
Sawari	Retinue.
Shukka	A royal letter.
Tayool	Land held in *Jagir* by a member of a royal family.
Tika	A mark of high rank.
Tusbeeh Khana	Hall of audience.
Walli Ahad	Heir-apparent.
Wasikah	Letter.
Zenana	Female appartment.

Selected Bibliography

A—Manuscript Sources

Manuscript records in the National Archives of India:

Foreign Department, *Political Consultations and Proceedings, 1800-1857; Secret Consultations and Proceedings, 1800-1857; Miscellaneous Series; Letters to the Court of Directors, Secret and Political, 1800-1857; Letters from the Court of Directors, Secret and Political, 1800-1857; Persian Department; Home Department, Public Branch Consultations.*

B—Published Records

Aitchison, C. U. (Compl), *A Collection of Treaties, Engagements and Sanads Relating to India and Neighbouring Countries*, Vols. III & V, Calcutta, 1932.

Bengal Regulations and Acts, Vol. III, London, 1854.

Bhargava, Krishana Dayal (ed.), *Browne Correspondence*, New Delhi, 1960.

Kaye, John William, *Selections from the Papers of Lord Metcalfe*, London, 1845.

Majumdar, Jatindra Kumar (ed.), *Raja Ram Mohun Roy and the Last Mughals*, Calcutta, 1939.

Martin, Montgomery (ed), *The Despatches, Minutes and Correspondence of Marquess Wellesley, K.C., during his Administration in India*, 5 Vols., London, 1836, 1837.

Prasad, Bisheshwar (ed.), *The British Government and the Kingdom of Oudh (1764-1835)—A Report prepared by Capt. J. Patan*, Allahabad, 1944.

Press List of Old Records in the Punjab Secretariat, Vols. I & II, Lahore, 1915.

Punjab Government Records, Vols. I & II, Lahore, 1911.

Ross, Charles (ed), *Correspondence of Charles, First Marquis Cornwallis*, 3 Vols., London, 1859.

C—Contemporary Publications

Busawanlal, *Memoirs of the Pathan Soldier of Fortune, the Nawab Ameer-ood-Doulah Muhammud Ameer Khan*, Calcutta, 1832.

Bute, the Marchioness of (ed), *The Private Journal of the Marquess of Hastings*, 2 Vols., London, 1858.

Francklin, W., *The History of the Reign of Shah-Aulum*, London, 1798.

Hastings, Marquess of, *Summary of the Administratian of the Indian Government*. Edinburgh, 1825.

Heber, Reginald, *Narrative of a Journey through the Upper Provinces of India from Calcutta to Bombay*. 3 Vols., London, 1829.

Kaye, John William, *The Life and Correspondence of Charles, Lord Metcalfe*, 2 Vols., London, 1858.

Life and Correspondence of Major General Sir John Maleolm, 2 Vols., London, 1856.

Malcolm, Sir John, *The Political History of India*, 2 Vols., London, 1826; *A*

SELECT BIBLIOGRAPHY

Memoir of Central India including Malwa and Adjoining Provinces, 2 Vols., London, 1832.

Metcalfe, Charles Theophilus (tr.), *Two Native Narratives of the Mutiny in Delhi*, Westminster, 1898.

Mill, James and Wilson, Horace Hayman, *The History of British India*, 9 Vols., London, 1848.

Prinsep, H. T., *History of the Political and Military Transactions in India during the administration of the Marquess of Hastings, 1813-23*, London 1828.

Sutherland, J., *Sketches of the Relations Subsisting between the British Government in India and the Different Native States*, Calcutta, 1837.

Thorn, William, *Memoir of the War in India Conducted by General Lord Lake, Commander-in-Chief and Duke of Wellington*, London, 1818.

Thrornton, Edward, *The History of the British Empire in India*, London, 1845.

Tod, James, *Annals and Antiquities of Rajasthan* (one volume ed.), London, 1950.

D—Secondary Works

Argyyl, Duke of, *India Under Dalhousie and Canning*, London, 1865.

Arnold, Edwin, *The Marquis of Dalhousie's Administration of British India*, 2 Vols., London, 1865.

Banerji, A. C., *The Rajput States and the East India Company*, Calcutta, 1951.

Banerji, Brajendranath, *Raja Ram Mohun Roy's Mission to England*, Calcutta, 1926.

Batra, H.C., *The Relations of Jaipur State with the East India Company*, Delhi, 1958.

Brooke, J. C., *Political History of the State of Jaipur*, Calcutta, 1868.

Buckland, C. E., *Dictionary of Indian Biography*, London, 1906.

Datta, Kalikinkar, *Shah Alam II and the East India Company*, Calcutta, 1965.

Fanshaw, H. C., *Delhi Past and Present*, London, 1902.

Griffin, H. Lepel, *History of the Principal States in the Punjab*, Lahore, 1870.

Gupta, Hari Ram, *A History of the Sikhs*, 3 Vols., Simla, 1952.

Hussain, Mahdi, *Bahadur Shah II and the War of 1857 in Delhi with its Unforgettable Scenes*, Delhi, 1968.

Kaye and Malleson, *History of the Indian Mutiny*, 6 Vols, London, 1906.

Lee-Warner, Sir William, *The Native States of India*, London 1910.

The Life of the Marquis of Dalhousie, 2 Vols., London 1910.

Martin, Montgomery, *The Indian Empire*, 3 Vols, London.

Mehta, Mohan Sinha, *Lord Hastings and the Indian States*, Bombay, 1930.

Ojha, G.H., *History af Rajputana*, 5 Vols. (*Hindi*), Ajmer, 1938,' 39,' 40 and' 41.

Pearse, Huge, *Life and Military Services of Viscount Lake*, London, 1908.

Sarkar, Sir Jadunath, *Fall of the Mughal Empire*, 4 Vols., Calcutta 1950,' 52,' 66.

Spear, Percival, *Twilight of the Mughals*, London, 1951.

Stokes, Sric, *The English Utilitarians and India*, Oxford, 1950.

Thompson, Edward, *The Making of the Indian Princes*, London, 1943, *Life of Charles Metcalfe*, London, 1937.

Wylie, Norman Henry and Young, Keith, *Delhi—1857*, London, 1902.

Index

Abhay Singh, 60.
Abu Kasim, 23.
Abu Zafar, 20, appointed the heir-apparent, 41; charges against, 22, 23; interview of the Resident with, 24; position of, 37, 39, 143.
Afrasaib Khan, 2.
Akbar Shah II, 7, 21, 22, 24, 115, 116, 119, 131, 134, 152, 182; accession, 20; death, 132.
Amherst, 124, 142, 144, 146, 147, 153, 156, 157.
Amir Khan, 45, 46, 47, 49, 52, 53, 56, 58.
Amrit Kunwar, 83, 88.
Amritsar, treaty of, 105.
Assaye, battle of, 9.
Auckland, 144, 145, 165.
Aus Kaur, 106, 107.
Bahadur Shah II, accession 132, 144, 158, 162, 163, 165, 166, 168, 170, 172, 173, 177, 179, 180, 182.
Baijnath, 83, 84, 85, 87.
Baij Rao II, 5.
Baldev Singh, 77, 83.
Balwant Singh, 77, 79, 82.
Barlow, Sir George, 19, 29.
Becher, Francis, 1.
Bentinck Lord William, 143, 144, 149, 152, 154, 158, 161.
Bhahadur Singh, 69.

Bhag Singh, 101.
Bhailal Singh, 100, 101, 106.
Bhairisal, 58, 70, 72, 75, 76, 89, 90, 93, 94.
Bharatpur, changes in the administration, 84, 85, 88; extent of British interference 85, 86; new administration, 83; succession dispute 77, 78; treaty with, 44, 67.
Bhathani Rani, 70, 71.
Brown, Major James, 2-4.
Bunga Singh, 101.
Bungail Singh, 109.
Canning, George, 176-178.
Churaman, 83-85, 87.
Cis-Sutlej States, British policy, 99, 100, 101, 109, 113, 114; British protection offered, 103, 104; revision of the policy 102; proclamation of protection 104–105; protection against mutual usurpations, 113, 114.
Colebrooke, Edward, 147, 160, 183.
Combermire, Lord, 82.
Cornwallis, Lord, 44.
Dalhousie, Lord, 134, 159, 171, 172, 176, attitude towards the royal stipend, 135; policy towards the Mughals, 168-169; proposal for final settle-

(196)

INDEX

ment, 169-170.
Dara Bakht, 166, 168, 169, 170, 171.
Daulat-ul-Misa Begam, 23, 24, 29, 35.
Delhi, Defence of, 10.
  Residency at, see Delhi Residency. Emperor of, see Mughal Emperor.
Douglas, Charles, 180.
Durjansal, 77, 78, 81-83.
Durmo, 111-113.
Edmonstone, 28, 55.
Ellenborough, Lord, 135, 145, 158, 165; proposals regarding the privileges of the Emperor, 162, 163.
Elphinstone, Montstuart, 49, 102.
Faiz Muhammod Khan, 139, 153.
Fateh Singh, 111-113.
Fenvick, Thomas Cavendish, 176.
Fouji Ram, 70, 74.
Fraser, Simon, 154, 176, 177, 180, 182.
Fraser, William, 154, 161.
French, designs of, 6, 7; Generals, 6.
Ganesh Narain, 90.
Govind Narain, 90.
Govindram, 84, 84.
Graham, Captain, 157.
Grant, Charles, 129.
Gujar Singh, 111.
Hakim Asanullah Khan, 164.
Hanumant Chela, 74.
Hastings, Marquess of, 31, 50, 61, 145; policy towards Indian states, 51; policy towards the Pindaris, 57, 58; See also Moira, Lord.
Hastings, Warren, 2, 3.
Hardinge, Lord, 159.
Hawkins, Francis, 148-151, 160, 183.
Holkar, 9, 10, 46, 52, 56.
Holkar, Malhar Rao, 152, 153.
Holland, John, 1.
Hukum Chand, 92.
  Assembly of *thakurs*, 93-96, application for *tika*, 141; British interference, 75, 89; Jaipur, condition of, 55, 68; dissolution of the treaty 44; negotiations for treaty 55, 56, 67; administration, 70; problem of succession 68, 69, 71; public appearance of the Raja, 93; reasons for interference, 89, 90; treaty, 43; withdrawal of interference, 90.
Jagat Singh, 68, 70.
Jai Singh, 70, 71, 141.
Jaswant Singh, 101, 106.
Jawaharlal, 83-87.
Jeet Singh, 111-113.
Jhota Ram, 89, 92, 93.
Jodh Singh, 110-112.
Khaim Kaur, 107.
Krishna Kumari, 45, 46.
Lake, Lord, meeting with Shah Alam 7; titles conferred, 7, 9, 13, 18, 19, 27, 42, 49, 152, 180.
Lockett, Major, 83, 84, 86, 88,

183.
Low, Captain, 91, 92, 93, 95, 96.
Madho Singh, 62, 81.
Malcolm, Sir George, 49, 102.
Man Singh, 46.
Martin, W. B., 161, 181.
Metcalfe, Charles Theophilus, appointed Resident, first term 49, second term 79, memorandum on Central India, 52, 54; negotiations with Jaipur, 55-58; opinion on the policy of non-intervention, 49, 51, 79, 80, 97, 98; opinion on Bharatpur succession 81; opinion on the royal stipend 125, 126, 130; opinion on the privileges of the Mughal Emperor 137; policy towards Indian states, 80; views on interference in Bharatpur, 86, 87, 89; views on non-interference, 61-63, 65, 66, 88, 92, 93, 95-98, 102, 122-127, 130, 135, 139, 140, 142, 147, 151, 160, 181, 183.
Metcalfe, Thomas Theophilus, 161, 167, 169, 170, 171, 176, 181.
Megh Singh, 68, 72, 90, 92.
Middleton, Nathaniel, 1.
Middleton, Samuel, 1.
Minto, Lord, 50, 102, 117, 118, 120, 125, 135, 152.
Mirza Bulant Bakht, 24.
Mirza Fakr-ud-Din, 133, 168, 170, 172-175, 177.
Mirza Fateh-ul-Mulk, 164.

Mirza Jahangir, 21, 24, 25, 27, 28, 32, 33, 36-40.
Mirza Jawan Bakht, 133, 172, 175.
Mirza Koesh, 175-178.
Mirza Salim, 132, 142, 143.
Mirza Shagi Khan, 2.
Mohammad Shah Khan, 52.
Moghal Beg, 180.
Mohan Ram Nazir, 68-73, 76, 90.
Mohan Singh, 68, 69, 71.
Moira, the Earl of, 50, 51, 137; policy towards the Mughal Emperor, 138, 139-142, 146, 155. See also Hastings, Lord.
Mughal Emperor, attempts to assure sovereign powers, 32; British policy 30, 31, conferment of *Khilats* 153, 154, forms of address, 145-147; meeting with the G.G. 143; position, 6, 26, 27, 36, 136, 137; presentation of *nazars*, 155-159; protection offered, 6.
Mumtaz Mahal, 20-24, 27, 31, 34, 36-38, 40, 41, 119, 143, 149.
Najaf Khan, 2.
Najaf Quli Khan, 2.
Ochterlony, David, appointed Resident and Chief Commissioner at Delhi, 8, 65; Governments censure, 78-79; opinion on Bharatpur succession, 73; opinion on Jaipur administration, 73; removal from

INDEX

Delhi, 18-19; resignation 7, 9, 10, 16, 17, 23, 27, 58; and death, 68-78, 91, 97, 100, 103, 106-108, 110, 112, 126, 136, 141, 160, 181, 182, 183.
Paget, Edward, 15.
Perron, 6, 7, 99, 100.
Phula Singh, 106.
Pindaris, 46, 47, 52, 57, 67.
Policy of non-intervention, effects 5; implications, 48-49; Metcalfe's opinion, 49-50; Seton's opinion, 48.
Policy of non-interference, 79-81, 82, 86, 90, 91, 97-98.
Pran Krishna, 119-121, 123, 182.
Pratap Singh, 95.
Qudsia Begam, 22, 24, 29, 34, 35, 122.
Raja Sher Mal, 31, 35.
Rajputana States Agency, 65, 167.
Ram Kaur, 109-111.
Randhir Singh, 77.
Rangit Singh, 101-105, 109-112
Rathori Rani, 70, 71.
Rao Chathur Bhuj Huldia, 68.
Rao Lachman Singh, 153, 154.
Rao Ram Rattan, 77.
Residency at Delhi, establishment, 8; jurisdiction, 2, reorganization, 65, 160-62.
Roy, Ram Mohun, 128-131, 144, 148.
Ripon, the Earl of, 165.
Rupa Bhanderin, 92.
Sahib Kunwar, 88.
Sahib Singh, 105, 106, 108, 153.

Salbhai, treaty of, 3.
Sangit Singh, 111.
Sawai Singh, 46.
Scott, Col. William, 10, 12, 15.
Seton, Archibold, appointed Resident 18, admonition, 29; adoption by Mumtaz Mahal, 37-38; attitude to the Mughal Emperor, 19, 21, 23, 30, 32, 33, 35, 36, 48, 122, 123, 136, 137, 160, 181, 183.
Settlement with the Mughal Emperor, decision of the Government, 14; Emperor's reaction, 16-17; final settlement, 177-78; nature, 14-15; proposals of Dalhousie 169-70; proposals of Ochterlony, 13; proposals of Thomas Metcalfe, 166-168; proposals of William Scott, 10; principle 12.
Shah Alam II, 2, 6, 7, 8, 17, 20, 22, 26, 27, 32, 115-19, 125, 152, 180.
Shah Haji, mission to Calcutta, 31; objects of the mission, 32; British attitude, 33; conduct at Calcutta, 34; failure of the mission, 35; results of the mission, 35; significance of the mission, 36, 116, 137, 182.
Shiv Narain, 55.
Sindhia, 4, 6, 7, 9, 27, 46, 52 53, 56, 97.
Sindhia, Daulat Rao, 7.
Sindhia, Mahadaji, 3, 7, 116, 118.

States of Rajputana, appeals for British protection, 47, 48; arrangement with Sindhia and Holkar, 45; British interests, 66; condition, 46-47, 67; reversal of Wellesley's policy, 43-44; strategic importance, 43; Wellesley's policy, 42-43.
Stewart, Captain, 14, 15.
Sriram Poojari, 87.
Surgi Amgangas, treaty of, 97, 125.
Syed Reza Khan, 14.
Sykis, Francis, 1.

Tagore, Dwarakanath, 164.
Tipu Sultan, 4.
Thompson, George, 164.
Tod, Captain James, 61.
Trevelyan, Charles, 160.
Umed Singh, 63.
Wellesley, Lord, 5, 6, 14, 17, 19, 26, 27, 31, 42, 44, 49, 51, 116, 118, 120, 125, 136, 167, 179, 181.
White, Lt., 106.
Zalim Singh, 62, 63.
Zinat Mahal, 133, 172, 174-176, 180.

Other Publications of Associated Publishing House

HEGEL AND THE MODERN STATE

An Introduction to Hegel's Political Thought

V.R. MEHTA

Few thinkers have exercised a greater influence upon the thought of their own and succeeding generations as G. W. F. Hegel. In philosophy, in politics and in historical studies, Hegel's influence has been all pervasive. And yet, paradoxical it may seem, the interpretation of Hegel has varied with the prejudices and predilictions of the critics. On the one hand, he has been regarded as the father of the concept of organized freedom, dynamic concept of constitutionalism and the nationalism and on the other hand he has been with equal vehmence dubbed and denounced as a charlaton and an opportunist and a demagouge who chained political speculation to the needs of the state of his times, as well as the father of modern totalitarianism, facism and jingoism.

Mr. Mehta tries to steer clear of these controversies and tries to present the complex political ideas of Hegel in brief but clear and intelligible form. How was Hegel related to the intellectual background of his own age? What were the basic promises of his system on which he constructed a ground edifice of his theory of state? Who were the essential character and disposition of his political theory? What influence shaped his philosophy? And, above all, to use Croce's expression, "What is living and what is dead", in his political ideas? This book endeavours to answer these questions keeping in view the problems of the Modern State. It makes a sincere attempt to help the reader to understand Hegel who has been one of the most misunderstood of philosophers in the history of Ideas.

THE RED REBEL IN INDIA

A Study of Communist Strategy & Tactics

V.B. SINHA

FOREWORD BY MORARJI DESAI

"The Communist Party of India is not a national party like other parties. It has roots not in India but outside." This statement of Jawaharlal Nehru was not made by him because he was a Congressite. It is an objective statement and a summing-up of the Communist Party in India. In the present book Mr. Sinha substantiates Nehru's point of view by giving an historical analysis of the Communists in India on the basis of data which he has gathered both from official and non-official sources. The author's analysis suggests that the Communists in India are loyal not to their country but to their masters abroad. Whether before independence or after, whether in peace time or during troublous times, the inspiration of the Communists has always come from outside. Such a political party cannot be anything else but be anti-national and a fifth-columnist.

The author calls his book **The Red Rebel in India**. It gives a dispassionate and objective analysis of the activities of the Communist Party in India right from its inception up to the events at Naxalbari. The book is divided into twelve chapters which are as follows: India—The Red Target, Communist Tactics Till Independence, Armed Struggle, Peaceful Strategy, In Kerala, Support to Chinese Aggression, Plan for Violent Revolution, And its Preparations, Raiding the Communist Dens, Red Rehearsals of Revolution—Bandhs, At Naxalbari, The Way Out.

FROM CASTE TO CLASS

A Study of the Indian Middle Classes

Y. P. Chhibbar

In this brief but comprehensive book Dr. Y.P. Chhibbar gives a socio-economic survey of the occupational structure of the Indian Middle-Class and the changes that it had undergone between 1945 and 1955. This book is based on the case-studies of three-hundred individuals from different caste levels. Dr. Chhibbar's enquiry reveals how the traditional caste which shaped, among other things, the occupational structure of the Indian society gradually began to give way to a diffusion of all castes into all occupations which were alien and at times even recalcitrant to it. Although the process of diffusion started in the early nineteenth century, the emergence of class from caste took long time and till the middle of the twentieth century the impact of caste on the occupational pattern was still prepotent in India. This book, then, provides an invaluable guide to the problems of the middle-class occupation pattern in India and its caste background.

INDIAN WAY TO SOCIALISM

KAMALA GADRE

FOREWORD BY V.K.R.V. RAO

"The affluent Americans, the acquisitive Englishmen, the assertive Russian, and the aggressive Chinese," writes the author, "may perhaps learn a thing or two from the philosophy of the Indian Revolution with profit to themselves and greater benefit to the entire world." And that philosophy is trusteeship—the Indian way to achieve a socialistic society based on truth and peaceful consent. Dr. V.K.R.V. Rao in his foreword says: "I would recommend this study to the careful attention of all those like myself who believe in the supremacy of means over ends, and in the need for a non-violent transformation of a feudal or capitalist society into a socialist society."

The uneven development of separate national units, particularly during the last century and a half in Europe and Asia, created apparent anomalies in the history of economic ideas, and it is thought by many in this country, as also in the West, that there was neither a doctrine of socialism nor any tradition of socialistic thinking in India.

The author of the **Indian Way To Socialism** dispels that misconception. She analyzes the meaning of socialism from the Indian point of view, and following Gandhiji's ideas of trusteeship, builds up a coherent thesis of socialism, and suggests a practical way of establishing a socialistic society in India. Dr. Rao says: "I have read Mrs. Gadre's book with both interest and profit if not also some heart-searching, and am confident that other reader will also get the same experience."

NAGALAND IN TRANSITION

MAJOR V.K. ANAND

Although Dr. Verrier Elwin and others have written many illuminating books about Nagas no fresh attempts has been undertaken to study the land and people of the Nagaland after the British left India. This book fulfils that want. The author toured all the three districts of Nagaland—Kohima, Mokokchung, and Tuensang—inhabited by tribes like Angami, Ao, Konyak, and Sema, and made a first-hand study of Nagas —the Nagas of the past—and what is more relevant to us—the Nagas of the present—how gradually they gave up their superstitions and not-too civilized past.

Dr. Verrier Elwin read the book in manuscript and commented as follow: "I read your book on Nagas with great appreciation......I do hope that you will go on with your anthropological studies for, if I may say so, I was greatly impressed with the work."

TRACTS FOR THE TIMES

This is a series in which the leading intellectuals of India will discuss the crucial problems which face us today. Its general title has been borrowed from that of the famous tracts of the Oxford Movement in England, carried on by John Henry Newman, R.H. Froude, John Keble, Dr. Pusey, and others. Confronted by apathy in religious matters on the one hand, and the challenge of materialism accompanied by atheism on the other, these men began a movement which was to bring new life into the moral and spiritual existence of the British people. The influence of the Tractarians, who made their Tracts very powerful instruments of their ideas, spread far beyond the circle in which they worked.

In India today there is a combination of apathy with sterility which is afflicting every field of activity—spiritual, moral, intellectual, and political. Even those who are aware of the bankruptcy are too depressed to revolt against it, and to try to rescue themselves and others.

The monographs and books in these series, for which the Publishers will enlist the best minds of India, will all deal the aspects of the contemporary situation—not only to analyse the present ills and discontents and lay bare their causes, but also to suggest remedies in a positive approach to all the problems.

The message of the whole series will be: "Fight it out until victory comes."

TRACTS FOR THE TIMES: ONE

THE INTELLECTUAL IN INDIA
NIRAD C. CHAUDHURI

In the first of the Tracts For the Times the author of **The Autobiography of an Unknown Indian, A Passage to England,** and **The Continent of Circe,** and a contributor to leading newspapers and magazines in India and abroad examines the situation facing the intellectual in India.

As Mr. Chaudhuri sees it, whether the failures are in the political or in the economic and social fields, the first and the most essential preliminary is to bring to bear the power of thinking on all the fields. The main cause of the failures seen in recent years is lack of thought, or incompetent thought.

But the man who would provide the thought, namely, the intellectual, is the man who is the most discouraged in India. Authoritarianism in politics and social life, hostility or apathy to intellectual activities, the precarious economic situation of the intellectual—all tend to make him feel frustrated, if not wholly paralysed.

In the second part of his essay Mr. Chaudhuri shows how the intellectual might conquer this frustration and get round the obstacles to exercise his proper function in contemporary India.

Mr. Chaudhuri's suggestions gain immense practical importance from the fact that he had to face all the difficulties and frustrations in their worst form in his own function as a writer, and has virtually conquered all of them.

A RAJASTHAN VILLAGE

BRIJ RAJ CHAUHAN

Here is a brilliant study of the life of the people living in a village in Rajasthan. It is a study of Ranawaton-ki-Sadri village in Chittorgarh district of Rajasthan, written by one who had initiated teaching of Sociology in Rajasthan and who had personally been observing various facts of rural life for seven years prior to the writing of this book.

The work brings out the nature of a **jagir** village and draws out clearly how a **Jagirdar** had directed the process of setting up of a village community. The stages of the village from a small hamlet to the medium-sized community have been traced along with increasing heterogeneity in the life of the people. Special studies of the local institutions of the **Hali** (the permanent plough man) and the **Chokhala** (inter-village networks of a caste subcaste) have been attempted for areas wider than the village. Some of festivals, specially the **Govardhan puja**, have been studied at the regional and even cross-cultural levels.

The book also examines the approaches followed in current scientific village studies and puts to test some of the formulations of the late Prof. Redfield of Chicago University and his associates in this connection. To the general reader in Rajasthan, the book opens out wealth of details. And for readers interested in studying the processes of rural life in Rajasthan, this happens to be the book they might have been waiting for.

PAKISTAN—HER RELATION WITH INDIA 1947-66

K.C. SAXENA

FOREWORD BY Y.B. CHAVAN

We must understand Pakistan; it is important for India. It is important for Pakistan too. Only then she may understand India, shed her fears and hatred and look at the world straight in its face. It is equally important for the world, more so, for the Afro-Asian world.

Why is this seemingly unending feud between the two sisterly countries? What were India's aims in the recent military conflict with Pakistan? Did she abandon in a day the policy of peace to which she had consistently adhered during the twenty years since her independence? Where did her idealism disappear when in 1948 she stopped her army almost at the point of her final victory, when she accepted the call of the United Nations for a cease-fire in Kashmir? Had she lost her conviction that victory was not won in the battle-field? Had she lost her faith in trying to live at peace with neighbour even when they constantly indulged in pin-pricks and uncalled for provocation? Had her fund of patience exhausted itself?

An effort has been made in this book to provide an answer to all these anxious questions. The book is armed with facts and figures, and marshalled in a manner which could be made use of equally both by the scholars of Political Science and the **Parliamentarians.**

ART & LETTERS SERIES

This series is intended to provide in a sequence of short essays a survey of artistic and literary activity of our time, both in India and abroad, and to place all the contemporary movements in their historical setting and interrelation.

The scope of the essays on art, painting, sculpture, or music, will be similar. All the art will be treated as part of a broad cultural activity, as also in their particular expression, so far as they are self-contained. The selection will be electic, and cover all significant movements and personalities. Apart from this, special questions affecting the history of literature and art about which critical or scholarly opinion has not as yet reached finality will be dealt with in the light of the latest researches and critical works of interpretations. As a rule, the series will attempt to provide a guide to general educated public with the object of promoting both enjoyment and knowledge of art and literature, and it will avoid extreme specialization and superficial popularization.

ART & LETTERS SERIES: ONE

SEALS & STATUETTES OF KULLI, ZHOB, MOHENJO DARO AND HARAPPA

J. P. GUHA

Here is a stimulating analysis of the well-known art objects from Kulli, Zhob, Mohenjo Daro, and Harappa. The author is unable to accept the views of such eminent authorities as Sir John Marshall, Stuart Piggott, Hermann Goetz and others. He proves his point of view not by furnishing new facts but simply by working in terms of particular analysis.

'I have confined myself to such practical conclusions as can be drawn by working in terms of particular analysis, that is, analysis of individual art objects, which alone should give rise to judgments. It is only by keeping as close as possible to the objects of art that I have defined and illustrated my point of view, and in this way, I have tried to guard against the errors which I find in the views I have inherited from my predecessors'.

AROUND THE WORLD ON A NICKEL

JIMMY BEDFORD

Around the World on a Nickel is Jimmy Bedford's own story of how he gave up the comfort and security of a good job and ventured into the unknown and saw a large slice of life in other parts of the world. The book follows his exploits from a "snatch" job in London to nine days in a Guinea jail and a ten-day visit with India's native "Peace Corps", Bharat Sevak Samaj. During his two-year tour, he slept in grass shacks, mud huts, goat sheds, on the ground, in palaces and a stable. He ate whatever was to be eaten wherever he went—whether baboon stew, hippopotamus steak, wret hog, gazzelle, or fricassed kangaroo, "These and other little experiences are what make travel interesting," says the author who doesn't believe in planning a trip. "The important thing is to get up and go if I had known all that was in store for me. I would have been afraid to start out!"

The author found India "One of the world's richest countries with people of every conceivable religious idea living harmoniously with one another".

Although he was impressed by India's togetherness, he was confused, bewildered and intrigued by all of the conflicting philosophies within the country. He concluded: "In spite of your faults; and lacking of malts, I love you still." In India, as well as the rest of world, Bedford found "hospitality unlimited." He was given food and lodging by doctors, lawyers, Indian chiefs, a streetcar driver, a welder, farmers merchants, street sweepers, mechanics, policemen, missionaries and carpenters.

KENNEDY THROUGH INDIAN EYES

EDITED BY RAM SINGH & M.K. HALDAR

To decide at what point and on which issue one will risk one's career, is a difficult and soul-searching decision. And this is true not only in the case of indviduals but also in the case of nations, Kennedy made for himself that decision. His life is a challenge to humanity to recognize and affirm its soul and personality so that equality, egalitarianism, peace and freedom may cease to be mere slogans and the world may yet have a chance to become the Parliament of Man, the dream of the great thinkers and savants of all countries down the ages.

This book is a selection of Kennedy's speeches and writings relating to the peoples of the developing countries. In the long introduction the editors have brought into relief what Kennedy's life and work mean for the world in general and India in particular. **Kennedy Through Indian Eyes** is a homage to the memory of Kennedy who knew that courage itself cannot be supplied to any one but his own self. "For this each man must look into his own soul," declared Kennedy: which is his message to the peoples of the developing countries.